Y0-BRH-371

WITHDRAWN
L. R. COLLEGE LIBRARY

MARRIAGE ENCOUNTER

a guide to sharing

by
Don Demarest

Marilyn Sexton
Jerry Sexton

CARL A. RUDISILL LIBRARY
LENOIR-RHYNE COLLEGE

A Giniger Book published
in association with

CARILLON  BOOKS

BX
2250
.D43
1977
157573
Dec. 1992

MARRIAGE ENCOUNTER
A CARILLON BOOK

Carillon Books edition published 1977
ISBN: 0-89310-052-8 (paperback)
Library of Congress Catalog Card Number: 77-88195
Copyright © 1977 by Carillon Books
All rights reserved.
Printed in the United States of America

Carillon Books
2115 Summit Avenue
St. Paul, Minnesota 55105 U.S.A.

DEDICATION

To Father Gabriel Calvo who first blew on the coals of this new revolution of love. And to all the 'thermonuclear' couples who have taken up the torch he handed them and passed it on to other couples and families through Marriage Encounter.

ACKNOWLEDGEMENTS

Apart from their inestimable debt to Father Calvo, the authors are particularly grateful to the team couples who graciously agreed to share their presentations—Len and Elizabeth Notto, Lynn and Gordy Boldt, Bob and Beth Barnes—and Father John Higgins, OFM CAP, who also read and made suggestions. To Sharon Doody who typed and critiqued (as did Roy Wolff). To Father Tom Hill, OFM CAP, who contributed, advised, inspired and cautioned. And to all the couples at the Dayton Conference who taught them the spirit of *eutrapilia*. We are also grateful to Robert Genovese, editor of *Marriage Encounter,* and to Sister Kay Leuschner, CSJ, National M.E. Publications Director, who provided the material for so much of this book and gave us permission to quote it.

TABLE OF CONTENTS

ABBREVIATIONS

AA: Alcoholics Anonymous

AFRO: Areas For Reaching Out

B.E.: Beginning Experience

C.D.: Couple Dialogue

CFM: Christian Family Movement

E.E.: Engaged Encounter

F.E.: Family Encounter

FIRES: Family Intercommunications Relationships Experiences Services

ICCFM: International Confederation of Christian Family Movements

J.M.E.: Jewish Marriage Encounter

Mar-Va: Maryland-Virginia Marriage Encounter

M.E.: Marriage Encounter

M.F.C.: *Movimiento Familiar Cristiano*

P.R.: Personal Reflection

10/10: Ten minutes of written reflection, ten minutes of Couple Dialogue.

"Some day after we have mastered the winds, the waves, the tides and gravity, we will harness for God the energies of love, and, then, for the second time in the history of the world man will have discovered fire."

—Teilhard de Chardin

"There is within each couple a divine energy of love, and, if it can be brought alive, it can loose a true revolution of love over the whole earth. But in order for this energy to produce a human 'thermonuclear explosion,' it has to be released by a deep sharing between husband and wife, through communication of their feelings and of their whole life together"

—Gabriel Calvo

INTRODUCTION
Who Are These People?

Imagine 1200 people crowded together in July on the small campus of the University of Dayton, sweltering in 90 degree heat in dormitories without air-conditioning, lining up in a serpentine that stretches for several city blocks to spend half an hour going through a cafeteria line, jamming auditoriums and classrooms to hear talks on such disparate subjects as Quaker Marriage Beliefs, Human Sexuality, the Joy of Critiquing, Love and Anger, Charismatic Renewal . . .

Couples in shorts and sandals, wearing T-shirts with slogans like "Virginia is for Lovers," wandering arm-in-arm across the ivy-encrusted campus, hugging and kissing strangers during the "Kiss of Peace" which is usually celebrated by a handshake in the parochial mass, joining hands to recite prayers during an interdenominational agape presided over by a rabbi, a priest and a husband and wife who are Protestant ministers of different denominations . . .

Couples who are mostly young, mostly middle-class, toting coolers of beer and tennis racquets, guitars and blankets, dancing to *When the Saints Go Marching In,* putting on irreverent skits that mock whatever institution has brought them together, wearing group fancy dress (cowboys here, farmers there, with straw hats and balloons that say "Watch Detroit, It's Ballooning"), breaking into song at the slightest provocation, exchanging family snapshots under a banner which proclaims TO FACE ONESELF OPENLY AND HONESTLY TAKES THE RAWEST KIND OF COURAGE...

1

Who are these people? What are they doing?

They are participating in a peculiarly American celebration which has elements of a class reunion and a sales conference, a democratic convention and revivalist rally. But there is an atmosphere you can almost touch of love and trust which is absent from the first two, of an openness and hilarity which seldom attend our political and religious gatherings. If it is a gathering of the clans, it is remarkably free of the exclusiveness and hermit-like insularity which usually mark such crowds. If these people are united, whom are they united against? A rival college, a competing firm, an opposing political party or sect?

Actually, this is the third National Marriage Encounter Conference, a get-together of the leaders of a movement which began in Spain in 1962, was brought to the United States in 1967, and now numbers some 500,000 couples, increasing at a rate of over 100,000 a year. Exact figures are hard to come by since National Marriage Encounter is an amorphous group which coordinates and sponsors affiliate chapters in most of the 50 states, which can then sponsor their own affiliates. A splinter expression, the "Worldwide (formerly "New York") Marriage Encounter," which is more aggressive in its recruiting tactics, could probably double these figures. Last year its annual conference accommodated 30,000.

In October, 1975, an International Marriage Conference was held in Rome with representative groups from Europe, Asia, Latin and North America.

Just what is Marriage Encounter? What is the secret of the spark that was kindled by an unpretentious Spanish priest in Barcelona fourteen years ago, which flashed across the world and which has spread across the United States in such a quenchless conflagration? Unlike Transactional Analysis, est, Group Encounter and other innovative (and manipulative) techniques of group dynamics and personal motivation, it is essentially religious in its orientation. Unlike the Catholic cursillo, the fundamentalist crusades of Billy Graham and other revivalists, it is fundamentally ecumenical—more than interdenominational, interfaith, with strong Jewish participation. (In the last four years, Jewish Marriage Encounter, which is affiliated with National Marriage Encounter, began in the East and has spread to 18 states.)

Marriage Encounter is an answer to the doom-cryers who

2

claim that monogamy is outmoded and that the nuclear family, like the extended family, is on its way out. It is a challenge to the statistics which demonstrate that the divorce rate in the U.S. is overtaking marriages (in 1922 one marriage in 7 ended in divorce, in 1972 one in 3, in 1975 for the first time one million couples filed for divorce). It is concerned especially with the rising divorce rate among people who have traditionally viewed the marriage vow and the family as partaking of the sacred. (It is estimated that in 1977 there are three to five million divorced and remarried Catholics.)

Marriage Encounter is an unabashed affirmation of marriage, a celebration of the family. Its founder, Father Gabriel Calvo, believes: "There is within each couple a divine energy of love and it can be brought alive. It has to be released by a deep sharing between husband and wife, through the communication of their feelings and of their whole life together. It cannot be done in just one moment. It is done, rather, through the sharing and dialogue of many hours and many days."

The core of Marriage Encounter (henceforth for brevity's sake to be referred to as M.E.), the initial experience, is a weekend in which 10-25 married couples are given an opportunity to examine their lives together, free from everyday distractions. They are urged to explore their relationship— their individual weaknesses and strong points, their hidden hurts, dreams, disappointments, their joys and frustrations— openly and lovingly in a face-to-face encounter with the one person they have chosen to live with for the rest of their lives.

The weekend is presented by a team of two or three previously Encountered couples and a minister, usually a priest. It runs from early Friday evening to late Sunday afternoon. And it consists of twelve team presentations which focus on various aspects of the marriage relationship. Each is followed by a period of reflection on certain open-ended questions related to the topic. Then, individually, husband and wife meditate on and write down their feelings about the questions. Next they share their written statements in private, and talk together in an effort to achieve more complete understanding. As masks are put aside and walls broken down, the couples learn to recognize the challenge, as well as the enormous potential, which their marriage offers—the growth in unity which is summarized in the Biblical phrase, "two in one flesh."

3

Although every weekend is different—as different as the couples presenting it and the couples sharing it—the result seems to be inevitable. It is expressed in statements like the following: "After eight years of marriage and six children, we have fallen in love ..."; "I suddenly realized that my wife is a mystery and I am going to devote the rest of my life to trying to appreciate her ..."; "Now each day is like opening a new gift ..."; "We have become the husband and wife, mother and father, the lovers we always wanted to be." It is expressed in gestures like buying new wedding rings or sending home a dozen roses addressed "To my best friend." It is expressed in the faces one sees emerging from the building in which the Encounter has been held—faces which reflect a new vision, an unexpected discovery. It is expressed in the behavior described above at the University of Dayton.

There is another word you often hear among Encountered Couples. It is the word "hunger." Their weekend, instead of filling them, has made them ravenous for more—more understanding, more closeness, more dialogue, more spirituality, more of God, more community, more sharing. And I think that, basically, is the secret of the Marriage Encounter movement and its snowballing progress. It isn't its techniques (as Father Calvo keeps insisting), its structure—there are other encounter groups with more innovative psychological approaches, more skilled direction by trained psychologists—or the answers (M.E. provides more questions than answers). It is that M.E. taps some universal hungers, hungers which our contemporary culture cannot satisfy, hungers which it often tries to suppress or deny.

In many ways we are like the people at the time of the coming of Christ, who were hungry and thirsty for something that their times could not provide. They flocked first to John the Baptist, then to Jesus, both of whom spoke to their hungers. And our Lord didn't provide many answers either that weren't already available in the Scriptures. He provided a direction. "I am the way," he said, "and the truth and the life."

And, surprisingly, Encountered Couples have a quality that distinguished the early Christians: "See how they love one another." This can't be faked.

The chief danger posed by the Marriage Encounter movement, especially the weekend, is that couples will turn in on themselves in their concentration on the restoration of their marriage. This is what Father Calvo calls the "sin of

4

conjugalism" and Edward Dufresne *(Partnership.* p. 65[1]) *egoisme à deux,* (shared egotism). But the opposite effect seems to be produced. Again, the words used by couples trying to describe their weekend show a remarkable unanimity: "I felt full to the top, overbrimming with love and I had to go out to find people to share it . . ."; "I found out love isn't love until you give it away . . ."; "Now I know what loving your neighbors really means . . .".

It can be summed up in the remarkable statement from Erich Fromm: "If I truly love one person, I love all persons, I love the world, I love life. If I can say to somebody else, 'I love you,' I must be able to say, 'I love you in everybody, I love you through the world, I love you also in myself.' " *(The Art of Loving.)*

This was brought home to me during the conference. During our weekend my wife and I had concentrated on each other. We couldn't help receiving some of the good vibrations that came from the other couples who were also discovering themselves and God. But at Dayton (which was a last minute decision and for which my wife, Betty, couldn't get away) the air was electric with *eutrapilia,* which is an ancient word for the spirit of playfulness, and with *agape,* which is plain loving kindness. Among these born-again couples, I was an odd man out (even the priests doubled up in the dormitories, but I had a room to myself). But even though most had shared the other two conferences, and in the Minnesota group had worked closely together as team couples for three or four years, I was never made to feel an outsider, an intruder. Wherever two or three couples were gathered together, I was invited in. And after the couples had embraced, they always had a hug and kiss left for me.

We shared the songs and prayers and jokes and talks. Marvelously human and warm and unpretentious discourses by Ed and Sandy Dufresne who bore witness to their marriage in separate Lutheran and Methodist inner city churches; Father John Powell, S. J., the theologian and best-selling author who didn't hesitate to warn us that he finds America on the verge of Dachau's contempt for human life; Ruth Youngdahl Nelson, wife of a Lutheran minister, mother of missionaries, grandmother of six, who urged us to go out and change the world; and Father Calvo, himself, who outstripped

1. Paulist Press, New York, 1975.

his translator but managed to convey, as eloquently as Marcel Marceau through his gestures and facial expressions, how M.E. couples can rake the cold ashes of 1976 into a blazing fire of love.

But when it came to the workshops there was too much to share. As a fellow conferee said, "It's like one of those huge handwritten menus at an elegant restaurant—there are so many tempting dishes you can't settle on one." So, in our yearning for new expressions and other apostolates, we split up and shared our notes on Yoga, Marriage and Scripture, Teenage Encounter, Parent Effectiveness Training, Marriage Enrichment Programs, Transcendental Meditation, Ministry to Divorced Catholics—whatever we could crowd into the three days. Again and again one heard during the question period, "My husband and I are hungry for . . . My wife and I thirst for . . ."

Jerry and Marilyn Sexton, my co-authors on this book (they have really provided the direction and I have only crossed the t's and added exclamation marks), have pursued a hunger for doing God's work most of their married lives. It has taken them to Africa, Mexico, Europe, to the Christian Family Movement and, almost from its beginning, Marriage Encounter which they now serve as National Executive Couple. They literally devote their lives to it. But they have acknowledged that they don't expect to be in it forever. Marriage Encounter will grow and change; they will grow and change. Right now, they feel, it is something very important for American marriages, and their own.

It was Marilyn, especially, who suggested that this book might serve as a guide to other couples for ways in which they might achieve a more open and creative marriage.

Since not everybody can or will want to experience a weekend (although this is a marvelous and inspiring occasion and everybody who possibly can should take advantage of it), we should try in this book to show how individual couples can achieve some of the same results in their own home.[2] Marriage Encounter is a sharing experience. It is some of the insights we have gathered—from many encountered couples—that we want to share with you.

---

2. Apparently Father Calvo himself, in his yearning to reach the poorest and neediest families, has come to a similar conclusion. He is currently preparing a series of correspondence courses about Marriage Encounter, of which more will be said later.

And we can begin our book by sharing the prayer with which Father Calvo opened the conference at Dayton:

May the spirit of God work in all of us. Lord, knock loudly on the door of each of our homes so that fire of your love may invade every house and heart—all our communities, organizations and movements—so that we can serve as docile instruments of your Revolution of Justice and Love throughout the world.

DD

Chapter
One

CHAPTER ONE

How and Why We Came to Make an Encounter— And How It Affected Us

The roots of the two most popular and effective lay apostolates in the contemporary Church in America came from Spain. The *Cursillo* (Little Course in Christianity) and *Marriage Encounter* both entered this country from Mexico during the 1950's and 1960's respectively. It is also coincidental that the authors of this book came to Marriage Encounter mostly because of their experiences in Mexico. We come from different backgrounds. I was born in New Orleans and raised in England. Betty is from the Virgin Islands. Jerry and Marilyn are from Minnesota. In Mexico we discovered something about the family and our faith that made us hungry for the experience that Marriage Encounter provides.

Betty and I lived in Mexico for eight years, early in our marriage. What we found there is something we have never achieved anywhere else, something we are still looking for—a real sense of community, a sense of wholeness. In Mexico there was practically no dichotomy between our family, professional, vocational and spiritual lives. Although we were foreigners we were readily accepted as friends, neighbors and fellow parishioners in the suburb of Coyoacan with its Franciscan Church of St. John the Baptist. There were no barriers of class, wealth, nationality or race that could erase our bonds of Christian community. We participated with our neighbors (my friends were mostly writers and Betty's friends, mostly teachers) in various forms of the lay apostolate— without any sense of intrusion.

This is probably because we participated as a family. Our little girls helped Betty with her catechism class. We served as godparents to many of our neighbor's children, rich and poor alike. We joined other families in parish outings and activities. As members of the Franciscan Third Order our children and their friends went begging door-to-door with Betty and the other mothers to raise money for the poor. And we discovered something of the solidity and solidarity of the Mexican's devotion to Our Lady of Guadalupe, their patroness ever since she appeared to the poor Indian, Juan Diego in 1531.

When we returned to the United States we realized something was lacking in our lives which once again became compartmentalized. I had my job, which was publishing books, and my vocation, which was writing. Church was a thing which we did on Sundays. Betty found that the Third Order in Fresno, California, was chiefly a discussion club. The children were strangers in a strange land—making the adjustment to a new system better than we did. But in their eagerness to learn the American way of life, they were often strangers to us, too. Betty missed the communal aspects of buying food in an open air market instead of a supermarket. Our neighbors seemed chiefly interested in our putting in grass so that the value of their tract home wouldn't deteriorate.

And then we discovered the cursillo. I made my cursillo the weekend President Kennedy was assassinated. Betty followed two weeks later. I made it with a Spanish working-class group, many of them grape pickers and migrant laborers from the San Joaquin Valley, the people that Cesar Chavez was later to organize under the banner of Our Lady of Guadalupe. Ninety percent of his leaders came from the cursillo movement. In our weekly meetings they provided the community of love and faith we had misplaced. When we came to Minnesota in the 60's, there was no cursillo movement. It is only recently that Betty and I returned to it.

But even in the cursillo, as wonderful as it is, we felt something was missing. Betty and I participated in the cursillo as individuals rather than a couple. With our weekly group, we examined our individual consciences and shared our individual religious experiences, without sharing them with each other. In a way, we even went to different churches. One Sunday Betty accompanied me to Our Lady of Guadalupe because I enjoyed the nostalgia that the hymns in Spanish provided. The next Sunday we went to St. Matthews, because

Betty enjoyed the sermons there. Obviously we were no longer involved in parish activities. We went to a Marriage Encounter because we had a suspicion that the reason we weren't finding the community we were seeking was because we didn't have it between ourselves.

The Sextons first became involved in Mexico because a former employee of Jerry's, Larry Dodge, left his job as managing editor of their suburban newspaper to join the Association for International Development. AID is an apostolate to help people in underdeveloped countries and existed long before the Peace Corps. Larry persuaded the Sextons to work within their parish to raise the money to support a young AID couple who were going to work in Mexico with a Maryknoll priest, Father Hessler. Incidentally, Marriage Encounter is full of what secular people call "coincidence." This was the same Father Hessler who introduced M.E. to the U.S. Having raised a considerable sum of money, the Sextons went to the town of Morelia, in the state of Michoacan, to see for themselves what was being done with that money. They were impressed with all that was being accomplished. There was a credit union, a center for folk arts and an export project that found buyers for the native crafts of twenty villages.

They were naturally disappointed when they returned to report to their fellow parishioners about the success of the project, only to find that the parish had lost interest and didn't want to raise any more money.

Father Hessler told them not to worry. He said that for him the main point of AID was not what the apostles brought to Mexico but what they discovered when they got there. He advised the Sextons to work hard in their own parish, because it needed what they had to bring more than the poor Mexicans of Michoacan did.

Later, when the Sextons had become involved in Marriage Encounter they went back to Mexico. Perhaps we should let them continue in their own words.

Jerry: In answer to your question about how we got involved in Marriage Encounter, it came about in this way. Marilyn and I were president couple of the St. Paul-Minneapolis Christian Family Movement in 1971. We had heard about M.E. and thought it might be a good adjunct for CFM—a breakthrough to the sort of community which was somehow lacking. At the time we weren't aware that M.E. had been started in Spain

13

under the auspices of the CFM and had been brought to the U.S. under the auspices of the CFM; in fact, by our friend, Father Hessler.

We made our weekend in Buffalo, Minnesota, at King's House along with the Barelas.

We had a good weekend. It wasn't the tremendous weekend we see some couples experience now, but we realized that it was a real solution to the stalemate we were going through in the CFM. That it really provided a sense of community. So we came back and recommended it to our friends in CFM, determined to work within M.E. to make it a vital part of CFM.

Marilyn: We made our weekend in November, 1971, the first M.E. Encounter in Minnesota. Then we went to Detroit for team training with the Otts and Barelas in January, 1972. While we were there we learned that M.E. was strong in Mexico and we decided to go down and see if there was anything we could learn.

Jerry: We went back to Michoacan, back to the city of Morelia, with two other CFM couples, the Doodys and the Joneses. And we stayed at the homes of local CFM leader couples. We wanted to arrange an exchange with them. We found that Marriage Encounter was very much part of their program, the four year program. The first year concentrated on marriage and involved making an Encounter. The second year the couples dealt with the family. The third year they worked in their parish. The fourth year they went out into the world. This struck us as a very logical process. It reinforced our suspicion that we were missing something. We found that in Morelia they had already presented fifty M.E. weekends. And the feeling of community there was tremendous. But when we came back to try and sell M.E. to CFM we didn't meet with much success. We decided to devote our full time to Marriage Encounter then.

And we are still learning from Morelia! What we saw in Morelia is just beginning to happen in M.E. here. At first there was chiefly a concern for marriage in the U.S. It was only when Father Calvo's manual was retranslated in 1973 that we discovered that this movement out to the community was part of the original program (the part that was called "Open and Apostolic Marriage" and in the 1975 translation is called "The Christian Commitment of Marriage"). Presently throughout the U.S., M.E. couples are concentrating on the family, putting on Family Encounters. This was the second step both in Father

14

Calvo's program and at Morelia. On the leadership level there is an increasing involvement with the parish—the third step. But we are still groping toward the fourth step—the world. It's still difficult to convince many people in the movement that the weekend is not an end in itself but just the first step!

Jerry: But you do have to make the first step. And then the second and the third, before you go on to the fourth. You have to become aware of yourself, your strengths and weaknesses, and change yourself before you can change the world.

Marilyn: I agree with Jerry, but I come at it from a different angle. I care about husbands and wives and the sort of family they have. I can't think of anything in life more miserable than to find yourself alienated from your spouse. In turn, the children feel the tension or the apathy between their parents. I guess I'm really involved in M.E. because I just care about people. I don't think we're going to change society until we change its smallest unit, the family. When a husband and wife find each other, and then their children, a Christian community is formed. When people find out the love they have for each other is more important than what they can buy, and they experience the joy of giving and see this reflected in others (which is what happens all the time in M.E. on the weekends and the follow-up) we have the new values that can change the world. Society can only be changed by people who care and are committed. And this begins at home.

Jerry: In other words, each of the steps has to be completed before you go on to the next. We have to create a good new marriage before we have a good family. And we have to have a good family before we can build a brave new world.

Don: Do you think that's why movements like the cursillo and Marriage Encounter have found such a tremendous following in the States? Is it because in the moving about of recent years, and the tremendous mobility involved in careers today—the necessity to change homes and even jobs—we have become a nation of strangers? We've lost the extended family and the old neighborhood roots, and we're looking for community. We're desperate for community. Is that it?

Marilyn: Yes. And for something more from our marriages. Marriages today have to carry an extra weight. And they're suffering from the strain.

Jerry: And there's the hunger for God, for spirituality. Don't forget that. All these new movements that the kids are flocking to—Hare Krishna, the Moonies, the Jesus Freaks. That means

15

something. That's a telling symptom that something's wrong with our society—with our families and the way they worship.

Betty and I had been married for 31 years when we made our Encounter at the M.E. Center on Rogers Lake in Mendota, a suburb of St. Paul. We made it on Mother's Day, May 10, 1976, because, as Betty finally admitted, she has always found Mother's Day a backbreaking chore and she was happy to find an excuse not to entertain the whole family. We thought we had a good marriage. We had five marvelous children who seemed to be well-adjusted, and a treasure of a granddaughter. But we soon realized that a great deal of the tranquility of our marriage came from evasion—from not facing up to the conflicts, from trying to ignore them. Or taking turns instead of sharing—like going to one spouse's favorite church one Sunday, to the other's the next. Betty was a little scared about making the Encounter at first. She was afraid that we would rip the scabs off long-healed wounds.

But the weekend taught us to do something we hadn't tried for years. It taught us to communicate. I realize now that this was mostly my fault. A person often becomes a writer, I think, because he finds it hard to communicate with other people except through the written word—at a distance. I was finding it easier to communicate to readers than to my own wife.

We still have a long way to go, but we are making the first steps. We are learning all over again to communicate with each other, which is like learning to walk again. It's hard. But exhilarating.

Jerry: You ask what Marriage Encounter has meant to us— if and how it's changed us? That's a tough question. It's tough to see our growth or where we were two, three, or five years ago. I came from a typical American background: "Work Hard, Save Your Money, Get Ahead." And I had reached the stage where I thought I had everything lined up. I knew where I was going and how to get there. I had all the answers. I was a self-starter, self-employed, had a successful business, beautiful wife, eight charming children. What more was there?

Now I don't have the answers any more. M.E. really shook all that up. It has shown me that feelings are more important than possessions; that there are wider horizons than the "American Dream." In a sense, M.E. has undermined my feeling of security. All right, that's healthy! But it's provided more questions than answers. It's jolted me out of my comfortable rut. And now I am more concerned with what

Marilyn wants than what I want. I'm concerned with what my family wants. What God wants.

Marilyn: I agree with Jerry. But we don't wallow in the depths any more. Oh, we still have fights. We have bad days when I think, "What's the use?" But we don't stay there very long. We've learned to let our feelings out and we know how important this is. Personally I've found out how to be more in touch with my feelings, how to be honest with them, to be comfortable with them, and it's made a difference.

For one thing I can talk in front of a large crowd now. Once, even the idea of sharing myself with a small group as a team member terrified me. M.E. has uncovered a lot of talents I never dreamed I had. I'm continually discovering my possibilities. And Jerry has changed. He's become a lot more sensitive. And our children have changed because of us. Because we're more accepting, they can be more outgoing.

Jerry: There's a certain frustration, all the same. We have all these tools—all this education in how to communicate, how to accept—all this experience of being open, of sharing. But it really doesn't help all that much. I think the difference is that before, we had all those fights and disappointments (and, of course, we still do). But now we know it can be so much better. We get impatient with ourselves sometimes.

Marilyn: The thing is that now when things go wrong, when we make mistakes, we have the ability to start again. We have a solid foundation to build on, to advance from. We didn't have this before our Marriage Encounter.

Jerry: It's been a growth process. Growth is usually painful. But it's better than stagnation. And when growth is shared— not just individual growth but the two of you advancing together—the possibilities are mind-boggling.

Betty and I, of course, haven't been working on our marriage from this new perspective as long as Marilyn and Jerry have. But we can see changes already. We can feel the growing pains. The children have noticed it. They feel more comfortable with us because we are no longer putting on a front with them either. We are beginning to build again that little community we had in Mexico when life wasn't so full of outside distractions, our own "Little Church." We are more aware of our dependence on God, on the need to share our prayers and spiritual experiences. We have learned to recognize the truth of Father Calvo's saying: "Our dialogue is the water. And Christ is the one who can turn the water into wine."

Later on we will be able to go out into the world and work on bigger communities. Right now we have some important restoration to do at home. There is a lot of gimcrack still in our marriage, something of the jerry-built and the second hand in our relationship. But it's comforting to realize that people who have been "Encountered" as long as the Sextons still have their problems.

One thing I, especially, learned from the weekend. I have to bring the same concern and concentration to my marriage as to the novel I am working on. It's a lot harder, but the rewards are potentially greater than any royalties or book club adoptions, or any rave reviews or letters from readers.

This is an aspect of marriage that Clayton Barbeau emphasizes in his new book, *Creative Marriage: The Middle Years:*[1]

> *"Marriage is an art form, the most challenging and complex of all the works a human being can be inspired to create. Unlike painting, poetry, the novel, architecture, or any other of the forms in which the essential creative element of our human nature finds expression, man-the-maker cannot lay down the tools of this art form, step back, and pronounce the work complete."*

---

1. Seabury Press, N.Y., 1976.

Chapter
Two

CHAPTER TWO

The First Stage of the Weekend: The Encounter with Self Or "Why Am I Afraid to Tell You Who I Am?"

PART ONE—FRIDAY NIGHT

Tolstoi's novel *Anna Karenina* begins with the oft-quoted words: "Happy families are all alike; every unhappy family is unhappy in its own way."

Like the other popular quotation from *Love Story*, "Love is never having to say you're sorry," this is, at best, a half-truth. There are many different kinds of happy families and happy marriages—so many that it is hard to pin down exactly what makes them this way. But unhappy marriages, as marriage counselors have pointed out, seem to follow a fatal and inevitable pattern.

Each Marriage Encounter weekend is also different. Because, even though a lot has been made of the slogan that M.E. is for "good marriages—to make good marriages better"—most people who attend an Encounter do so because they think that their marriage lacks something.[1] And the discoveries made during a weekend vary widely from couple to couple, just as the team presentations, which form the nucleus of the weekend, offer many different sorts of insights. The encountering couples take what they need from an enormously varied menu. These include a long list of "Subjects for Under-

---

1. Father Calvo has said of "this commercial slogan" that it is against the Spirit of the Gospel and foments feelings of pride and pharisaism: "I have always thought of M.E. as a service for all marriages, especially those in most need ... those which are conscious of their weaknesses, their faults and inadequacies."

standing " (including Money, Time, Sex, Relatives, Work and Religion) on which happy marriages have reached infinite gradations of agreement and compromise, but on which ill-adjusted marriages seem inevitably to founder. These are listed also as "Symptoms of Spiritual Divorce."

The following chapters are based largely on the weekend Don and Betty Demarest made, although the Sextons have added material from the many others they have participated in as team leaders. The presentations, or topic talks, have been taken mostly from those given by three team couples and a Capuchin priest. Len and Liz Notto are a Catholic couple, aged 50 and 48, married 31 years, who have six children (one adopted). Gordon and Lynn Boldt are Lutherans, aged 36 and 35, with two children and 14 years of marriage. Bob and Beth Barnes are both 29, married 8 years, without children; Bob is a Baptist, Beth a Catholic. Father John Higgins has been a priest for 22 years. (Most of that time has been spent teaching high school religion and coaching. The religious dimension is provided on most weekends normally by clergy such as a priest, brother or sister, a rabbi or a minister.)

They represent a typical cross-section of the three hundred or so Minnesota couples who have been motivated by the success of their Encounter to share their experiences with others on a succession of weekends. Together they have given over 30 Encounters. Although, as will become apparent, their marriages had suffered from almost identical faults and failures, they have won through to a happy family life that is quite unique and geared to their special circumstances.

Their talks have, of necessity, been extremely condensed for the purpose of this book. They can be fleshed out by reading some of the material listed in the bibliography. Each chapter is followed by a Postscript in which the Sextons and Demarests have dialogued—much as team couples do when they prepare their talks—about their own marriages and what M.E. has contributed to them. Father Tom Hill, the third member of the National Executive team, also participated.

* * *

It was a balmy Minnesota May afternoon with thunderheads hovering on the horizon when the Demarests drove to the Marriage Encounter Center in Mendota Heights, a southern suburb of St. Paul. They did so with mixed emotions— the gaiety of getting away together for the first time in three years, without any housekeeping or writing (sic) to worry about; the apprehension of having to face up to emotions, and especially feelings of inadequacy, that had been carefully buried and bricked over for years. It reminded Don of going to college in a foreign country. It reminded Betty of leaving her family in a Washington suburb to go to Don's native New Orleans on her honeymoon. Both had an intuition of entering strange and possibly dangerous country, full of unexpected obstacles, with wild animals lurking in the undergrowth.

The red brick building on the edge of a lake behind a high school, with its baseball diamond and tennis courts (the Center used to be a dormitory at St. Thomas Academy), also brought back mixed memories, which weren't entirely alleviated by the burly white-haired man who bustled out to greet them and take their bags. In his faded sweatshirt and sneakers, he looked like a Christian Brother in mufti.

As he led the Demarests along the corridor to their bedroom on the second floor, they noticed that each door had a gaily colored placard with figures modeled after the "Charmers" cartoon and appropriate slogans: "Love Is—John and Joanne Thanking God for Each Other," "Don and Betty— A Gift to Brighten Cloudy Days."

" 'Abandon Hope All You Who Enter Here,' might have been more appropriate," Betty wisecracked. Her smile was tense.

"We'll be meeting in the conference room at the bottom of the stairs in 15 minutes," the husky guide, who had introduced himself as Len, told them. "There are coffee and cookies, if you're feeling in need of nourishment."

When they entered the big, sunny room, most of the other couples were already there sitting stiffly on the metal chairs which lined three walls. Mostly they were young, handsome, wearing embroidered jeans, or expensive-looking jumpsuits, and *adidas*. There was only one couple older than the Demarests. A red-faced man with an Irish Boston accent sitting near them was telling his neighbors that he was 68, that he and his wife were celebrating their fortieth anniversary at the Encounter as a present from their children. "Marriage Encounter," he chortled. "If I don't know Mary after forty years, I never will. But this is my gift to her instead of spending the weekend on the golf course."

The walls were hung with banners. The Demarests read them as the last few chairs were being filled. WE CAN ONLY LOVE WHAT WE KNOW. TOGETHER WE CAN MAKE THE

23

DIFFERENCE. IF YOU LOVE SOMEONE TELL THEM. YOU CAN FLY BUT THAT COCOON WILL HAVE TO GO. A stubby, pixie-faced man wearing a flowered sport shirt over black trousers, introduced the team couples. "And I'm Father John, a Capuchin priest and soccer coach." He looked like Friar Tuck. "Now, perhaps we can go around the room for the rest of the introductions. When each of you present your spouse, you might tell us what you particularly like about each other, or what first attracted you to him or her."

When it got to the Demarests, Don said that what appealed to him most about Betty was her freshness, "the way she faces life with a child-like wonder and delight." Betty said she liked Don's intelligence, "the way he always questions things and looks for answers." The Boston Irishman said he appreciated his wife's reliability, "she never does anything unexpected."

Len, who seemed to be the leader of the group, explained the nuts and bolts of the weekend. There were cigarettes, toilet articles, coffee and snacks available at all times. The team members would make any necessary telephone calls. Finances would be discussed on Sunday. This infernal weapon (he tinkled a small hand bell) will regulate your comings and goings.

As he did this, Don realized why he looked familiar. With his wide, swarthy face, broad shoulders and furrowed forehead he could have been a stand-in for Lorne Greene, the patriarch of the Ponderosa. His wife, another Elizabeth, was petite, brown-haired, with a shy but engaging smile. She offered a short prayer for the success of the weekend: "Lord, inspire us to merit the titles of 'husband' and 'wife'. Help us to look to you and to one another to rediscover the fullness and mystery we once felt in our union. Help us to be honest enough to ask 'Where have we been together and where are we going?' Brave enough to question 'Where have we failed?' Foolhardy enough to say, 'For me we come first.' Help us together to believe how fragile, yet powerful, how impossible yet attainable our love can be. Above all, Lord, give us each as 'Husband' and 'Wife' the courage to be for each other a person rather than a title."

Another team couple, Gordy and Lynn Boldt, took turns giving a brief history of the Marriage Encounter movement and its purpose. Gordy, a short, tidy man with a neatly-trimmed black beard and intense eyes, quoted Father Calvo's purpose in founding the movement. "The Marriage Encounter (he has stated) is designed to give married couples the opportunity to examine their lives together—their weaknesses and strong points, their attitudes toward each other and toward their families, their hurts, desires, ambitions, disappointments, joys and frustrations—and to do so openly and honestly in a Christ-like, face-to-face, heart-to-heart encounter with the one person they have chosen to live with for the rest of their lives."

He outlined what a Marriage Encounter was not. "First of all, it's not a retreat, a withdrawing from the world of home, family and neighborhood. We are going to be very preoccupied with those things. Above all, Marriage Encounter is not any sort of T-Group or sensitivity session. There will be no group dialogue or group dynamics, no sort of brain-washing or confrontation or emotion manipulation."

Lynn, a serenely handsome red-haired woman in her mid-thirties, told them, while her husband passed out notebooks and pencils, that these would be the tools they were going to use on the weekend, the life-rafts that would take them on a tremendous voyage of discovery. "The word *encuentro* in Spanish means more than a casual meeting. It has the implication of exploring, plumbing depths, of making discoveries. This is what you'll be doing with each other this weekend, if you are open and honest and really work at it."

Then the babies of the team took over to explain "The Rhythm of the Weekend"—what would actually take place and what it was hoped would be accomplished. Bob and Beth Barnes were fresh-faced, incredibly young looking, and brimming with zest and joie-de-vivre. They were obviously very much in love and seemed genuinely to enjoy being there, sharing what they had found in their own marriage. For the first time Betty began to relax and Don to lose his initial skepticism.

"Beth and I talked often," Bob said, "two years ago of making a get-away weekend and how great that would be just to pamper ourselves. Go to a fancy resort motel and have a ball. Then we heard about M.E. and Beth said, 'Wouldn't that be fun? Just the two of us for a whole weekend, concentrating on *Us* and what we mean to each other.' But I thought, 'What the hell are we going to talk about for a whole weekend? And what am I going to *do* with her all weekend, with no music or entertainment?' "

"Well, I found I had lots to say. And we're still saying it. And it was a very full weekend. Instead of making a get-away, we found we had a come-together weekend."

Beth pointed to a poster over her head which showed a mouth and two ears. "You might wonder," she said, "why God gave us two ears and just one mouth. Part of the problem of our marriage was that I talked too much and did too little listening. Our weekend gave me a chance really to listen to Bob for the first time. You won't believe how much I learned. Not only about him, but about myself. And we want to give you the same chance this weekend."

Taking turns, the two explained what was going to happen. The team couples, they insisted, including the religious members, were only there to start things going and keep them running. They would give some talks about various areas of marriage and share some of their own experiences—"not because we are in any way experts, but in the hope that in revealing some of our own mistakes and struggles you might see some of yours reflected." This was called the Presentation part of the weekend. But the heart of the Encounter, the only important part of it, was what the couples did on their own, with the help of their notebooks. After each presentation they were to be given some questions to reflect on and write about separately—the Personal Reflection, or P.R., part of the weekend. Then they were to come together as a couple, exchange notebooks and read what their spouses had written, then discuss them in the Couple Dialogue, or C.D. stage.

"There are two things we want to suggest," Beth said. "It's terribly important to be completely honest in what you write. Don't just put down what you think your spouse wants to hear. On the other hand, of course, don't use the notebooks simply as an outlet for your gripes and frustrations. Then, when you read what your partner has written, read it carefully—first with your mind, then with your heart. It's a love letter you're reading, for heaven's sake, even though you probably haven't written each other love letters for years. Finally, when discussing what you've both written, listen carefully to hear what the person is saying behind the words on the paper. A risk has been taken. Trust and understanding are essential."

Bob added, "I didn't want to write in a notebook when Beth and I made our Encounter, because I thought it was a waste of time. I thought we'd get a lot more done just talking together. But I quickly learned the value of the notebooks. I found I had to think out what I wanted to say instead of just blurting what I could before I was interrupted. And I was amazed at how much Beth had to say without my help or pointing out where she was wrong."

Beth stressed that what the couples should be dealing with in their writing and discussion was *feelings,* not thoughts or judgments. Early in life we learn to suppress our feelings, they said, so that we can fit into acceptable social patterns, and to avoid giving ourselves away (the most terrible of social sins). "When we fall in love," Bob said, "feelings take over. When we both feel the same way we get married. Then we start to think again and make judgments. But we want you to go back to those early feelings, to identify and understand them again. So, in your P.R., if you can substitute the word 'think' for 'feel', you're not making an encounter. You're not rediscovering each other."

Don's thoughts had wandered; he was snatched from his reverie by something Beth was saying ". . . brief explanation of the rhythm of the weekend, we are going to give you a chance to try it out with a short 5-minute P.R. and 5-minute C.D. Open your notebooks and write down:

   1. Why did I come here?
   2. What are my feelings about being here?"

After they had separated, Don to the bedroom, Betty to a bench by the lake, Don scribbled in his notebook:
   1. Apart from my curiosity about M.E., I wanted to get to know you better. In spite of our love, and all the time we've been married, we still don't know each other too well. Or, perhaps, we do know but don't want to take the trouble to do anything about it. I hope this weekend will be an opportunity for us to get closer—to understand each other's needs and hopes and fears.
   2. I guess the important things haven't started to happen yet. We've been talked at, instead of talking to each other. But I already feel close to you just because we are out of our usual rut. By ourselves in a group of strangers, instead of being surrounded by the kids and dogs (for whose affection, perhaps, we tend to compete.)
   Here it's just you and me, lonely, unsure of ourselves, like that night in the hotel in Washington, after our families and friends had left, and we were alone together for the first time.

27

Underneath it all, there's still some suspicion and skepticism. Are we being manipulated? Will anything worthwhile come out of the high hopes?

Betty wrote:

1. I came because I wanted to get away from Mother's Day. I wanted to be quiet and find me. I wanted to get to know this other you. I want my spirit to feel again.

2. Nothing much about being here. No anticipation. I'll try and be open. I'm so weary. And I'm so hungry.

This was read later, since the Demarests didn't get a chance to share their notebooks. The bell summoned them back to the conference room after only five minutes. Perhaps, they thought, this is only a dry run, a way to get us used to writing.

Some new posters had been added and the team couples began to explain more fully what they meant by feelings, and why, as a new banner proclaimed, "FEELINGS ARE NEITHER GOOD NOR BAD—THEY JUST ARE." Len said, "We focus on feelings because they make our dialogue more intimate and immediate. My feelings are a response to a person or situation, revealing where I am right now. Feelings are 'I' statements, '*I* feel this way,' '*I* am in this mood.' When we say, 'I feel that . . .' then we are in danger of making a judgment. Similes and metaphors, especially those involving such images as colors, foods, weather and animals, are helpful in clueing your partner in on what you mean. You should recognize that feelings often cover up other feelings. When we start with surface feelings we should dig harder to try and find out if there are deeper emotions below the surface that the superficial feelings are hiding."

Lynn and Gordy role-played some typical marital dialogue, starting with the judgmental, moving to the purely personal or neutral, and ending with the open and accepting.

"You're always buried in your newspaper," Lynn said. "You never pay attention to what I'm saying. It's like talking to a brick wall."

"But I am paying attention. I can repeat every word you said."

"You're not thinking about it. If you can read and listen to me at the same time, you obviously can't take what I'm saying too seriously."

"I'm sorry. It's a bad habit."

"Whenever you do that I feel rejected. Unimportant. Like excess baggage. Like the time you forgot to tell me you were

28

spending the weekend fishing with your boss, until I'd made other plans."

"I didn't realize that. I guess my problem is that I've been listening to people at the office all day, hundreds of problems. I really feel tense, like an overwound clock ready to spring. I want to relax for a few minutes before dinner."

"But I haven't had a chance to talk to a soul all day. There are some things I really want to discuss with you."

"And I want to talk to you, too. I do value what you say. There are some things I want to ask your opinion about. But I'm really not up to it, right now. Can we have a real talk after dinner? I can make a much better contribution then."

"You're right. I ought to go out and see how the dessert's coming, anyway. After dinner, then. I can't tell you how much I've missed you today."

At this point Lynn had begun to tune up her guitar and Gordy had passed out some song sheets. As the couples, tentatively at first, and then as fervently as the team couples, began to sing along to "Got to Get in Touch with the Way That I Feel," the invisible wall that seemed to separate some of them began to disappear.

Someone had turned out the lights and the faces reflected from the single candle in the middle of the room were relaxed and sharing.

The chords died away and Father John picked up a book that was lying on the table beside the candle. Father read Michael Quoist's "Lord, I Have Time." He bade the couples goodnight and suggested that they meditate about what they had heard and experienced since their arrival. For the Demarests nothing had ever seemed as welcome as the Charmer cherubs prancing on their bedroom door.

POSTSCRIPT

Don: A great deal was made on our weekend about feelings being neither good nor bad. I don't believe this is in the Calvo Manual. It seems to me that M.E. can encourage people to wallow in feelings like anger or sadness, rather than dealing with the one thing that can be changed or improved in a marriage—that is, attitudes.

Jerry: When you indulge too much in feelings you are being self-indulgent. I think it was Brother Don Byrne who said that a feeling that lasts for more than five minutes is no longer a feeling but an attitude.

Father Tom: The problem is talking too much about feelings. When we put on an Encounter for Indians (it's a very simple program that follows Calvo), there isn't too much stress on feelings, but rather intentions and behavior.

Marilyn: I disagree. There's more to dialogue than feelings, but feelings are terribly important. I have to make Jerry aware of my feelings, honestly, before I can reach any sort of honest dialogue with him. When I tell Jerry I feel tired or bad-tempered, he can understand my attitude or my behavior better by understanding the cause for it.

Jerry: But there can be too much made of feelings. If love is a feeling, rather than a commitment or an attitude, then when I fall out of love, lose the honeymoon illusion, there's nothing left.

Tom: The same thing applies to what happens after the weekend. When couples try to recapture that Second Honeymoon feeling, it can be false and lead to a big let-down.

Don: That Cloud Nine high?

Tom: Right. It's a tremendous problem for the clergy. When you take the M.E. model and try to use it in the parish, people expect the high they've heard about on the weekend and they're disappointed.

Jerry: Now we're talking about after the weekend. The first step in any communication process is learning how to share feelings. It's a lot easier to hide behind attitudes and ideas. Carl Rogers (in *Becoming Partners*[2]) says that the first step in discovering yourself is to become truly aware of your feelings. Then, when you share your deepest and most vulnerable feelings with your partner, it almost always draws a similar sharing. He says something about "such sharing provides an enormous body of sensitive, quivering data (I think I'm quoting him right) which the two of you can use to improve the quality of your relationship."

Don: But Rogers also deals with attitudes and ideas.

Jerry: There has been a big controversy in M.E. about this. Father Jerry Haladus' article in *Agape*[3] about the need to think about our feelings brought a storm of protest.

Don: All the same, Father Jim Friedel's talk at Dayton on the importance of attitudes was immensely popular. It seems to me he was saying that although feelings are neither right nor

2. De'acorte, N.Y., 1972.
3. November, 1975.

30

wrong, the attitudes underlying the feelings and the behavior which comes from them can be moral or immoral.

Tom: It's legitimate to recognize, he says, that "I've got a lousy feeling because I've got a lousy attitude." If the attitude is what is causing the conflict, then it's got to be examined if the relationship is going to be improved.

Don: It's the same point Ed Golden is making in his article.[4] He's against judging anyone else's feelings, but he suggests that in order to grow we have to take a close look at our own feelings and the attitudes behind them. Some of my feelings are downright destructive, not only for myself but for the people I live with. Should I simply say (he says) "Well I can't help it, that's how I feel," and go my merry way?

Jerry: Ed may have something when he says that in the traditional M.E. approach there is almost an Eleventh Commandment: Thou shalt not judge any feelings, not thy spouse's, nor thy neighbor's, nor even thy own.

Tom: Yes, the temptation is just to say, "I have strong feelings about this and I told you how I feel. You'll just have to accept me as I am." If I've revealed my feelings, I'm absolved from blame or any need to make any accommodations.

Marilyn: All right. One should be aware of the attitudes behind one's feelings, esecially if they are counter-productive. But if you start analyzing the other person's feelings, you start making judgments and begin the vicious circle all over again.

Tom: Ed, and Jim, too, are only suggesting that we try to uncover the attitude behind any of our own feelings that seem destructive. Not to judge or analyze our partner's feelings.

Betty: For me the big highlight of the weekend was discovering Don's feelings. After thirty years of marriage I know a lot about his ideas and attitudes. But I didn't really know how he *felt* about a lot of things, including me.

Jerry: The first step in learning to communicate is getting at the real, gut feelings. If this doesn't happen on the weekend, probably nothing else will. But after the weekend, there are other avenues you can explore. Marilyn and I took part in the Interpersonal Communication Program, and we learned to be aware of sensations first, then interpretations, feelings, intentions and actions, with the help of their "Awareness Wheel."

4. February, 1976.

Don: Father Friedel holds up the Beatitudes as the sort of attitudes that Christians should strive for. He says that if you make these a part of your life, your feelings and emotions will fall into place. You'll be able to relate to others in a happy, healthy, positive way.

Tom: And this is really what Gabriel Calvo is saying. He talks about Dialogue *in* the Lord. About communication on all levels—intellectual, sexual, spiritual as well as emotional.

Jerry: I guess the key to the Encounter is not to exaggerate any one aspect, or to stay too long in any one stage, but to move along with the flow, as Calvo planned.

PART TWO—SATURDAY MORNING

The next morning birds were singing but the couples were mostly silent—a comfortable talked-out silence, as they wolfed down platters of ham and eggs.

Back in the conference room the candle had been relit, although it was hard to distinguish its wavering flame in the bright sunlight. Beside it were a single rose in a long-stemmed vase and a paperback Bible. Father John picked it up and read the passage from Ecclesiastes which begins, "For everything there is a season and a time for every matter under heaven." In the background the cassette player, which had been providing background music, was turned up and the words became distinguishable. They were Pete Seeger's song, based on the passage Father John had just read—"Turn, Turn, Turn" sung by the New Seekers.

"As the preacher said," Father John remarked, "there is a time for everything and now it's time to look at the most basic element of the weekend and that is myself. The most difficult person I have to come into contact with each day is that image that glares back at me from the bathroom mirror each morning. The raw facts before I have a chance to make it ready for the world by shaving off its whiskers, patting on skin bracer, practicing a smile."

He spoke of all the roles he was preparing to play during the day—priest, teacher, coach, member of the archdiocesan school board, chaplain to the K of C, superior, son. But somehow he found it difficult to find the real person behind all the roles. And if he did manage to find it, could he accept it, be at peace with it, love it? That was the hard part. "Because," he said, "before I can love someone else—before I can be a loving priest, teacher, chaplain or coach—I must be able to love

32

myself. Until I can look in the mirror and smile at what I see, I will be afraid to smile at anyone else."

But sometimes, he said, it was hard to find his true self among all the roles, the masks he wore to keep people from seeing his weaknesses, his failings, the places where he bled. "I guess my safest camouflage is my Roman collar."

Gordy told them that as far back as he could remember he had trouble showing his feelings. It was a way of avoiding conflict. In most cases he would go along with the crowd—go to the movie or restaurant someone else suggested, without making his own preference known. This persisted into his marriage. "If some unexpected invitation came up—to play bridge or go to a ball game—Lynn would be excited, but I would resent it. Perhaps I'd planned to work in the garden or watch TV, but I wouldn't say anything. It didn't seem important, and we'd go. Lynn would catch my resentment and after it was over, a quarrel would flare up. All because I'd hidden my real feelings in order to keep things cool."

"If you were to ask me right now how old I am," Lynn said, "I probably couldn't tell you. I live in the memory of yesterday and the expectation of tomorrow and seldom appreciate the glory and beauty of just today. For some reason I find little satisfaction in the present. The result is I wallow in feeling sorry about yesterday's spilt milk and anticipating tomorrow's splendor. But I build such high hopes for it that I'm almost always disappointed. It's a vicious circle." Lynn, who'd given the impression of such serene self-assurance, admitted that the reason she had so much trouble accepting the present was that she had a poor self-image. "Because I don't accept myself, I find it hard to accept what happens. I find it hard to accept the fact that this is the Lord's day and that it's a clean slate on which to accomplish something worthwhile."

"Speaking of masks," Bob said, "my two favorites were my Little Boy mask which I use in stores to get better service from old ladies and the other was Joe Macho which I put on when people put me down because I look so young. Then I go back to the vocabulary and strut like I did when I was a sergeant in the Marine Corps." His Marriage Encounter had done away with the necessity for masks. When Beth told him that she had rediscovered the person she'd fallen in love with, the person she'd always thought of as the real Bob, he realized what a waste of time his play-acting was.

Beth grinned at us impishly. "For a long time I didn't think it was necessary to encounter myself. I was satisfied with coasting along and never knowing why I was happy or sad, angry or bored. For years I just accepted my fluctuations of mood as heredity. My father is an extremely moody man and everyone accommodates to his moods. For years that was my rationalization. I was my father's daughter. Bob made it very clear that he wasn't marrying my dad."

Beth admitted that it had taken her a long time to grow up. Even after her marriage she played house and when things went wrong she'd revert to her little girl roles using the tricks that had always worked: being winsome, or, if that failed, tears. Then, one day, she had looked in the mirror and had been terrified at what she saw. Bob walked in on her and found her crying. When he asked what was wrong, she had exploded: "I'm old and fat and ugly." He'd let her sob for a while, then he asked, "What would you do if I died?" "I'd be lost." "Right! And that's exactly what I'd be without you. Don't you know that I love you and that you're the most important person in my life and even when you do get old you'll still be beautiful to me?"

"For me," Beth said, "that was the turning point. I began to look at myself more objectively. At last I began to accept the things that made me different from everyone else. The things that Bob had recognized all along as I went swinging up and down like a yo-yo."

Father John summed it up: "Somewhere along the line we learn that there is something shameful about loving ourselves. Yet Jesus told us to love our neighbor as ourself. Real self love is not a selfish love. Real self love is an honest acceptance of my personhood. I have been created in the image of God. And God doesn't make junk."

This time the couples were asked to answer three questions in their notebooks for themselves alone. These questions would not be shared. They were: *What do I really like about (a) myself, (b) you, (c) us?*

Betty wrote:

1. At the moment I can't think of anything I like about myself. Perhaps something will come to me later.

2. I like your strength. I like your opinions. I really do like your knowledge. I like your capacity to be yourself. I like your tolerance. I like your willingness to learn. I like to hear you laugh. I like your tenderness to the dogs.

3. I like the way we dance together.

34

Don wrote:

1. That I have overcome the feelings of being unlovable that my father instilled in me. That I have learned to accept love (not as easily as most people do). That I was finally capable of loving you and the kids. On the whole now, I'm capable of liking people and trusting them to like me back. I guess this makes me less selfish and self-centered than I used to be.

2. As I said before the group, I like your freshness, your ability to enjoy things in a simple way, your openness, your honesty. The fact that, unlike me, you don't view everything in relationship to yourself. You aren't questioning and adding up people's reactions, wondering if they like you or whether you're lovable. (Maybe this isn't always true, but I think you're a lot more open and less self-conscious than I am. And when you aren't, it's been my fault. It's been what I have done to you.)

3. As D.H. Lawrence said of his marriage, I'm proud that we "have come through . . ." a lot of heartaches, misunderstandings, hurt feelings. Perhaps at last we're beginning to grow up a bit and can now (finally in our 50s) begin to start adding to each other instead of picking away. I think this is quite a recent thing, but I trust it. I'm almost beginning to think that we're headed for a (not serene, we could never be *serene)* cantankerously happy, joyfully battling, 'we're in this together, luv,' old age. (Perhaps we're getting close to being able to laugh at ourselves. As a pair, instead of as individuals.)

When they went back to the conference room, Lynn was tuning her guitar again. The words to "I Wish I Knew How It Feels to Be Free" seemed appropriate, especially "I wish I could break all the chains holding me."

They were presented three more questions—this time to be shared definitely with spouses. They were:

1. *What are my masks and fears?*
2. *When do I use them?*
3. *What do I like about myself?*

Betty wrote:

1. My best mask is being so damned thoughtful, trying to anticipate everyone's needs, when actually I'm hoping that other people will wait on me. I want people to do things for me, to fulfill my needs. But I really don't know

35

what I need. My latest mask is unselfishness, when, underneath, I'm really terribly greedy.

2. Constantly.

3. I like my thoughtfulness, I like my unselfishness—when these are my real feelings and not my masks. I like my capacity for love. I like my capacity for hate. I like my ability to listen.

Don wrote:

1. Again, because of my childhood, I have a terror of being unloved—so my main mask is one of indifference: "I care for nobody, no not I, if nobody cares for me." And so another mask is anger. If someone encroaches on my private island, if anyone asks anything of me—especially love, or a sign of affection, or just help with the housework—I put on my mad mask, or my mask of cold disdain. And the mask behind this mask is Hurt Feelings. When, repulsed by my mask of indifference or contempt, people don't ask me to join them, ask me to love them, tell me they love me, I put on my martyr mask.

2. and 3. I am using them less and I like myself when I recognize them as masks, or try to do something about the feelings that prompt them. In spite of the emotional scar tissue and the habits of my childhood and adolescence, I can still show emotion. Increasingly I'm able to put out a hand without being scared that it will be rejected. Basically, I think I am a warm, caring person. Or, perhaps, the masks of being warm and caring are getting more natural and honest, less of an act.

I like myself when I'm honest and natural, just as I hate myself when I'm either reserved and withdrawn or (even more so) when my outgoingness is a big, phoney Chamber-of-Commerce Glad Hand. I guess I am suspicious of the times when I seem warm and friendly only to get equal amounts, carefully measured, of love in return. What is hard, especially, is to be outgoing and loving just for their own sake and not to get something in return. To love you for you and not just so that you'll love me back.

When the Demarests met in their bedroom and read each other's notebooks as appreciatively as if they had been love letters, as carefully as if they contained the clues to a treasure hunt, Don said to Betty, "One thing seems obvious about both of us. Our masks are often the same as our virtues, the things we like best about ourselves. So what's wrong with wearing a mask, if it's a pleasant one?"

Betty: "I can recognize when you're wearing a mask. And even when it's a nice one, it's a put down."

Don: "Think about this, though. Even when being kind or caring is a mask, it can grow into a habit or an attitude. So the right masks can become flesh and a permanent part of our faces. There's nothing we can do about our emotions. But we can change our attitudes and habits. If I put on a smiling mask consciously, my behavior tends to match it. Just as if I put on an angry mask or a disdainful mask, my behavior follows."

Betty: "Because people react to your mask. If it's a threatening one, they are scared. If it's a humorous one, they're amused."

Don: "So, a good mask is better than an anti-social emotion. Emotions may be morally neutral. But they can be modified and channeled. And they can start a chain reaction. So many of our fights come from misinterpreting a gesture or facial expression. Then one over-reacts to a fancied slight or presumed lack of concern."

Betty: "But if we express our feeling, we don't need masks. I like your naked face best, even when it's sad, which it often is in repose."

Don: "All right. Naked, unguarded, spontaneous, trusting. These are the opposites to masks. And they're bridges we can build on."

Betty: "I like the face you have on now. It's excited, interested and unself-conscious. Like a little boy's. The way you looked on our first date."

POSTSCRIPT:

Don: Earlier we were discussing whether feelings could be good or bad. Should all masks be condemned? Or are some necessary? Like good manners. White lies. I guess what I'm trying to say is: Should we ever hide our feelings?

Jerry: I suppose you should seriously ask yourself, "What masks do I wear? And why?" How do I really want people to see me? I used to wear the masks of the Perfect Father, Loving Husband, Successful Provider. Then it changed. I wanted people to see me as a Christian, someone who cares about others, who reaches out a hand.

37

Don: But is that a mask? If that's what you mean to be, even if it's not completely realized, I'd say it was a role rather than a mask.

Marilyn: You don't have to get rid of masks. Just recognize them. If Jerry's mask is being the "Perfect Father" or the "Good Christian" he should be aware that he is doing so.

Betty: During our weekend we almost decided that choosing the right mask, the "Concerned Christian" to use your example or the "Friendly Face," is almost a step in the right direction. If you try to live up to the mask you've chosen. And it doesn't hurt anyone.

Jerry: As long as you don't take the mask for the reality. As long as you remain open and vulnerable.

Father Tom: As long as you aren't playing games.

Marilyn: Or trying to manipulate your spouse. If Jerry comes home from work and the house is a mess because the kids were supposed to clean it up, I can put on my martyr mask. I can whine and say, "I can't do anything with those kids. They promised to clean the house, but just look at it! I suppose I'll have to do it all by myself." I'm trying to manipulate Jerry into taking over. Probably he'll lose his temper and shout at the kids, and everybody will be resentful. But if I admit honestly, "I'm exhausted. Do you think you can talk the kids into cleaning up," things will then probably work out with a minimum of friction.

Jerry: Encounter with Self is finding out how you feel and laying the cards on the table.

Marilyn: Yes, recognizing and admitting the hidden agenda is essential for any worthwhile relationship.

Don: First of all you try not to play games with yourself. Then you play honestly with your partner.

Tom: You have to become child-like, as Christ said, instead of childish. To be childish is to indulge in moods. To be child-like is to be open, without guile.

Betty: I remember our daughter Marie with her wedding gown. Suddenly she dropped all her defenses. She was entirely open and vulnerable, but happy and trusting. I hadn't seen that side of her for years.

Tom: The person is a mystery, like God and the universe. A continuous revelation. M.E. tries to encourage and perpetuate the revelation—to oneself and others.

Marilyn: One weekend I heard the perfect example about what encountering yourself means. This wife said (I can't remember if it was a team couple), "If you wanted to give someone a marvelous gift, you wouldn't wrap it in a beautiful box with ribbons and ornaments, unless you knew what was inside."

Jerry: That's why Calvo starts with the Encounter with Self. You have to know yourself before you can be of any use to anyone else.

Tom: Kierkegaard talks about the danger of losing yourself. You notice the loss of an arm or a leg immediately. But you can lose yourself without being aware of it.

Don: Carl Rogers says that first you must discover yourself, then accept yourself. The most important discovery, he says, is that "the thing which can't *possibly* be revealed to the other *can* be revealed, the problem which you *must* keep to yourself *can* be shared."

Betty: The three big moments of the weekend for me were personal discoveries. 1. That I wasn't as bad a person as I thought I was. 2. That Don accepts me for the person I am. 3. That I don't have to play games with God.

Don: Carl Rogers quotes one of his clients as saying, "I've found out that the horrid black ball inside me is the most lovable part of me; the part that I thought was ugliest is the most beautiful because I've learned to share it."

Marilyn: It's a tremendous release not having to carry the burden of yourself. To find someone willing to share it.

Don: Are there any exercises apart from those on the weekend that can help a couple to discover themselves and share themselves? Something that anybody could do at home?

Jerry: You can take a sheet of paper and divide it into two columns. List all your good points in one column. Your faults in the other. Usually the negative list is much longer.

Marilyn: Tom taught me to look at it like a batting average. What is Rod Carew of the Minnesota Twins hitting? 400? That means he is wrong 60% of the time. Ask yourself, "How often do I behave like this? Do I lose my temper six times out of ten?" It's more likely one in ten. And then look at the percentages of your good points. Are you kind four times out of ten? It's liable to be at least six out of ten. We underestimate our virtues and exaggerate our faults.

Jerry: Let your spouse list your good points. You'll find that he or she comes up with a lot more than you do.

Don: What about the "Emotional Inventory" they run every now and then in the magazine?

Marilyn: Anything you do together is reassuring. Your parents, spouse and children know you best. And they love you in spite of your faults. It's only you who expect yourself to be perfect.

M.E. Materials
GUIDELINES FOR DIALOGUE*

W 1. Make your reflection a love letter.
2. Do your written reflections separately but with your partner foremost in mind.
3. Describe feelings in fullest detail to trigger partner's memory.
4. Refer to partner with direct address frequently in the letter, using name or endearing term, but avoid sentimentality for its own sake.
5. Be honest, but make it attractive; invite your partner to feel it—even though feelings can be shared with gentleness.

E 6. Exchange notebooks lovingly, and without comment; go to your partner's notebook seeking the person, not information.
7. Work at the reading and dialogue proper with as much intensity as the written reflection.
8. Read the reflection twice, once for the feelings and once seeking the person behind the feelings.

D 9. After two readings, identify and share the feelings triggered. Begin conversation with, "What are your feelings now that you have read my letter?"
10. Select the feeling(s) most meaningful to the relationship which should be explored so the relationship may grow.
11. Describe your partner's feelings back to him, suggesting tentatively what you're picking up, giving him/her an opportunity to share more of himself/herself.
12. Search through your partner's feeling until you live it as your own, working along with your partner—word pictures, intensity, duration, a time you felt the same way—manifesting a desire to know the person more.
13. Avoid attacking or judging your partner's feelings or defending your own.
14. If any decision comes in dialogue, it's not a dialogue.

S 15. Select question for next dialogue.

*W = Writing; E = Exchange; D = Dialogue; S = Select Question for next Dialogue

40

SOME STATEMENTS THAT CAN SET UP
BARRIERS TO COMMUNICATIONS

1. PERSUADING WITH LOGIC, ARGUING, INSTRUCTING, LECTURING *("Do you realize . . .," "Here is why you are wrong . . .," "That is not right . . .," "The facts are . . .," "Yes, but . . ..)*
Such responses provoke defensiveness and often bring on counter-arguments. Persuasion, more often than not, simply makes the other defend his own position more strongly. A reaction can be, "you always think you're right." Having logic on your side does not always bring forth compliance or agreement.

2. ADVISING, RECOMMENDING, PROVIDING ANSWERS OR SOLUTIONS *("What I would do is . . .," "Why don't you . . .," "It would be best for you . . ..")*
It is not true that people always want advice. Advice implies "superiority" and can make the other feel inadequate and inferior. If the advice does not seem sound, then the person has to argue against it and spend time dealing with it rather than think up his own solutions.

3. EVALUATING, JUDGING NEGATIVELY, DISAPPROVING, BLAMING, NAME-CALLING, CRITICIZING *("You are not thinking straight.")*
More than any other type of message, this makes one feel inadequate, inferior, incompetent, bad or stupid. The response is very defensive—nobody likes to be wrong. Evaluation cuts off communication—"I won't tell them what I feel if I am going to get judged." Another response to evaluation is to evaluate right back—"You're not so good yourself."

4. DIAGNOSING, PSYCHOANALYZING, INTERPRETING, READING-IN, OFFERING INSIGHTS *("What you need is . . .," "What's wrong with you is . . .," "You don't really mean that," "Your problem is . . ..")*
To tell someone what he or she is "really" feeling, what his/her "real" motives are, can be very threatening. If your analysis is wrong, there is resistance; if it is "right," the other can feel exposed, naked, trapped. The "here-is-what-you-need" message implies superiority. People get resentful and angry when someone interprets their motives.

41

Interpretations, more than likely, will stop communication rather than encourage him/her to tell you more.

5. KIDDING, TEASING, MAKING LIGHT OF, JOKING, USING SARCASM *("When did you read a newspaper last?", "Get up on the wrong side of the bed?", "When did they make you President?")*
Such responses effectively cut off communication, make the other feel you are not interested and show lack of respect. They often will produce an angry response. Or the other may feel you really don't understand how seriously he/she feels about something. Responses such as these often stem from hostility in the speaker; consequently, they may provoke counter-hostility.

AN EMOTIONAL INVENTORY

One of the surest ways of achieving personal identity is to record and report your emotions and feelings. We must learn to listen to our true feelings and report them in a mature way, refraining from all temptations to moralize our feelings as good or bad, reasonable or unreasonable. We must not try and tell our feelings what they should or ought to be, but we must let them tell us what they are.

The following is a partial list of emotions which the normal person feels from time to time. It is suggested you use pencils or pens of two different colors to indicate your ability to **record** and your ability to **report.** Draw a line from the margin line on the right of the emotion through and into the box that most approximately describes the frequency of your experience of the emotion listed and put an X there. Then, with a different color pen, draw a second line under the first to indicate the frequency of your reporting this emotion to others and put an X in the appropriate box. There may be a variation, e.g., I may feel angry frequently, but never show it. After you have finished the inventory, share it with your spouse.

The only questions or discussions that are in order are those that invite fuller description of the emotions that are felt, or the possible, factual reasons why some emotion is never felt. Stay away from "should" or "ought" where feelings are concerned. Stay with what is factual. There is no such thing as a moral or immoral emotion, no such thing as a reasonable or unreasonable feeling.

EXAMPLE

	never	*rarely*	*often*	*very often*
Accepted	|	| X |	X |	|

Interpretation of example: I often (box 3) feel accepted by others, but I rarely (box 2) express this feeling to others.

FEELINGS	*never*	*rarely*	*often*	*very often*		*never*	*rarely*	*often*	*very often*
Accepted					Creative				
Affectionate					Cruel				
Anger					Curious				
Anxious					Defeated				
Anxious to Please Others					Dejected				
Apathetic					Dependent				
Beautiful					Depressed				
Bewildered					Deprived				
Cheated					Desperate				
Compassionate					Disappointed in Self				
Competent					Disappointed with Others				
Confident					Dominated				
Confused					Domineering				
Cowardly					Eager to Impress				

43

FEELINGS

	never	rarely	often	very often		never	rarely	often	very often
Easily Manipulated					Inadequate				
Embarrassed					Incompetent				
Fatalistic					Inconstant				
Fear					Indecisive				
Flirtatious					Independent				
Frustrated					Inferior				
Generous					Insincere				
Grateful					Isolated (alone)				
Gratified w/personal accomplishment					Jealous				
Grudge-Bearing					Lonely				
Guilty					Loved by another				
Happy					Loving of others				
Hatred					Loyal				
Homicidal					Manipulated				
Hopeful					Manipulative of others				
Humorous					Masked				
Ignored					Masochistic				

44

FEELINGS	never	rarely	often	very often
Melancholy				
Misunderstood				
Optimistic				
Passionate				
Peaceful				
Persecuted				
Pessimistic				
Phony				
Pity for others				
Pleased with others				
Pleased with Self				
Possessive				
Poutish				
Prejudiced				
Protective of others				
Proud of others				
Proud of self				

	never	rarely	often	very often
Rejected by others				
Remorseful (sorry)				
Repulsive				
Sad				
Sadistic				
Self Pity				
Sexually Aroused				
Shy				
Sinful				
Sluggish				
Sorry for self				
Stubborn				
Superior to others				
Suspicious of others				
Sympathy				
Tender				
Terrified				

FEELINGS	never	rarely	often	very often		never	rarely	often	very often
Threatened					Used by others				
Tolerant					Useless				
Ugly					Violent				
Unappreciated					Weary of Living				
Uncertain of others					Wishy-Washy				
Uncertain of self					Wishing to die Suicidal feelings				
Ungifted					Youthful (exuberant)				
Unresponsive									

MARRIAGE ENRICHMENT AT HOME*
Thinking Together

Individually, complete the following sentence stems. Then compare your completed sentences. How were your sentence completions alike? How do you account for any similarities or differences? What can you learn from discovering your own ideas, your partner's ideas, and your partner's perceptions of your ideas on subjects such as these?

1. When I wake up in the morning, I feel _____

My partner feels _____

This often results in _____

*Reprinted from *Marriage Enrichment,* the ACME newsletter, Nov.-Dec. 1976.

46

2. When we go to parties, crowds always make me feel ____

   In crowds, my spouse feels ____

   So we ____

3. I want to spend our vacation time by ____

   My partner thinks we should use it for ____

   Generally, we ____

4. In terms of personality traits, my partner tends to be ____

   I think I am inclined toward ____

   This is reflected in ____

5. I look around and compare what we have with what other couples our age have and I feel ____

   My partner feels ____

6. With respect to privacy, I enjoy ____

   My spouse needs ____

   We meet these needs by ____

7. We occasionally discuss "living for today" versus "saving and planning for the future." My partner says ____

   I tend to think that ____

8. Our life goal together is _____

   _____

   My spouse's life goal is _____

   _____

   And mine is _____

   _____

9. I believe the most effective way to keep a marriage growing
   is to _____

   _____

   My spouse acts as if the most effective way to insure a
   growing marriage is to _____

   _____

10. If I could change any one thing about our marriage, I'd
    change _____

    _____

    I suspect my spouse would change _____

    _____

Chapter Three

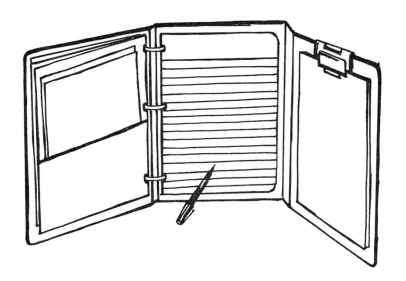

CHAPTER THREE

The Second Stage of the Weekend:
The Encounter with Each Other
Or "Does Our Marriage Indicate
Symptoms of Spiritual Divorce?"

PART ONE—SATURDAY NOON

After a quick coffee-and-cookie break, the couples found themselves back in the conference room. The sun was pouring through the windows like a benediction and children were yelling gleefully across the lake. But, inside, the atmosphere was as purposeful and concentrated as a conference on world peace.

Bob and Beth were unexpectedly serious, almost somber, as they discussed the state of marriage in the modern world. In 1922, they said, one out of seven U.S. marriages ended in divorce. In 1972 it was one in three. In 1975 there were 2,133,000 marriages and 1,077,000 divorces—which means that almost every other marriage will be dissolved. But these represent only the legal dissolutions and don't take into account separations and the much larger number of marriages in name only—marriages which are continued for reasons of convenience or laziness, for the sake of the children or through economic necessity.

Father John spoke of the Vatican Council's document on *The Church in the Modern World* in which it is stressed that marriage today is under terrible stress: "Serious disturbances (he quoted) are caused in families by modern economic conditions, by influences at once social and psychological, and by the demands of modern society."

51

Falling in love, he told them, is as easy as it ever was. Staying in love these days is much harder—without the support of custom, the extended family, the support of one's community. Most of us, when we get married ("which includes my marriage to you, the Church") believe that it will last forever, that ours is the exceptional case: *Love Story* without the leukemia, a tale of devotion to astound a cynical world.

"The crisis of modern marriage," he said, "also affects our own marriages. However, a marriage crisis is not the death of love, but the proof. As gold is proved in a crucible, love is proved in crisis. Perhaps you have reached the bottom of your selfishness, but you haven't gotten to the bottom of your love. Instinct is exhausted but not the mind or the heart. Now that you have experienced your full capacity for selfishness, it's time to experiment with your capacity for love."

Gordy took up the dialogue. "As you can tell from Father John's talk, we're beginning to talk about marriage now, talking about her and me, talking about us—not just me. This is the beginning of the second stage of the weekend, the We stage. This is where we examine our relationship as a couple, take the risk of being open with each other through dialogue, in order to realize the full potential of our marriage. The take-off point for this stage of our Encounter is the Basic Law of Growth, with its three stages: Illusion, Disillusion and Joy. A lot of marriages come apart because they fail to reckon with the Basic Law."

According to Lynn, the first or Illusion stage of our marriage is when we see our partners as we would like them to be. Perhaps for a girl he is that knight on the dashing charger who will whisk her away from her dull world of textbooks and family chores to a fairyland of eternal bliss. Expectations play a major role, and expectations are usually a search for self-gratification in which the Other exists only to fulfill my needs. This is the person I see in the family album.

"Back about 15 years ago, Gordy had been out of college a year and I was a junior. Some of our friends were already married and we thought this would be a great adventure. I dreamed of going with Gordy to golden autumn football games, returning to an apartment right out of *House Beautiful* to celebrate the victory with our friends, of all the independence I would have as a wife and student, with no dorm curfew, and all the hours I would have with Gordy at my beck and call."

"I had a different dream," Gordy admitted. "While I was at

work somebody would be doing all the cooking and cleaning I'd come to loathe as a bachelor.

"Then our evenings would be free for fun and romance. There might be slight money problems, but surely Love Would Conquer All."

The next step, however, was already upon them. Once a couple begins to recognize that one's spouse is just a human being, and the world outside the dream cottage is cold and practical, that dream of "living happily ever after" breaks down into three realities:

1. *I am not what I thought I was;*
2. *She is not what I thought she was;*
3. *Communication between us on all levels is more difficult than we thought.*

Liz and Len had been married even younger, while they were still in high school—with similar illusions. Len thought that "apart from being married to the prettiest girl in the world" he wouldn't have to answer to his parents for his conduct, could do anything he wanted, and stay out as late as he liked. The disillusion set in when the first two babies came right after each other. Len had to spend long hours at work to support his family and Liz seemed entirely preoccupied with the house and the children.

According to Len, "The honeymoon really didn't last very long. I found that my wife was even more demanding of my time than my parents had ever been and that the world didn't owe me a living." Because home, with the baby bottles and diapers, wasn't anything like he'd imagined, Len worked at two jobs—"partly as an excuse for not having to be there." Then, after four children, he still felt a loner. His main preoccupation was, "Why can't Liz understand me? She's certainly not the person I married."

The turning point in their marriage came when their four-year-old boy suddenly shouted in the middle of the night: "Hey, you guys cut that fighting out!" It was a warning sign and a roadmark in their lives. They began to communicate better, and as they did so, they learned that they both really wanted the same things, but hadn't been able to convey that longing.

"Now we're in the joy stage of our marriage," Len said. "I have found that Liz exceeds all my expectations. Now she is not only my wife and lover, but also my best friend. Of course, we don't stay on that plane, we still fight."

Liz pointed out that long before the actual legal divorce a marriage can show signs of dissolution. Although we may be living closely together, we are simply co-existing, sharing the same quarters, as "married singles." There are certain symptoms to watch for, she said, which signal the onset of "Spiritual Divorce"—which can be summarized as "a closeness of bodies but remoteness of souls," with external agreement but deep mental and emotional disagreement.

Among the symptoms she had recognized in her own marriage were: mutual sentiments of disillusionment, boredom and competition; indifference to the other's problems; frequent quarrels; feelings of being alone and misunderstood.

Len provided an example of a crisis in their married life. After he and Liz had been married for eight years he went into business for himself, operating a service station. Although he had a mechanical background, he knew nothing about business management. As the problems piled up and the time he had to spend on the job increased, he found it impossible to communicate with Liz. Spending many fourteen-hour days, eating and sleeping much of the time, at his place of business, he looked on Liz as a live-in baby-sitter, cook and house-keeper.

"I was leading the life of a loner," he admitted. "Our communication was zero. I was even beginning to resent the kids."

"Len and I lived in the same house," Liz added, "were the parents of the same children and even shared the same bed. But we were becoming strangers, with almost nothing in common. I really hated that damned service station of his. When he came home from it he was too tired to do anything but sleep. I had almost forgotten what it was to have an adult conversation."

It was evident from the pain on Liz's face that she wasn't enjoying reliving this painful period. The warm sunshine flooding the conference room seemed to belie what was being said. As Len clutched his wife's hand to give her the strength to go on, several other couples were exchanging glances and nodding in acknowledgement of similar experiences.

"This was the period of my selfishness," Liz went on. "I had MY home, MY kitchen, MY children, and I thought I was doing everything that could be expected of a wife and mother. But I was feeling very neglected. When I told Len of my loneliness he would answer with his financial problems. We were so wrapped up in our own troubles that we had no time for the other's tale of woe. Even God seemed distant. I went to Mass frequently and taught the children to pray—but it was a matter-of-fact, dry, spirituality. The poster on that wall sums it up." Liz pointed to: WHEN GOD SEEMS DISTANT, WHO MOVED?

Gordy and Lynn next shared some moments of the spiritual and emotional crisis in their marriage. Gordy pointed out that once we recognize the symptoms of spiritual divorce, admit that our marriage is not everything it should be, we've crossed the first high hurdle. "It's like an alcoholic. He can't be helped until he admits he has a problem. We have to find the infection that is causing the fever—isolate the symptoms and then treat them."

"Our problem wasn't lack of love," Lynn said, "or even a diminution in our affection. It was simply an inability to communicate this love, which was interpreted as indifference. When this feeling of indifference has reached a certain stage, the symptoms of divorce are at fever pitch. Real divorce may be around the corner."

Father John demonstrated that the symptoms could exist in a religious community as well as a marriage. When the superior doesn't listen to the grievances of his fellow priests and brothers, when personal habits and preferences conflict, when there are arguments about the cooking and cleaning up, the community is faced with *its* symptoms of spiritual divorce. "What I'm trying to say is that behind those mysterious walls we have the same problems you do. Community life can be a disaster without dialogue and communication."

At this point Bob and Beth handed out a blue sheet headed by a cartoon of couples shouting at each other and the title, SYMPTOMS OF SPIRITUAL DIVORCE. (See end of chapter). As this was being read, the cassette player gave forth with Simon and Garfunkel's "Sounds of Silence."

Don read some of the symptoms to himself: "Almost habitual sadness in the married couple and the family; mutual sentiments of disillusionment, boredom and emptiness, indifference to each other's problems; frequent or habitual coldness in relationships . . . "

(Deep chords, "the words of the prophets are written on the subway walls and tenement halls, and whispered in the sounds of silence." More guitar chords. A profound hush.)

Don and Betty took the next questions off to their private lairs—Betty beside the lake, Don to a sycamore tree behind the tennis court. In answer to 1: What symptoms of spiritual divorce do I find (feel) presently existing in our marriage? Betty wrote:

I suspect that we have too little time for each other. We always seem to be in a rush and when we have to talk about something important I feel I have to make it as short and essential as possible so I won't waste the time you need for your writing. This makes me feel terribly inadequate and frustrated. I know your writing is important, but does it have to exclude me and the children? Is our life together completely unimportant compared to your dream world?

In answer to question two, what do I think (feel) is causing these symptoms, Betty wrote:

I think that I'm too wrapped up in myself. What you have to say about your day—even if it's only that you had the same bus driver both ways—is important enough for me to stop my dishwashing or vacuuming and listen. What drives me up a tree is that damned TV set. The few moments we might have for each other we are taken up by IT. I think that it stands between us like a sinister demon. Sometimes I have a terrible urge to take an ax to it.

Don wrote:

1. I feel abandoned and lonely in the things that mean the most to me. I feel (sense) that you aren't really interested in the novel which, for me, is a terrible struggle to express who I am and what I believe in. You aren't really interested in me, even to the extent that my students are. At the same time I have a hunch that I don't really appreciate all you do to make my writing possible, the cooking and cleaning. I fail to recognize—or communicate—all that you've taught me, that you contribute to the novel as well as to my whole life. I feel that you feel I don't appreciate this. I recognize that my being tied up every evening and weekend on the book is unfair. That it doesn't give you a chance for shared recreation and your right place in our marriage. This leads to mutual feelings of coldness, bad humor and anger (or, what's worse, a silent, pregnant resentfulness).

2. Sometimes I have a hunch that I can share my hopes and fears more easily (at least safely) with my students. I guess the wall I have built up here is because I don't really trust you to understand what I'm trying to do and how

hard it is. My writing is such a naked, desperate thing, that it is very touchy ground for us to meet on, and so I've been unwilling to share it with you.

When I'm unhappy, or touchy, or *scared* to be touched, my reaction (it goes back to my childhood) is sarcasm. This adds more stones to the wall between us, more feelings of hurt to excuse my hiding behind my little barricade of words. And silence.

They have been talking about the *macho* complex—about it being hard for a man to show tenderness or appreciation by touch, by words, by giving thanks. This is compacted for me by phony demonstrations of affection in my childhood. Unless tenderness and gratitude are expressed spontaneously—without forethought, almost unconsciously—I tend to suspect they are hypocritical. When we are close, I find it easy to touch and thank. The minute the wall is up I find it impossible.

When the Demarests had read each other's notebook, there was a feeling of distress and empathy and a longing for openness and communication. They made a pact to try to break down the walls between them—"the silly walls (as Betty put it) that come from being too wrapped in our private cocoons, longing to break out and meet the butterfly in each other, but too scared or lazy to do so."

She told Don that the reason she didn't like to discuss his novel was because she felt unequipped to do so. She wasn't a literary critic. He had told her that he didn't need technical criticism. He could get that from his editor and his students. What he needed from her (as the person who knew him best), was to point out when he was being phony, or untrue to himself. Above all, he needed some reassurance from her that what he was doing was worthwhile.

They agreed about television, which had become a drug like alcohol ("electrical dependency" was Betty's phrase), and a wall rather than something to share. They made a pact to find more time to do things together and with their children. Betty promised to play tennis with Don and the boys and he promised to take her dancing.

After a hurried smorgasbord lunch the inevitable bell summoned the couples back to the conference room. Fresh posters had been hung on the walls. I LOVE YOU FOR WHAT YOU'RE NOT, TOO. THORNS HAVE ROSES. CAUTION:

HUMAN BEINGS HERE: HANDLE WITH CARE. LISTEN
AS IF YOUR LOVE DEPENDED ON IT.

POSTSCRIPT

Don: You three have been involved in so many Encounters.
Is there any way a couple can use this book at home and get
some of the same results as they would on a weekend?

Tom: I doubt it.

Don: David and Vera Mace have a new book that strikes me
as pretty sound. *How to Have a Happy Marriage*[1] actually
makes a guarantee that if a husband and wife will do the
exercises and tests together they can achieve a satisfying
relationship.

Tom: It isn't the same as the weekend at all. Even the Weekends for Couples Groups the Maces present are different.

Jerry: I am convinced that if a couple sat down together and
went through the same process as they do on a weekend, P.R.
and C.D. about the same questions, a discovery will take place,
then a sharing and an increase in communication. That's what
we hoped for when we decided to do this book.

Marilyn: We thought it could help the thousands of couples
who will never make a weekend. We didn't think of it as a come-
on for making a weekend, P.R. for the movement.

Tom: There's no guarantee that the actual weekend will
work. So many things can go wrong. And part of the success of
the weekend, if it is successful, is the ambience, the community,
the sense of sharing with the team couples and others. To say
nothing of the praying that's going on.

Betty: Still, I wish I'd known more about it beforehand. It
took me quite a while to get over my anxiety and to really
understand what it was all about.

Jerry: I'm sure that there will be growth if a couple follows
Father Calvo's dynamic.

Tom: If they become aware of God's plan for them. If they
balance couple dialogue with couple spirituality. If they realize
that dialogue alone isn't enough.

Marilyn: And as long as they don't see this book as *the*
answer to all their problems. I was horrified when the
publishers wanted to subtitle it "A Survival Manual." But a
"Guide" is all right. And M.E. is a sharing experience.

Jerry: We don't want to delude people into thinking that

---

1. Abingdon, Nashville, 1977.

58

M.E. is the only solution. It's a way to go. It's a search for answers.

Tom: You can't tell people How to Have Perfect Sex or teach them how to pray, just as you can't tell them how to have a happy marriage. You can show them what a good marriage looks like and the way some people have achieved it.

Marilyn: Christ said "I am the way."

Tom: Yes, but there's almost no theology of marriage (apart from Caffarel who influenced Gabriel). However, Calvo's approach is good psychology and sound spirituality. And if you follow his lead—without staying too long in one stage or exaggerating any one aspect—you're bound to get somewhere.

Don: And thousands of couples have found that "somewhere" is a lot better than where they were before.

Marilyn: But there's no point in skipping around. Or doing it solo. If a couple (and the Maces insist on this) read this book together, preferably aloud and P.R. and C.D. about the questions, they will be communicating.

Jerry: If they manage to absorb even a little of Calvo's spirit, it will be a worthwhile experience.

Marilyn: Gabriel talks about "blowing on the coals" of a dormant marriage. It's a wonderful image. I would hope that reading this book would blow on the coals of any relationship.

Don: So reading this book can be an approximation of the weekend, if the couple does the exercises. At least the next best thing.

Tom: Ideally it will interest them in making a weekend. And then finding a support group. That's almost essential. I wonder what sort of follow-up readers will have.

SATURDAY AFTERNOON

"Did everybody have a good lunch?" Bob asked. (Groans). "Is everyone ready for a nap?" (Cries of assent.) "I hope no one feels overworked because the weekend is just beginning. And here are some more questions. Is anyone starting to feel a little depressed or frustrated or anxious about this weekend? So far we've been dealing with some pretty heavy topics and perhaps you're beginning to feel that nothing good is going to come out of this—that this weekend is going to be a pretty negative experience. (Murmurs of "No," and smiling faces contradicted him.) 'Wow, man!', you've probably been thinking. 'What other clunkers do they have to throw into our marriage?' As Beth told you last night, this weekend isn't an end-all, it's a beginning. You have to start all self-evaluation with an honest awareness of your faults and problems. We need to keep in mind that marriage isn't the easiest way to live. But it is one of the best. And we must recognize those symptoms of spiritual divorce, so we can understand the feelings causing the symptoms and work through them to that state of joy."

He explained that we were going to reconsider some of the topics which had been listed as Symptoms of Spiritual Divorce and include some others in the session on "Subjects for Understanding."

"Just as each of us is unique," Beth chimed in, "in his/her individuality, so each of our marriages is unique and different from every other marriage. But there are some subjects that almost every marriage has to face: children, sex, work, relations, money, death. They affect all of us and provide the basis for lifelong discussion. It's how we feel about these areas that makes us unique."

Again she stressed that we are raised to suppress or deny our feelings. Boys are told not to cry and "be a little man." When we give way to our feelings we are told to "grow up." ("Does that mean that we equate growing up with suppressing our feelings?") Feelings are expressed in direct and indirect ways. "You didn't take out the garbage again" is an indirect way of saying, "You make me furious." But indirect expressions of emotion hinder depth communication, just as direct expression helps it.

"One of the biggest blocks in my communication with Bob was that he didn't have the same feelings about some important subjects that I did. However, I recognized his potential and realized it was only a matter of time before he would see the light. When we made our weekend I learned that we don't have to justify our feelings. That gave me a new freedom. But, wait! It meant that Bob was also allowed to have his own feelings. It was no longer a case of his wrong and my right ones."

Feelings, she explained, are complicated. They have reverberations. ("I may have feelings of resentment about Bob's work. But each time I express them he gives me a lecture on how lucky we are that he has this job. Pretty soon I begin to feel guilty about resenting the time he spends at work. Now I have a feeling about my feeling.") The only way to communicate completely is to put all the feelings on the table, and sort them out through mutual give and take.

Gordy and Lynn spoke about the various forms of dialogue

and which lead to the best communication. The first response is *Rejection:* "You can't feel that way ... Nobody feels like that. .. Mature people don't feel that way." This is a dead-end. The second response is *Toleration:* "It's okay for you to feel like that, but I'm not having any part of it ... (Don remembered his grandmother saying, 'Darling, you're entitled to your opinion'—meaning that she wouldn't take it from anyone else.)" The third response is *Acceptance:* "If that's the way you feel, it's all right with me, BUT ..." This sort of acceptance is often present when a husband accepts his wife's childish fears of mice and bugs, or a wife accepts her husband's need to watch football on TV. It's the recognition of the other's right to behave in strange ways with which we cannot identify. It's a step beyond tolerance. It is a recognition of the other's uniqueness and lovability, warts and all.

Finally, there is *Empathy:* "I understand. I often feel that way myself." This is the most creative and productive kind of communication. It is reaching out completely to one's spouse; entering fully through imagination into another's world. It is being totally present to the other—sharing the unity of one flesh. It turns a You into a Thou.

"Sometimes," Len said, "complete understanding demands questioning on the part of the listener. It involves queries such as 'What do you mean by ...?' 'Tell me more about that feeling.' It may involve feedback. When Liz has some intuition about the children that I don't quite understand I might say, 'It sounds as if you are worried about Jeff having the car. Are you trying to tell me that I should put my foot down?' "

The team couples took turns dialoguing various topics which had been listed. "It is by this sort of open communication," Liz said, "that we turn what had been areas of disagreement into Subjects for Understanding."

Again the encountering couples were given a list to think and write about in private, and then to share. (P.R. to C.D.) They were told to put a check mark against the subjects on which they felt their feelings were least understood by their spouses, to read them again and pick the two or three subjects on which there seemed to be the most misunderstanding, to write out their feelings or attitudes about these two or three, and if time allowed, to continue with the other subjects checked. Len explained, "Two things will probably be going on. You may begin to discover something about your own reality and then will come recognition of your feelings about this discovery."

There were fourteen subjects: 1. Money, 2. Health, 3. Time, 4. Work, 5. Rest, 6. Sex Relations, 7. Marriage, 8. Children, 9. Relatives, 10. Relationship to God, 11. Atmosphere in the Home, 12. The Big and Little Talents in Our Home, 13. The Apostolate, 14. Death. (For the complete sheet and its explanations, see the end of this chapter.)

Don ticked off six subjects, but only had time to write about three of them (although each involved two others.)

Time and Work: This seems to be our major Subject for Misunderstanding. Perhaps we should discuss some sort of realistic time table which allows for more sharing. Plan outings. Read books which we can discuss. Make a more conscious and worthwhile use of television. Go to the Guthrie Theater and the Walker Gallery more often; out to dinner and then to a play, movie or art show. Plan and allocate household chores, so that there isn't the continual bickering or feelings of guilt or martyrdom. We are more wasteful of time than we are of money. And there isn't that much left. ("At my back I always hear Time's winged chariot hurrying near." Remember the Marvell poem I used to court you with?) Discuss what we're going to do and where we're going when I retire. These are all just check lists and jump-off points to practice the kind of dialogue they've been talking about.

God and the Apostolate: Better planning is involved here, too. We really should make more time for praying together. How much do we actually share? So much of our spirituality seems to be a private, Me and God, rather than a God and Us relationship. I feel guilty about how little we do in terms of acts of charity, rather than taking the easy way out with a check book. Can we live more Christian lives, sharing with the poor? (Remember our fiasco with the Blind Indian?) We moved to the West Side so that we could recapture the community we felt at San Juan Bautista, the Franciscan church in Mexico. But we haven't really become involved that much with Our Lady of Guadalupe and the Chicanos. We should get more active in the Cursillo again. And try to set up a Spanish-speaking group. That could solve a lot of the above problems.

Relatives and Children: Although they're marvelous about sharing themselves with us, coming over on weekends, etc., I think we are more on the receiving than giving end with the kids. How much do we really know about the relationships between John and Ruth, Marie and Lee? About what John and Pepe really want to do with their lives? Since Pepe shares so many of my interests, perhaps I'm more involved with him than anyone. But Johnny is the odd man out. And he probably needs us most. He and Dana, who is way off by herself in Arizona. Perhaps we should plan to spend our summer vacation there.

Death: Time's winged chariot is getting closer. But we haven't discussed this for ages. Where is our will? Should we write a new one? What kind of funeral service do we want? (I'll haunt you if you let them show me in an open coffin.) Should we think about donating our bodies to science—or specific parts, like eyes, liver, etc., to save a life? The finances involved. Should we buy pine boxes now? Join a Burial Society? Have we thought at all about the survivor? I worry, especially, that there might not be enough money for you.

Betty wrote:

Money: Such a root of evil! My idea of money is to have loads of it and then settle back and never think of it again. I do think we should do bills together, so I'll have a better idea of what there is and where it goes—although I really prefer to remain in ignorant bliss. What are we going to do about John's and Pepe's college expenses? What sort of insurance do we have? How much will there be for retirement? If a crisis struck—medical or otherwise—could we weather it?

Death: I have often thought about this. And I always feel how useless I would be without you. But now I almost suddenly know that you are so much a part of me that even though you were dead, and no part of me was—you'd always be with me. Life would be dull plodding, but somehow I would not be alone.

God: I believe I still have my private God. But I do feel that we are learning to be more like the babes in the wood and hand in hand we are going toward Him together. One of the many things I'm still trying to learn is how to share you with God and God with you. My love of God used to make me frustrated because I wanted to be perfect *now*. (My love for you was the same. I wanted to be what I thought you wanted me to be.) But now I am beginning to

63

accept the fact that God loves me as I am, with all my imperfections. He understands me better than I do, so now I can concentrate on my love for you. More and more I am learning to love you truly. Now I have to learn to love me. Not to be sorry for myself or for my faults, but to be glad God made me, so that we both can come to Him. We can give glory to Him even with our imperfections. Because, as a pair, our imperfections tend to cancel each other out.

POSTSCRIPT

Don: I have trouble with the Three Stages of Growth: Illusion, Disillusion, Joy. It's almost as if you can attain a state of Joy, like Nirvana. You've gone beyond illusion and disillusion and reached a plateau of pure happiness. Almost the Beatific Vision.

Jerry: It's a part of the weekend we've been reconsidering. We've substituted "Decision" for "Joy." Of course, it's a continuous cycle, not something static.

Marilyn: The Paschal mystery is a better category. Birth, death and resurrection.

Tom: I prefer Expectation, Reality, Choice, to describe the marital cycle. There's the stage of hope. Then the recognition of the Other as a Thou. The acceptance of that reality, which is an act of the will.

Marilyn: It's the decision that is fulfilling. It doesn't have to be joyous. Perhaps there's a sense of relief, a feeling of peace, once the commitment has been made. But it can be painful, too.

Don: In some of the books I've read about M.E., and the way some encountered couples talk about the weekend, it sounds like a sort of eternal honeymoon. Built-in bliss. It seems almost a sacrilege to admit that things can slip back to where they were before. Or that an encountered couple can still fight and be unhappy.

Jerry: The truth is you continue to have illusions (or expectations) and disappointments, but there is knowledge that with what you have discovered you can move ahead. There is growth, real growth. The fundamental situation hasn't changed. We're still the same people. But we realize we can do something. You don't become Perfect Lovers over night, or perhaps ever. But even if we fight we are more aware of why we do so. We can choose not to. We can move on.

Marilyn: There is a change after the weekend. It can be a dramatic change.

Jerry: An encounter has been made. A discovery.

Tom: M.E. gives people hope. A realization that things can be different. Then there is the faith element.

Betty: It can be pretty shattering to go back to where you were. Even for a short time. You thought you were over that sort of thing, done with those silly games.

Marilyn: But you can recognize them as games, admit your part in it, try again together to be honest and open.

Jerry: Take the Subjects for Understanding. These are all potential Symptoms of Spiritual Divorce. You have to dialogue on the areas where you have most conflict—sex, money, relatives, work, whatever. Then they become Stages of Growth.

Marilyn: You shouldn't always try to solve problems. Just to share them is often enough. There was a couple on one of our weekends who had a real problem because of the father-in-law. There was nothing they could do about him. They didn't want to avoid him. But just recognizing that he was a problem, especially for the wife, provided a handle for managing the situation. He was still a devil. But he was "their" devil, not just an occasion of guilt.

Don: What about the Symptoms of Spiritual Divorce? Are they too negative? Can they be dangerous if the couple spends too much time on them?

Jerry: Symptoms should be taken for what the word implies. We have certain physical symptoms, an ache or an irregularity, and we go to a doctor for a checkup. A symptom is a sign of potential danger. Something to be reckoned with.

Betty: But it's like the physical symptoms. If you worry too much about them you can become a hypochondriac. I'm a terrible hypochondriac.

Marilyn: We have some new sheets for Subjects of Understanding that explains this better.

Don: Let's put them in the book.

Jerry: Of course, the dialogue isn't enough. There must also be forgiveness.

Marilyn: I remember a couple on an anniversary weekend we gave. They'd had a hell of a marriage, a real, living hell. One question we put, for sharing, was "What was your happiest moment of the past year?" She said, "I don't have a happy moment, apart from the M.E. weekend. It was then that we learned to forgive each other." It was a tremendous occasion, especially for the husband, to learn that he had been forgiven.

65

Don: Father Capon says, "A man and a woman schooled in pride cannot simply sit down together and start caring. It takes humility to look wide-eyed at someone else . . . to praise, to cherish, to honor."[2]

M.E. Materials
SYMPTOMS OF SPIRITUAL DIVORCE

1. Almost habitual sadness in the married couple and in the family.
2. Mutual sentiments of disillusionment, boredom, and emptiness.
3. Dissatisfaction.
4. Indifference to each other's problems.
5. Frequent or habitual coldness in relationships.
6. Lack of sweetness and small courtesies.
7. Lack of tenderness.
8. Climate of insincerity and of mutual distrust.
9. More confidence in third persons than with own husband or wife.
   A. Nagging
   B. Lack of planning things together
10. Lack of dialogue and intimate communication.
11. Most communication mechanical, routine, and on the surface.
12. Feeling of being alone and not understood.
13. Frequent bad humor and tension.
14. Mutual aggressiveness.
15. Frequent quarrels: in their bedroom . . . in front of the children . . . in front of anybody.
16. Ridicule of each other.
17. Insults, rude words, sarcasm, and ridicule.
18. Superficial life and continuous escapes (liquor, drugs, vices).
    A. Never able to think deeply
    B. Evasion
19. A life of selfishness and sin.
20. Individual spiritual life (each soul in a "closet").
21. Personal apostolate causing conflict.
22. Lack of enthusiasm—do not appreciate all spouse does for you.
23. Lack of or loss of the capacity of wonderment.
24. Lack of faith in love and in matrimony.

2. *Bed and Board*, Simon & Schuster, N.Y., 1965.

SUBJECTS FOR UNDERSTANDING

This is a list of "subjects for understanding" ('areas for reaching out'), followed by short phrases, each of which should be preceded by the question:

"HOW DO I FEEL ABOUT . . ."

It is hoped that the phrases will help you identify your feelings about these subjects during your personal reflection.

Money—the role it plays?—how we spend it?—how much we save, give, borrow, loan?—how we/you/I keep track of it?

Health—the way we care for ourselves?—our eating and sleeping habits?

Time—how we value our time?—the way we use it?—how much time we spend together, apart, with our children, watching T.V., reading, learning, playing, loving, praying, doing nothing?

Work—its priority in our life?—sharing the successes, the failures, the challenges, the frustrations, the tensions, the details of my/your work?—the interest exhibited for your/my work?

Rest and Relaxation—our vacations?—the ways we relax?— the recreation we practice?

Sexual Relations—the intimacy of our sexual relationship?— the sensitivity to each other's sexual needs and hangups?— my/your response to my/your affections?—how we handle our sexual frustrations and failures?

Marriage—our commitment to each other?—the support we display for one another?—the authority, submission, dominance, indifference, obedience, tolerance we act out in our relationship?—the depth of understanding we display to each other regarding temperaments, likes, dislikes, hopes, dreams, faults?—our friends and their influence on our relationship?

Children—the example we are setting for them?—the respect we show them?—the relationship each of us has with each child?—the goals we have set for them regarding their education, their religious training, will, liberty, responsibilities?—the consistency of our discipline?

Relatives—our involvement with our relatives?—their positive/negative influence on our relationship?

Relationship to God—His importance in our life?—the time spent communicating with Him through prayer and deepening our knowledge of Him through His word?—our ability to share our personal relationship to Him with each other?—our willingness to encourage each other to develop our personal relationship with Him?

Atmosphere in the Home—the positive/negative vibrations our home reflects?—the confidence and dialogue that is/is not present?—the community of love, openness, honesty, equality for all our home generates?

The Big and Little Talents—the opportunity we provide to recognize the talents and special interests of each other and our children?—the way we help one another to develop our talents, special interests, hobbies?

Our Apostolate—our witness to those around us?—the time spent serving Christ through church and/or community related activities?

Death—my death and/or you dying?—being a widow/widower?—the provisions that have been made for our children?—the knowledge we each have about the other's desires regarding funeral arrangements?

Chapter Four

CHAPTER FOUR

The Third Stage of the Weekend: The Encounter with God
Or "Dialogue Alone Doesn't Save"

SATURDAY EVENING

The shadows were lengthening outside and tantalizing smells of cooking distracted the couples as they were summoned by the bell to one more session before dinner. The all-purpose coffee table had been converted into an altar, with two candles and a crucifix.

Father John began talking in a low, quiet voice. "Every spring," he said, "the farmer prepares the soil of his fields for sowing. He takes care to cultivate it, to fertilize it, to use weed killer and nutrients so that the soil will be ready for the seed. With this preparation he hopes for a fruitful harvest in the fall."

During the previous hours, he said, the team had been helping the couples to prepare the soil of their hearts through the parables of the mustard seed, the leaven and the treasure in the field. They had been discing it with the sharp harrows of marriage in the modern world and spiritual divorce. They had cultivated it with dialogue about the subjects that most need understanding.

"Now," he said, "the team and I would like to share another parable with you. A parable is a story Jesus used to help us understand His Great Good News. A parable is like a mirror. In it we can see our lives—our flesh and blood and spirit. In this parable we shift from "We" to "We and God." God has a plan for marriage, a new way of looking at an old relationship which has infinite possibilities. If we reflect on this parable, it can teach us a great deal about what marriage can be, what each of your individual, and unique marriages can be."

71

Then Father John read the parable from Matthew 13 . . . "Other seeds fell on good soil and brought forth grain, some a hundredfold, some sixty, some thirty. He who has ears to hear let him hear."

In some marriages, Father explained, we have the *hard ground* of a refusal to be open, to listen. In this impenetrable soil, love dies. The *shallow soil* is when a couple who had begun with enthusiasm, gradually lose interest, demand to be served, become self-centered, striving for its own needs. Love withers. There is no room for it to spread its roots. When the soil of a marriage is *thorny,* the original caring is smothered by "worries, riches and pleasure." When love is calculating, fearful, anxious, irresolute, the marriage is in danger. These obstacles block out the light of one's partner and the light of God's Word.

The *fertile soil,* however, is generosity of spirit, complete openness to each other. It is a willingness to share, a dying to self. "Jesus told us that the seed must die before it can develop and blossom—two into one, rooted in a shared Yes to God's plan. Reflect for a moment on this message and pray that we, as couples, may be open to receive the seed of God's plan—which actually comes from Him in the words and actions of our spouse."

The couples were given 20 minutes to answer one question, with 20 more to C.D. about it. The question was: *In what ways do I feel you giving a part of yourself to me?*

Betty wrote:

You give yourself to me when you share your opinions—when you let me inside your thoughts, wishes, when you tell me what you had for lunch, when you call out to me when you get home from work.

When you give me your manuscript to read and I'm afraid. (It's a part of you I'm not sure of. A stranger I can't face. It's like a child you had by another woman.)

When we pray together, you give yourself to me.

I guess I really like us to make love because then I *know* you give yourself to me.

Don wrote:

In your gaiety and enthusiasm, you renew my life. When you are being a little girl, open-eyed, full of wonder and joy, you make me a little boy again, alive to all the marvelous sights and sounds and smells in the world.

72

Perhaps I treasure particularly those parts of yourself that you're shyest about sharing: the books you like, your sharp reactions to strangers, the memories of your childhood in the Virgin Islands, your secret likes and dislikes. After all these years of being with you (when I allow myself to completely BE with you, entirely aware of you), I still find new hidden prizes, little delights that pop out from some unexpected corner or hidden depth. And I'm struck again by how much there is, your range and complexity.

But the most important thing you have done for me is giving me back God (as the heroine of my novel does to the narrator). And, in continually revealing your God to me—the God you discovered for yourself but Who was handed to me—I find my God, our God. The terribly sad thing about my novel is that, when this girl Haidee who gave Johnny so much is taken from him, he has nothing left. It would be the same with me.

The candles were lit again on the altar-table; the paperback Bible lay open on the white cloth stitched with crosses. Len picked up the book and read the passage from Genesis about God creating man in his own image, giving him dominion over nature: "then God looked over all that he had made, and it was excellent in every way."

Liz read St. John's First Letter: "No man has ever seen God; if we love one another God abides in us and his love is perfected in us. God is love, and he who abides in love abides in God and God abides in him."

Father John read the other passage from Genesis, the one about God creating a helpmate for Adam, because it was not good for man to be alone . . .

> This at last is bone of my bones
> and flesh of my flesh;
> she shall be called Woman,
> because she was taken out of Man.

"God entrusted the world into the keeping of two people. Salvation has to come to the world in this union of male and female. Both man and woman reflect the living image of God in complementary and blending ways. They reflect His healing, liberating, forgiving and protecting tenderness. We are told that Adam and Eve were 'naked and unashamed.' There was nothing between them to hide, or cover up. God seems to be

73

suggesting in Genesis that marriage can be Paradise. This was His plan, this community of love. And so marriage becomes the unit on which we can build all society. This is a model for all human relationships."

"We aren't aware of our nakedness until we look outside our marriage," he went on. "The forbidden fruit represents those things that can destroy a marriage, break up community, poison love. When we are aware of our naked separateness, we try to cover this up with plastic fig leaves—the various masks we have discussed, the games we play to avoid encountering each other in trust and openness."

"It is the same with my priesthood as your marriage. Once our first parents discovered their nakedness, dissension arose—between themselves, between their children (Cain and Abel), between nations (the Tower of Babel). But it's God's plan for marriage to be a paradise. We can find our way back to it, if we have lost it. We can strip ourselves naked and build the relationship over and over again—going through the cycle of birth, death, resurrection, or illusion, disillusion, joy."

Liz told them that when she was growing up her family provided the example of unity she needed. They prayed together after dinner every night. When something good happened to one member of the family, all rejoiced. If misfortune struck one, all shared the grief. But the closeness she had achieved with Len was much greater. "In the New Testament Matthew gives us Christ's message that 'a man must leave his father and mother and cling to his wife and the two shall become one body. They are no longer two therefore but one body.' We discover in the scriptures that marital love is the highest form that human love can take."

"In the early years of our marriage our togetherness was superficial. But gradually, as we began to share joys and heartaches, our unity became deeper. Unity is total sharing and caring, acceptance of the other person, warts and all, loving even the warts. Unity is saying 'Everything I have is yours.' And 'You are my better half.' It is total self-surrender. We believe that our unity has a spiritual element. It's a triangle that includes Len and me and God. Within this triangle our children feel protected. As Father said, it's a return to the Garden of Eden. We are not ashamed of our spiritual nakedness. We have no secrets from God or each other."

Father John emphasized the theme of God's love for His people throughout the Bible. In the Old Testament God is

74

revealed as a jealous lover of Israel—he provides for their physical well-being; he guides them and shares their everyday life; he protects them from their enemies and leads them out of temptation. Israel is like the tender vine that God plants and cares for. The relationship of God and Israel becomes that of husband and wife, as the prophet Hosea describes it. Because God has chosen this most profound human relationship to describe his relationship with us, human marriage takes on an unsurpassable dignity, sublimity and personal depth, that no other relationship can match.

"The priesthood and marriage," he said, "share a oneness and are complementary to each other. Both are designed to give life. Husband and wife mirror God's creative love in giving life to their children and to each other. My priesthood is designed to give spiritual life through the preaching of the Word, and especially, through the giving of the Eucharist. Both vocations are meant to build the kingdom of God on earth—to tend the tender vine of life and make it grow."

Lynn and Gordy provided examples of the unity in their marriage and the ways it had helped them grow spiritually. "In John 3:36," Lynn said, "we read that Jesus sets you free to become all you were meant to be. I know what this freedom means. Through his loving kindness Gordy allows me to be the person God meant me to be. He opens so many gates for me. He allows me to use my talents even when it means that it is time taken from him. He understands my longings, he accepts my frustrations. He takes me as I am, no matter how undeserving. Through this love and acceptance I am growing, and we are growing together, toward a more perfect life in Christ."

"All that promotes real marital unity," Father John summed up, "persons, circumstances, things, is in accordance with the plan of God. All that endangers or corrupts marital and family unity is directly opposed to God's plan. It works the same for me. What builds up my priesthood and my relationship to the Church and to God is God's plan. What does not is not from Him. It would seem that you and I have a need for one another. As we work out God's plan in our lives, we are a Sacrament for everyone to see."

At this point the couples were returned to their notebooks and three questions:

> *1. What are the two or three events in our married life that united us the most? (Please describe.)*

75

2. What type of unity do we have now?

3. What hinders or builds unity in our marriage?

Betty wrote:

1. I think that time in New York shortly after we were married and your mother wanted you to go somewhere with her, although you'd promised to do something with me, and you said, "From now on, in all the important things, my wife comes first." That was the first time I realized we were really married. Then when Pepe had polio as a 30-day-old baby in Mexico City. And when Dana had to leave the convent.

2. I think we now have a working unity that stops our quarrels from becoming fatal. That makes each of us try to catch the other before we fall into the ripping-apart trap.

3. My exhaustion. My passion for keeping the house immaculate. Your writing and tennis. My selfishness in failing to see your kindness. These hinder it. Our struggle to be honest with each other helps to build it.

Don wrote:

1. The three moments of utter terror and despair in my life were: 1. when we thought Dana had polio, 2. the death of Haidee at 4 months, 3. Pepe in the iron lung. If I hadn't had you beside me at those moments I might have cursed God. Instead they brought us closer together—not only to each other but to Him. I remember the last two occasions especially. Riding through those dreary stretches of the Bronx to take Haidee's body to the cemetery. The death watch over Pepe in the *Hospital Infantil* in Mexico City (and then the joy at his miraculous recovery). Holding your hand as tight as a life-line on both occasions... Then you were the strong one. You helped me keep my faith in God because yours didn't falter.

2. Our unity is solidly founded on memories like these. A bit battered, bruised and tarnished at times, it still reflects a closeness I never came close to with anyone else. It's conceivable that I could temporarily fall in love with someone else—or you could. But I could never leave you because it would be leaving the biggest chunk of my life behind.

3. I guess those memories are the glue that keeps our marriage together—as well as memories of the good times:

our wedding, the weddings of Ruth and Marie, the birth of all of them (my being there for Johnny and Pepe's might rank with the moments of terror). The various homes in so many cities. The shared pride in the triumphs of our children. And now our grandchild, Kelly, to watch grow up together. What hinders unity is forgetting all this. The feeling that we are alone; that I am self-sufficient, that I don't really need anybody else, not even God—that is my temptation occasionally. And that's forgetting who I am. Because you are a part of me, just as those shared traumatic experiences are. Carelessness, selfishness, forgetfulness, lack of awareness are the things that work against our wholeness, that corrode the unity—forged in pain and delight—that are Donald and Betty Demarest in the Year of Our Lord, 1976.

As they read these words, the Demarests were reminded of a remark that Liz had made that morning: "When Len and I made our Encounter we found that many of the things we wrote in our notebooks were very much alike. We also found that on some issues we differ greatly. Even though we have identity in our marriage, each of us still has our personal unity and marital unity doesn't take that from us."

Dinner Saturday night was a special occasion and lived up to the delectable odors which had tantalized the couples while they were doing their P.R. and C.D. Instead of sitting together at long tables, boarding-house style, they were seated at individual tables, with immaculate table cloths, the best silver, roses, wine and candlelight. The team couples waited on them with t.l.c. (It reminded Don of the restaurant in Puerto Rico where he had blown a month's pay as an Aviation Radioman 2/c to propose to Betty.)

As they re-entered the conference room, the Demarests looked for new posters and noticed these: YOU TOUCHED ME, I HAVE GROWN. CONFIDENCE IS A DECISION, A GIFT TO BE GIVEN. AND THE WALLS CAME TUMBLING DOWN.

"We call this presentation Confidence and Dialogue," Bob said. "It's a step forward from the 'We' stage of the weekend we studied this morning. We are back to talking about how a husband and wife can relate to each other on a day-to-day basis. But we are talking about ways to achieve the unity that is God's plan for marriage."

Confidence, he said, is the key to dialogue. Confidence is more than trust. It is opening up completely to another person. It is not just the communication of the big issues, problems, joys. Instead, it is a mutual and constant revelation of intimate thoughts, desires, fears, the small everyday preoccupations.

"*Our Town* by Thornton Wilder," Beth continued, "is a fascinating play about small town life and everyday occurrences: birth, marriage, death. It has some especially good insights about marriage. I remember one line, particularly, which is spoken by Doc Gibbs on the eve of his son's marriage to the girl next door. He says, 'Julia, when I married you, do you know what one of my terrors about getting married was? It was that we'd run out of conversation ... I was afraid we'd run out, and eat our meals in silence. But you and I have been conversing for 20 years without hitting any dry spells.' Well, I chatter a lot. But it used to be the kind of conversation that covers up the important things. I didn't want to worry Bob about my real fears. I sold our chance at understanding and deep communication for a mess of pottage—the old bromide 'peace at any price.' It's a terribly costly kind of peace."

"Real marital communication," Lynn said in her turn, "involves taking a big risk. It's based on the confidence that what I have to say will be accepted. I think of that rose on the table or daisies in the spring in my garden. I won't know what their beauty is until they bloom. I can only hope and imagine. When they do open up, they may have a defect, a bug or a misshaped petal. But their over-all beauty is the main thing. It is the same with dialogue. I can blossom for Gordy, confident that he will accept me in spite of any bugs or misshapen petals. Finally, I've learned to trust him when he says that he finds me beautiful."

"I have to develop confidence in myself," Gordy said, "before I can be truly open to Lynn. I have to be honest with myself. I have to encounter myself *daily*. There is no way I can open myself to Lynn if I don't know who I am. At the same time I must have confidence in Lynn if a meaningful exchange is to take place. I must realize that she is continually encountering herself and accepting herself and is willing to share herself with me as she finds herself at that moment."

Lynn added that we also have to have confidence in the marriage relationship itself. If we have confidence in ourselves and in God, this confidence grows so that we can handle all our relationships openly and honestly. With our children, our parents, our in-laws, with friends.

"This wasn't always true," she said. "Because of my fundamental lack of self-confidence, I often found it easier to communicate with one of my girl friends than with Gordy. I always thought that Gordy and I could be helpers, lovers, partners, but that friendships were to be found outside our home. But since our Encounter I have found that Gordy can be my best friend as well as the other things."

"And now that we're friends," Gordy admitted, "I can finally share my friends with her and accept her friends without jealousy."

"Dialogue," Lynn continued, "is essential to confidence. We *confide* in someone we trust. (The word comes from the Latin, and means 'with faith.') Because we trust that person, we are eager to share our most intimate feelings and ideas. This dialogue can take many forms—verbal, non-verbal, body language, intercourse. This weekend you have been experimenting with a form of dialogue that may be new to you: Personal Reflection and Couple Dialogue. Later on we'll talk about using it in your daily life. What we call 'Ten and Ten': ten minutes P.R., ten minutes C.D. We have discovered that 10/10 can be a real tool to ensure our personal growth."

"A lot of the time Gordy and I communicate non-verbally. We know each other so well that a certain look in his eye can tell me more than a book. But we still need the written dialogue to get at those hard-to-express feelings. We use 10/10 for those occasions when we feel ourselves holding back, or failing to understand, or when we have fears or jealousies we're ashamed to admit openly."

"And then," Gordy said, "we have a written record of our feelings. We can re-read our notebooks and discover how much closer we've grown over a period of time."

The encountering couples were given three more questions to practice their P.R. and C.D. They were:

1. *What kind of confidence do I really want with you? What are my expectations? (Describe in loving detail.)*
2. *What areas in our married life do I find are difficult to share with you?*
3. *How have I made it easier or harder for you?*

Don wrote:

1. I guess I would like to reach the state where we don't have to share through the spoken word—that we would instinctively know what the other wants and feels. But we aren't angels. Besides, words are exciting, if difficult and dangerous weapons. I wish you'd ask me to explain things I say or write that you don't understand.

2. Again, my writing, I suppose. A lot of the thinking and reading I do. Perhaps this is because the only way I can encounter myself with any depth is in fictional terms.

3. I know I make it hard for you because I expect you to understand something that's been extremely difficult for me to write (in my novel, I mean). Also, because I have a phobia about coercing people. I don't want to force my novel on you unless you're really interested in it.

Betty wrote:

1. I want the confidence that you can correct me and I won't feel like a dimwit. I want the confidence that I can correct you and not sound as if I'd scored a point.

2. After all these years I still find sex hard to talk about. But then most of the things I talk about I worry to death and they lose all the magic.

3. I have made it hard for you because I often see dialogue as debate. But I do try to make you feel confident that I will be there functioning the best I can, no matter what happens. If I can't show confidence in my words, perhaps I can show my confidence in you by what I do.

When the Demarests went back downstairs, Lynn was playing the guitar and the other couples were sharing glasses of wine or pop. Lynn played "The Wedding Song," an old favorite of Betty's:

... A man shall leave his mother and a woman leave her home and they shall travel on to where the two shall be as one. As it was in the beginning, is now and 'til the end. Woman draws her life from man and gives it back again. And there is love . . ..

"Now," Len said, "you've got about half an hour to be by yourselves with nothing planned, nothing programed. You can go to your rooms or take a stroll by the lake or stay here and listen to music. Lynn will try to play any requests you might have."

Betty and Don walked around the lake, arm-in-arm, a thing they hadn't done since their courting days, talking very little, content to listen to the silence broken by the occasional splash of a fish, the chirping of crickets, the eerie query of an owl. The moon seemed to fly through the clouds, creating tremendous chiaroscuro effects of black and silver; the light one moment as bright as a photographer's flash followed by an intense and complete blackness, in which they felt like the only people left in the world.

They were on the other side of the lake when they heard the bell, a clear and irrevocable summons. When they reached the conference room, Father John was in the middle of his talk.

"Remember that other passage in Genesis," he was saying, "which goes 'God created man in his own image, in the image of God he created him, male and female he created them. And God blessed them, and God said to them, 'Be fruitful and multiply and fill the earth and subdue it . . . And God saw everything that he had made, and behold, it was very good.' "

It's tragic, he said, that in every age some people have found this body that God made evil (some very pious people at that) and the act of marital intercourse—which mirrors the unity of Christ and his Church, which is the most creative and intimate way a couple can share themselves—as something necessary but not quite nice. As something shameful. (A feeling that was instilled in a lot of us, Don thought wryly, in our parochial schools. He remembered the crack he'd heard at a Catholic conference on Marriage, "We were taught this in the eighth grade. 'Sex is dirty. Save it for someone you love.')

"Today," Father was saying, "we have gone to the other extreme. Sex is exploitation. Sex is a sales gimmick. The Girl Next Door is the subject for a *Playboy* centerfold. They're even using little children in the slimy movies they show in the sex ghettos. On the other hand, adultery is depicted in the mass media as something as ordinary and meaningless as a smile and a shake of the hand. The miracle of marital intercourse is degraded into something as mechanical as chewing gum."

"Some people blame God, or the Church, for this negative attitude toward our bodies and sex—which they claim they are freeing us from. But people have been reading this Biblical passage for thousands of years. The words and the message are clear enough. We have come forth from God's creative hand. He made our bodies, as well as our hearts and minds. He commands us to be fruitful. He looked at everything he had

81

made and said it was very good."

"From the beginning," he explained, "God gave us an additional blessing, a helpmate to save us from loneliness. And this helpmate was not only bone of our bone but also a fascinatingly different sort of person, a part of His mystery. We joke about it, write songs about it ('How Do You Handle a Woman?' or 'Why Can't a Woman Be Like a Man?'). Yet the fact remains that a man can never fully understand a woman. Any more than a woman will ever totally comprehend the thoughts, feelings and actions of a man. Yet, together, we form a marvelous blend. Like two halves of a separate fruit, we complement one another; together we fulfill each other's needs, make up our mutual deficiencies. In a phrase, we are equal but different."

"To love," he summed up, "is to see and cherish our partner as a unique person—rich, deep, complex, mysterious. It is to view him or her as the missing piece of the puzzle of our lives. The better half, perhaps, but at least the half which, lacking, we are less of a person. Less whole, less strong, less capable of loving."

The other team couples then shared some of their marital experiences—the embarrassing or wonderful, sometimes funny, sometimes tragic experiences that most couples find in the privacy of their bedrooms. The repetitious mistakes and false attitudes they had acquired from their parents or teachers. In his delightful book, *Bed and Board*,[1] Father Robert Capon, the Episcopalian priest, wrote: "It was not enough for the Creator to make us human. Absurdly, he went further. Male and female created he them. The truth of our being is that we are one species, but just barely. Even without counting porpoises, this planet houses two different sorts of rationality, two different kinds of freedom, and two different brands of love: men's and women's. But nowhere are we more confused about our roles than we are in the matter of sexuality."

This observation was reinforced by the frank, rueful witnessing of the team couples. Most commonly it had been a feeling on the part of the wives that they were missing something ("No bells rang. The earth didn't turn over.") that novels and marriage manuals had told them they should expect. And the husbands felt needlessly guilty. Or tended to

---

1. Simon & Schuster, N.Y., 1965.

blame their wives for making them feel this way. But they spoke, too, of the gradual coming together, of learning to discuss what had been a forbidden topic, and of at last finding in intercourse not only another means of communication, but the best way to get close to their beloved, to experience and share their love. They got to "know" one another in the way the word is used in the Bible: "And Isaac *knew* Rebecca."

In between the talks some more cassettes were played. "Annie's Song," by John Denver and "The First Time Ever I Saw Your Face."

The final questions of the day were presented for P.R. and C.D. They were:

1. *Do you think that sex has become routine in our marriage? And if so, why?*
2. *Are trust and confidence expressed in our sexuality?*
3. *What is there about you that arouses me sexually?*

What the Demarests wrote in their notebooks was too personal and erotic to reproduce here. In fact the rest of the evening is most decently conveyed by the favorite (and perfectly meaningful) convention used by Victorian novelists . . . (Three dots.)

The conference room, when they re-entered it, was in darkness, until Father John lit the tall Paschal candle beside the altar-table. Each of the couples had been handed an unlit candle when they came in. Len and Liz were sitting behind the table. The Paschal candle threw shadows on their faces and made Len look more than ever like an Indian or a frontiersman. After several minutes of silence he began to talk.

"Earlier we heard about God's plan for us as married couples. He wants us to live united with each other and to Him. If God is present in our marriage—if He is a vital part of our lives—only then will we know true unity in our relationship. We have heard scripture quoted this afternoon telling us that God approves of marriage. That He smiles on marriage. Liz and I would like to take turns reading you another passage of scripture, from the Gospel According to St. John, Chapter 2, Verses 1 through 10 . . . "

"This, the first of his signs, Jesus did at Cana in Galilee, and manifested his glory and his disciples believed in him . . . "

As he finished his verse, Liz said, "Christ was present at a small-town wedding in Galilee to celebrate the wedding of a young couple. When they tell him that the wine has run out,

Our Lord hesitates. He doesn't feel that this is the right moment for a miracle. Then he looks at the young couple and becomes concerned about this beginning, this celebration of theirs. This passage tells Len and me that Christ stands beside all marriages. It also tells us that a celebration now and then is good for all of us. We have Christ's approval."

Len said, "Married Love is like this rose. It cannot be taken for granted. It must be nourished and cultivated before it can bloom in all its beauty. The candle beside this table represents the love that Christ has for each of us. He brings light into our lives through his love."

He asked the couples to come forward and light their candles from the Christ candle.

"The room is brightly lit now. Our love, together with Christ's, can illuminate the whole world. So often, though, we say things that hurt each other—things that make our love a little dimmer. Let's each of us think of some moment during the past week when we said or did something that hurt our spouse. It doesn't have to be something big, perhaps just a cross look or a grudging 'okay.' Often little things like this hurt more than the big ones."

"Now let's quietly tell our spouse that we're sorry for the hurtful thing we did. And then let's blow out our candle."

After a pause Len continued, "Our candles have gone out. But the room isn't completely dark. Notice the Christ candle is still burning. That's how it is with Christ's love. It never dims. No matter what we do, he continues to love us. He forgives us and wants us to forgive each other. He wants us to keep the light of our love burning so that the whole world can see it and be lightened."

Liz looked at her husband across the candle. She thanked him for all that he had done for her. ("I love you for forgiving me the weak, foolish things I sometimes say . . . I thank you for discovering the good things in me that no one else ever notices . . . I thank you for giving me the joy of Joan, Lenny, Daniel, Jeff, Carla and Randy . . . .")

Len said, "I love you, Liz, for the quiet efficiency with which you tend our home. I love you because your happiness makes me happy; I love you because you're a very nice person; I love you because you think I'm a nice person; I love you because together we make a good team."

Meanwhile another team couple had turned on the recorder. The song was "My Cup Runneth Over With Love." The

84

sincerity of the Nottos, who had been married as teenagers and whose love had survived so many years, had weathered so many storms, obviously touched some of the more recently married couples. Their expressions as they turned to each other indicated, "If they can do it, so can we."

"Forgiveness is so important," Liz said. "That's why the famous quotation from *Love Story* is so ridiculous. Love, in our marriage, has been remembering to say 'I'm sorry' over and over. It's forgiving and being forgiven as many times as God forgives. So let's tell our partners that we're sorry for the episode we've just mentioned. Let's say 'I'm sorry I hurt you. Please forgive me.' These are the truly healing words for Len and me."

"After we've done this," she suggested, "after we've both apologized and forgiven each other, let's all come and light our candles again from the Christ candle." "We would like to end this meditation on a positive note," Len said. "Let's each of us think of something our spouse did for us during the past week that made us feel good to be alive. Again, it doesn't have to be something big. It could be an encouraging smile when it was needed, or a pat on the shoulder. When you think of something your beloved did for you during the past week, tell them about it and say 'Thank you.' "

Don Demarest no longer felt that he was being manipulated. If this was corny (and, of course, it was), he decided that too often in their marriage he and Betty had avoided moments of intimacy because of their terror of being 'sentimental.' He thanked Betty for coming on the weekend, even though she hadn't really wanted to. She thanked him for letting her pick the date, so that she wouldn't have to spend Mother's Day cooking and cleaning.

POSTSCRIPT

Don: On our weekend the creative and liberating aspects of marital fidelity were barely touched on. And yet this is something that the most humanistic and free-thinking marriage counsellors are beginning to stress.

As a matter of fact, it goes back to D.H. Lawrence, who is often looked on as the first outspoken advocate in fiction of free love, but who devoted his life to perfecting his marriage to Frieda. He wrote that without a deep commitment to fidelity, no relationship between the sexes can be meaningful. (Incidentally, although he is often violently anti-Christian, he also speaks of Christianity as "having brought marriage into the world, marriage as we know it. It is marriage that gives man his *little kingdom* (I don't believe he'd read St. Chrysostom) of his own, within the big kingdom of the state ... It is a true freedom because it is a true fulfillment, for man, woman and children.")

Carl Rogers in *Becoming Partners: Marriage and Its Alternatives*[2] has many interviews with swinging couples, couples who have tried shared sex in communes, and various unmarried unions. Almost all speak of the discovered need for fidelity. One wife, who had experimented outside with her husband's approval, is quoted: "The sexual act between a married couple is *sacred* and unto itself and when that's shared with another person that diminishes the original sanctity (my emphasis)."

Masters and Johnson in *The Pleasure Bond*[3] conclude that the only truly joyful unions, the only completely satisfying sexual relations, are between married couples who are faithful.

Marilyn, you brought this to my attention along with the *Redbook* poll. I'd like to ask you two questions:

1. How important do you think fidelity is for marital success?
2. Do you think the mountain of sex manuals that have been published in the last decade have helped or hindered the average marriage?

Marilyn: Well, to begin with, I think that the more people learn about sexuality the more obvious it becomes that it doesn't depend on mechanics, or manipulation, but a relationship. The *Redbook* survey of 100,000 women discovered, to its surprise, that religious women were the sexiest. That women with a religious orientation were the best adjusted in this as in other areas.

Jerry: Everyone today is looking for self-fulfillment. The singles' bars are crowded (often with married men). And all the time the old-fashioned route is the most rewarding.

Don: What the married lechers are looking for is right there at home.

Marilyn: Sexual fidelity is part of the marriage commitment. The commitment to God, to one's spouse and the

, 2. Delacorte, N.Y., 1972.
3. Little, Brown, Boston, 1975.

community. M & J say in *The Pleasure Bond* something like, "Trust has been asked for, trust has been given and trust has been repaid." And that sex is a physical expression of emotional unity.

Jerry: And that's what couples discover on the weekend. For anything to be believed there has to be a model. The team couples provide this. And parents can provide it for their children.

Marilyn: All the talks and statistics and sermons can accomplish nothing unless people can see and touch an experience. Unless kids can see what a good marriage can be in "living color" in the lives of their parents, they will look for heroes in the soap operas.

Betty: Perhaps M.E. can make marriage believable, provide new heroes.

Jerry: God and sex are the great mysteries of our time.

Marilyn: And you can't learn about either just from books. The sex manuals have frequently confused people and made them more dissatisfied.

Jerry: On the weekend the Cana ceremony is a key moment. It provides the balance not only between couple dialogue and couple prayer, but shows that couples need Christ's active presence in their marriage.

Marilyn: Father John Higgins has done some historical reseach on Cana. The miracle was not only changing water into wine. It was taking some pretty filthy water right out of a cistern and changing it into a vintage beverage. The water of our past relationship often contains a lot of sediment and just plain mud and garbage. Forgiveness and renewal through Christ's presence is the conversion process.

Jerry: This is where Worldwide M.E. doesn't go far enough. They tend to imply that the conversion is in the dialogue, that the dialogue is enough.

Tom: "Does dialogue save?" Calvo asks. "No, God saves. Then, what does God want? Dialogue."

Don: It's a paradox. Or rather, like most paradoxes, a completed circle.

Jerry: Calvo recognizes that more is needed than human communication and human commitment. Revelation should take place at the Cana Service on Saturday evening and is covered by the Sacrament of Marriage talk Sunday morning.

Tom: "Sacrament and Its Graces." The word is a problem, not only in ecumenical and inter-faith settings, where there's a lack of agreement, but especially with Catholics where the word has become such a cliche. We know the Baltimore Catechism definition but the word often gets in the way of the reality of God working.

Jerry: The Hebrew word "Hesed" might be better. It means God's loving kindness—the loving kindness between husband and wife and God and his people.

Don: According to Rabbi Kligfeld the Jewish word for santification, blessing or making holy is "Kiddush." "Kiddushin" is the Sanctification of Marriage, which he substitutes for the Sacrament of Marriage. A Jewish marriage, he says, is a contract between the couple and God. The gold ring is simply something of value, to seal the contract.

Marilyn: When Vic Barela was retranslating the Manual, he picked up on what Calvo means by confidence in "Confidence and Dialogue." Confianza in Spanish has the sense of commitment, the same root as fiancée. It also signifies the special relationship between godparents which is so important in Spanish culture, the *compadrazgo* relationship. A *compadre* in Spain or Mexico is prepared to do almost anything for the person he has this relationship with.

Betty: He will bail him out of jail or lend him money. He is committed to do this. It's almost stronger than a blood relationship.

Don: We only have the godparent relationship between godparents and godchildren. But even this should be more than an honorary relationship. A godparent should look out for his godchild and protect it against its parents if that's necessary.

Tom: Henri Caffarel, who has had an enormous influence on Calvo, writes about this in his book, *Marriage is Holy.*[4] God's commitment to the family should be matched by the family's commitment to God, the community relationship.

Marilyn: Vic says this commitment works both ways. The *compadre* will be furious if the *confianza* isn't used. If he isn't called on, when the other is in trouble.

Betty: The *compadre* has the duty to call his *compadre* (co-father) on the carpet when he is drinking too much, for instance, and neglecting his family. If he doesn't do so, he isn't fulfilling his *confianza*.

4. Fides, Notre Dame, 1957.

Jerry: And because of our marriage commitment, as Calvo says, I have the right to expect intimacy and trust from my wife, as well as sex, the so-called 'marital right.'

Don: So we have come full circle, back to all the implications of sexual fidelity.

M.E. Materials
SELF-EVALUATION QUIZ ON HUMAN SEXUALITY
By Gene and Mary Lou Ott
Edina, Minnesota

*(Reflect and write in private—
Exchange with your spouse if you wish.)*

1. If you had just one word to describe yourself what would it be?
2. If you had just one word to describe your spouse what would it be?
3. What physical feature of yourself do you like the most and why?
4. What physical feature of the one you love do you like the most and why?
5. Describe yourself looking in a mirror.
6. Describe your feelings about your body.
7. Describe your feelings about your sexuality.
8. What events in your past do you think influenced your sexuality as you now experience it?
9. Are you becoming freer as you grow in your self-awareness?
10. Are you willing to give up memories or hangups in order to grow sexually?
11. How honest are you about your sexual needs and would you like to be more open?
12. Is there anything you sometimes pretend to be that you are not?
13. What do you feel when you're alone and think about your spouse?
14. What do you need most from your sexual relationship with your spouse?
15. What would you like to change, if anything, in how you and your spouse relate sexually?
16. Rate yourself as to how loving you are on a scale of 1 to 10 and give an example to show this.
17. Describe how your body language may reflect your sexual mood.

18. Rate your comfort level with touch on a scale of 1 to 10:
    a) with your spouse
    b) with other people.
19. What are your feelings as you answered these questions?
20. Are you satisfied with your answers to the above questions or are there areas in which you would like to change? Which ones?

MARRIAGE RATING SCALE

Rate yourself and then have your spouse do the same by placing a check mark in the appropriate column. The column under "1" is the poorest and each column is better till you reach "6" which is the very best.

	1	2	3	4	5	6
LEISURE TIME:						
We spend enough time together as a couple in social activities and recreation						
This time is enjoyable						
Our family recreation includes enough activity with the children						
Neither of us objects to the other's independent social life and interests						
We share and accept each other's ideas about leisure activities						
SEX:						
For my part I think our sexual life is good						
I believe my partner thinks the same						
We can discuss our sexual feelings and needs frankly						
MONEY:						
We've worked out a satisfactory budget or management system						
I'm satisfied we manage as well as we can on our income						
We can discuss money matters comfortably						
We consider each other's wishes on how the money should be spent						
Our income supplies our basic needs and leaves some for enjoyment						

IN-LAWS:

My in-laws aren't a source of friction or argument					
His/her relatives cause no problem					
We accept each other's relatives sufficiently					
We even enjoy being with at least some of the relatives or in-laws					
We can talk about our relatives without becoming angry					

CHILD REARING:

We agree on methods of child discipline ..					
We share equally in making rules for the children					
We both enforce these rules					
Our children feel free to discuss anything with either of us					
As a family, we feel free to discuss any subject					

ROLE EXPECTATIONS:

We have a balance of privileges and responsibilities in our marriage					
My spouse meets my expectations of a marriage partner					
I'm satisfied with the organization and structure of time, work and responsibility in our family					

Total your score by adding up the value of the check marks you've made.

If your score is between:

     51 and 70, emergency repairs must be made.

     71 and 90, you really need a tune-up.

     91 and 110, you have a satisfactory, but ho-hum,
             performance.

    111 and 130, you're winning the race.

    131-plus, wait 24 hours and retake the test. This mood
             can't last.

Now compare your score with that of your partner, if the scores vary more than 30 points in either direction, you're not communicating.

Then compare each of your scores for individual items. If you vary more than two points from each other, you aren't tuned in to each other in that particular area.

A CREED FOR MARRIAGE ENCOUNTER

We Believe

That God didn't and doesn't make junk or trash. He created all of us good and made us in his image, both male and female.

That we can't love what we don't know—especially ourselves. And since we are what we feel, we have to discover or recognize feelings to know ourselves and others.

That feelings are neither morally good or bad. They simply are. (What we do with our feelings, however, can become a moral question.)

That the state of marriage in modern society is in a crisis situation.

That marriage and the family are the basic institutions, the main building blocks, of all society.

That each person is unique. So, each relationship between two unique persons is also unique. Because of this, there can be no universal norm to follow nor any marriage expert who can tell me what my relationship with my spouse should be. It is up to the two of us to discover, to grow in, and to live out this unique relationship.

That marriages need support of other married couples to survive. These other couples provide the support given formerly by the extended family.

That a love relationship, marriage, is a dynamic, growing reality. It can have no limit, because love, like God, has no limit. So, a love relationship never reaches its final stage or ultimate plateau.

That dialogue, the continual and mutual self-revelation of feelings, is the life blood of a marriage relationship.

That the "Basic Law of Life" is the continuous series of stages, referred to as Illusion—Disillusion—True Joy. This is the natural ebb and flow of life and describes how we grow. Likewise, this "Basic Law of Life" is similar to the biblical theme of Birth-Death-Resurrection.

That it will be very difficult for children ever to learn how to love if they do not experience love in the home at an early age—mainly between their mother and father. So, the most important thing a father can do for his children is to love their mother, and for her, to love their father.

That discovery and belief in God comes through a human love relationship for most of us. The most natural place for this experience is in marriage. And this seems to be God's plan.

That the marriage relationship between husband and wife and the spirit of love between them is the living image of God. Marriage is a community of love and is God's plan, or model, for unity among unique human persons.

That the joy and beauty planned for us by God in the sacrament of Marriage is far beyond our wildest imagination.

That the nature of married love, like all love, is apostolic. If it is real, it cannot be contained, but must be open to the whole world. For it is of the nature of love to reach out beyond oneself.

That you can't give to the world what you don't have. How can anyone attempt to solve the problems of the world, communicate with others, or heal the wounds of an alienated society, if he or she can't communicate with or is alienated from that person he or she has chosen to live with until death?

Chapter

Five

CHAPTER FIVE

The Fourth Stage of the Weekend:
The Encounter with the World
Or "A Sign for All to See"

Sunday morning the sun was sparkling on the lake which was whipped with little whitecaps like a succession of ice-cream cones. The breeze bent the willows which surrounded the dormitory and the Demarests could hear children shouting as they fished from a pier on the opposite side of the lake. Someone was sailing a boat which skimmed across the surface like a white butterfly.

Again, the breakfast was enormous, and genial, sleepy-eyed couples passed the syrup for the pancakes with a minimum of conversation. One wife looked at her husband with a grin and catching his eye giggled like a schoolgirl. The atmosphere reminded the Demarests of a honeymoon hotel.

The Catholics had a chance to go to Father John's Mass. After they were assembled again in the conference room at nine o'clock, Father John reminded them of the parable of the Kingdom of Heaven being like a treasure hidden in a field which a man found and covered up, then went out and sold all he had to buy that field. Marriage, he said, is like that. A treasure is something that grows more and more precious as time passes. It is something we have to search for, to discover for ourselves—and sometimes we don't even know we've found it until another person points it out to us.

"Marriage is also a sacrament. More than a contract, which is based on one person's word—a giving over of certain rights to another. To place all of one's honor and dignity in another

97

fragile and free human being is no small ideal. But marriage is more than that. Marriage is more than a religious ceremony, the priest's blessing or the exchange of vows before the community. In marriage the husband is a sacrament, the symbol of Christ, and the wife is a sacrament, the symbol of the Church. This is a tremendous and abiding mystery."[1]

Above all, he emphasized, marriage is not just a legal way to have sexual relations. It is a sharing of God's creative powers. But even more, it is a means of grace which two Christians possess in virtue of the sacraments of Baptism and Confirmation . . .. In this sacrament the husband gives graces to the wife and she gives him other graces. "It goes both ways, husband to wife and wife to husband."

Father John beamed on the couples, like a Santa Claus opening his sack of Christmas treasures. Because he seemed so excited about what he was sharing, the encountering couples had to smile back at him. They were beginning to accept his loving concern, to identify with him as a genuine spiritual father.

"Marriage is not just between two people," he said. "There is a third person involved, a person (as John the Baptist said) who may be living in our midst and unrecognized. How many Christian marriages stumble along without the awareness that Jesus is the third person in their alliance—ever present and ready to provide help and guidance? The deepest revelation a wife will receive about Christ's love for her is the expression of her husband's love. Similarly, the husband in giving himself to his wife gains some understanding of how Christ gives himself and identifies himself with the people he loves. But it is more than understanding. It is also sharing and participation."

"In a very real and tangible way marriage is a symbol of the God who inserted himself into human history. It is an incarnation, a putting on of human flesh, which brings the ineffable down to the human level. When you think about this it really blows your mind."

"The thing to remember is that God works in and through human beings. One phase of revelation is human experience."

Continuing his talk on the Sacrament of Marriage and its graces, Father John pointed out that the word Sacrament is

1. See Chapter Nine for a fuller explanation of Sacrament and Mystery.

from the Latin meaning to "make holy." Therefore, whatever the couples do together in love is sacramental—whether it is just washing the dishes, or painting the bathroom, all the way to sexual intercourse or sharing in the care of a sick child. Husband and wife living in the lasting communion of love are a sign—a revelation first of all to each other, then to their children, and finally to the community and the whole world. Married couples reveal the mystery of God's love. And the fact that this love brings forth children reveals the close link between love and creation. Only those who are married can appreciate this mystery completely.

The Demarests noticed that the team couples had hung new banners and put up new posters. WHO YOU ARE IS GOD'S GIFT TO YOU; WHAT YOU MAKE OF YOURSELVES IS YOUR GIFT TO GOD. LOVE IS A MYSTERY TO BE LIVED, NOT A PROBLEM TO BE SOLVED. A long banner in brilliant colors, with butterflies and balloons, depicted a triangle with GOD, I and We at the three corners, and the legend LOVE TAKES THREE.

Bob and Beth demonstrated how a sacrament works: the transition from the material to the spiritual, from the visible to the invisible, the external to the internal. Hugging, they explained that "This is the external sign which signifies the internal meaning of our love. The words 'I love you' clarify the meaning and bring about a deeper reality. The words are creative and change the everyday reality to the sacramental as ordinary water is changed into holy water and bread and wine are changed into the Eucharist."

"That Christ is in your marriage," Father John said, "(as he is in my priesthood) is completely real and capable of proof. It's just as real, perhaps more so than the chairs and tables in this room. Jesus said very clearly 'When two or three are gathered in my name, I shall be there with them.' He goes through his birth, death and resurrection in each marriage which has been sanctified. Your love for each other makes him present. He is crucified in your fights and discord. He dies in couples who are in serious sin, who have broken off their relationship with God and the community of believers. He comes back to life when couples make up after a quarrel and return to unity with each other and with the community."

"Several years ago, there was a movie called *God Needs Hands*. He needs married couples, especially, to go into the world as representatives of his creative love. When they are in loving unity, when they trust and share and communicate in a truly loving way, they present the water which Christ turns into the 'best wine' of sacramental love. Then you make Christ present to your neighbors and the world."

"There are graces involved in every sacrament. In marriage we find the grace of healing, of unity, of sanctification, of witness and many more which may be discovered when you evaluate your own marriage."

"To get back to the symbol of marriage as a treasure, we must remember that a treasure which remains hidden is worthless. Much of the beauty of precious elements can remain dull and lifeless until they are constantly polished and taken care of. The treasure of marriage is enriched and maintained by frequent use of the other sacraments—especially the Eucharist—by shared prayer and works of corporal mercy. Sometimes the whole point of a treasure is lost when it is put away behind glass in museums or in a bank vault. The tremendous joy of the marriage treasure is that it can be rediscovered again and again. Search in the field of your relationship for those extraordinary prizes you first saw in each other. When you sold everything you had to buy the field and live as one life, one unity, one faith, one trust, one love, one happiness—the unique experience of sharing your love with God who is also Three Persons in One."

The team couples took turns to share the many graces they had discovered in their marriages . . . as a testimony of the way God touches individual lives; the grace of healing—not only the wounds of selfishness and laziness and lying and jealousy in their own union, but in the lives of their friends and neighbors. The grace of parenthood (and grandparenthood) was mentioned frequently. Liz and Len bore witness to how their own children had grown up to trust the reality of their love and how they had shared this love with an adopted child.

Lynn said that she especially appreciated the graces she received from Gordy to be herself. "He understands my longings, he prompts my friendship, he accepts me as I am, and gives me the freedom to pursue my special talents and interests." Gordy acknowledged the graces he received from Lynn's gifts as a homemaker and mother, as well as the freedom she provided him to concentrate on his work.

Bob and Beth revealed the grace that each had provided the other in discovering Christ, respecting the other's faith and sharing it without any attempt at coercion or proselytizing.

Liz testified to the graces of discovery and admiration that Len had shown her and their children in exploring the wonders of nature and the surprises of everyday life. Len thanked Liz for helping him break out of his shell of coldness, for melting his reserve. ("Liz has given me the grace to let my emotions show. She taught me to laugh and cry and not be ashamed of either.")

Finally, the encountering couples were given a sheet of Marriage Evaluation questions to fill out. Beth emphasized that this was known as "The Grand Dialogue." "This moment is so important," she said, "that many other couples who have made a weekend are praying for each of you individually. They have sent these prayer cards addressed to each of you."

Then the couples were urged to devote serious and prayerful consideration to the printed sheet, starting with the first questions and not skipping, but going into each with as much depth as possible and being as specific as they could in describing their feelings about each. The sheet was divided into eight Subjects: Self, We Two, God, Children, Relatives, Neighbors, Our Home and Social. (See end of chapter.)

There were sixty questions to be answered in ninety minutes of P.R. (the longest session yet) and ninety minutes of C.D., three hours altogether. The Demarests found some of the questions repetitive and the time inadequate to deal with all of them in depth, but that they were good springboards for the longest and most intimate examination of their lives together that they had ever had. (See end of chapter.)

After lunch, there was a brief discussion of the finances of the weekend and couples were urged to think about volunteering for training as team couples.

Gordy and Lynn invited the couples to write a love letter to their spouse when they had time. It might be based on such topics as 'What is my partner's most endearing quality?' and 'What has been the most significant event or experience of the weekend? How do I feel about it?' These letters, they said, would be addressed to one's spouse, then placed on the table with the scripture between two lighted candles. They would be mailed by the team in a few weeks.

Then, to the accompaniment of Lynn's guitar, the couples sang some of the songs they had already learned. They were given a few moments to meditate about what the weekend had meant and what they would write in their letters, as they

CARL A. RUDISILL LIBRARY
LENOIR-RHYNE COLLEGE

listened to "Yahweh, the Faithful One," from the album, *Neither Silver or Gold* by the St. Louis Jesuits.

Then they were dismissed to write the love letters on special stationery the team provided. "This is going to be the best love letter I ever wrote," the Boston Irishman announced. "It will sweep Mary off her feet." He winked at the others.

Back in the conference room for the final presentation of the weekend, the couples found the walls completely covered with posters and banners. Among the new ones the Demarests noticed were: TO CHANGE IS TO GROW, TO CHANGE OFTEN IS TO GROW MUCH. LOVE ISN'T LOVE UNTIL YOU GIVE IT AWAY. TO LOVE IS TO BRING GOD AND THE WORLD TOGETHER. MARRIAGES AREN'T MADE IN HEAVEN, THEY COME IN A KIT AND YOU HAVE TO PUT THEM TOGETHER. The afternoon sunlight was literally bursting through the open window, bringing out all the color in the large bunch of red roses on the altar-table.

Lynn was playing, "They'll Know We Are Christians" softly. When she had finished, Liz asked, "How often is it said of us as it was of the early Christians, 'See how they love one another'? And just what is Marriage spirituality? This is the topic we are going to explore now. Is it a life spent in church, on one's knees as the organ plays ethereal music and one almost hears the sound of angel wings? This is what I used to think being spiritual was as a child. A state of bodiless ecstasy, of complete detachment from the world."

Now, Liz affirmed, she finds Christ where he told us he could be found: "Whenever two or three are gathered in my name." She finds him in her house, in her kitchen, in her bedroom. "Every act of love I perform for my husband, my children, my neighbors is a prayer. But the best prayer is when we all do it together, sharing the work and the joy and the love."

"Marriage spirituality," Len chimed in, "is not being on Cloud Nine. It is not just me and God. It's Liz and me, the two of us, and the two of you. It's a blend of the worldly and the spiritual. Marriage spirituality is the two of us being ourselves: me being a husband, father, businessman; Liz being a wife, mother, homemaker; the two of us being friends to each other and sharing that friendship with our neighbors. Spirituality is understanding our self worth and that of all God's children. Marriage spirituality is us, here and now, with God's help sharing ourselves and reaching out to you. It's building bridges instead of walls. It's giving life, God's life."

"Before we were married," Bob said, "I had a great feeling of independence. I thought I could do everything myself, without relying on outside help. I fell on my face a lot of the time but I was too proud to ask for help. Now I realize that I need two other people, God and Beth. When we got married, we added a new dimension to our love—a new unit which is better than either of us could be alone. We are responsible to God for our actions and to our spouse as well. I can't go to God alone anymore to ask for his forgiveness and blessing. But Beth and I can go together, because we are 'one flesh.' "

We are bodies and souls, minds and emotions, Beth continued. When we fall in love, it's not just a physical attraction. God opens our eyes and let's us see the inner person. That's why God is the greatest asset to any marriage. He thought it up in the first place. If you include him in every part of your marriage, he will add another wonderful dimension.

"When we were married people wondered which would convert the other—Bob the Baptist or Beth the Catholic. It seemed impossible to many of our friends and relatives that we could stay close in spite of our religious differences. But we managed. We both decided we weren't going to convert or be converted. Once we agreed, we never discussed it again. We swept it under the rug. Oh, I would spend an hour on Sunday 'practicing my religion.' That was the sum of my marriage spirituality. Often I longed to pray with Bob, but I was afraid that he would feel threatened. Prayer, instead of being a solution, had become a problem."

It was during their Marriage Encounter that Bob and Beth began to realize that God was absent from their marriage—that so far they had been married on the physical and intellectual level, but were almost entirely lacking a spiritual dimension. They had admitted a longing to pray together. They went home with a spiritual commitment.

What happened next was typical of many mixed marriages. "The first times we tried praying together," Beth admitted, "I let Bob do all the talking. I would chime in with an occasional Amen. The only prayers I knew were the mechanical ones I'd learned in my Confraternity of Christian Doctrine classes. But Bob was patient and encouraging and, soon, I found myself talking to God as a person, as our friend, as our partner. Now it's the great moment of our lives when we put our arms around each other and talk to Our Friend."

Every morning before they go to work, the Barnes sit in their car and offer up the day to come. They pray together spontaneously before they eat. And every night before going to sleep, they thank God for the good things that happened that day. ("There are moments when I feel closer to Bob spiritually than I ever did physically.")

"The question of who is going to convert whom," Bob said, "no longer seems to matter. What is important is that we have a mutual belief in Our Heavenly Father. It's how we live that matters. And for us that is Marriage spirituality."

Liz closed this presentation with further witness on the spiritual progress they had made in their marriage since their Encounter. "Our weekend brought us closer to each other and to God. We realized that it was just a small beginning in the life cycle of becoming a better Christian couple. As the song says, 'They'll know we are Christians by our love.' We start each day with the awareness that 'Today is the first day of the rest of our lives.' "

Len took up the thread without a pause. "For us, Marriage spirituality is living out our Encounter beyond the weekend. It's a continuation of the dialogue we started then. It's a continual awarenss of the need to be open with each other and our children. We believe that our Encounter was a special gift from God. And because, through it, we learned to experience the strength of our love for each other, we feel the need to share what we have with others."

The next questionnaire the couples were given for twenty minutes P.R. and twenty minutes C.D. was as follows:

1. *How do I feel life would be without God?*
2. *How much is God part of what we feel about each other?*
3. *Who or what is nourishing our religious faith?*
4. *My love for you and God makes me want to . . ..*

This is how the Demarests answered:

1. Don: Life would be meaningless. It would be a world in which Evil triumphed and there was no hope for justice or mercy or truth. I would join the mad scramble to get my share like everyone else. All my selfishness and lack of concern for others would come to the fore.

Betty: I can't imagine life without God. Because there would be no life. There would be no me.

104

I am learning (reading Thomas Merton) that even sin is an acknowledgement of God. Our imperfect selves can give glory to God just as the animals and stones do. If God wanted us perfect, He'd have made us that way. Even when I'm frustrated, I can imagine how much fun the angels have watching me, then maybe I'll smile, too.

2. Don: My love of God is so bound up in my love of you (discovering you was discovering God) that I feel it would be very hard to keep my faith if you weren't there to share it. This really scares me.

Betty: I guess what I am trying to get at is that even my guilt, and my impatience with us, can give glory to God. More and more I am learning to love you truly. I have to learn to love *me*. Not be sorry for myself, or about myself, but to be glad God made me and found you for me—so that together, as a completed pair, as part of His Plan, we can give Him greater glory. This idea thrills me. It reaches a secret place deep down inside me and tingles.

3. Don: The cursillo, going to Our Lady of Guadalupe with you, seeing our children grow up so well (especially Pepe) always reminds me how much we owe to Our Lady. Reading Merton's autobiography (and lately his biography) reminds me how similar our backgrounds were and how lucky I was to meet you.

Betty: Thomas Merton (and I'm so grateful to him—I only have to read a few lines and I'm immediately in the presence of God) helps me grow spiritually. I guess converts tend to think alike. And all my old—I thought dead—faith comes to life. I am so grateful for this strange gift of faith. Why me? But then, why us? This millionth second chance God keeps giving us. What scares me is that every second we can also choose to become either saints or devils.

4. Don: Share it with the world, help Johnny and Marie see what they are missing. Perhaps we should try to get John and Ruth to make an Encounter. Get some of this feeling into my novel (without preaching). It also makes me want to be more thoughtful of you. I feel so sorry when I see how tired you are at the end of the week. (But it's also hard for

me to show this honestly. You'll have to be patient with me.)

Betty: In *The Sign of Jonas,* Merton, in writing about God's love for man and man's love for God, says (sort of): God does not need our love. We need His. We must therefore, love God and one another, for their own sakes. We must serve, try to please, enjoy—not so that our love can be returned, but just because we do love. If we love and serve each other, our co-workers, etc., then we're serving Him. Right now I feel freshly and deeply in love with you and with God. (The two feelings are mixed.) And because of this I love everybody—even the ugliest and nastiest who reflect part of me. Because of you and God I can even love myself. (On reading Betty's notebook, Don was impressed by how well Betty was beginning to communicate, especially since she had always been scared of the written word and had started the weekend by writing only a few terse statements.)

"We are in the final stage of the weekend," Liz announced, "the WE-GOD-WORLD stage. Until this afternoon the emphasis has been on you as a couple, on your love relationship, your unity with each other and with God. Now we'd like to suggest that married couples have a special call and opportunity to build a more Christian world for their children to inherit. Our first apostolate is to our children and then to the community. Because we have an open and apostolic marriage and an open and apostolic family, we should be concerned with the needy others outside our little circle of relatives and friends. We have to allow the love which we have discovered to overflow and reach others who are in desperate need of our little treasure."

"There are many immediate apostolates," Len said, "right in your own parish and neighborhood. Making sure not to neglect your children, you can contribute to your religious community by serving as a lector or usher, by decorating the altar or sewing vestments, by singing in the choir. And there are all sorts of volunteer organizations that are crying for help. Offhand I can think of the Boy and Girl Scouts, Big Brothers, coaching Little League, hospital aides and Meals on Wheels for the shut-in."

106

He added that it was because he and Liz had been so inspired and helped by a particular team couple during their weekend that they had decided to take training and become team couples themselves. Now, he said, their pastor had asked them to organize an in-parish program for engaged couples.

Liz testified to another rewarding experience. After their oldest son and daughter had married, their family had seemed suddenly to have grown smaller. And for almost the first time in their married lives, they had an empty bedroom. They discussed the possibility of adoption with the three boys who were still at home. Everybody voted for adopting a baby girl. However, when she and Len had attended a meeting at the adoption agency, they discovered that the majority of the other couples—mostly younger and many childless—wanted to adopt newborn babies. They also learned that older children living in foster homes were crying out for adoption. They decided that since they already knew the joy of a newborn they would ask the agency for an older girl.

"Finally," Liz said, "we met our little girl, Carla. She was seven and a half (two years older than our youngest boy). She was a shy, withdrawn child who captured our hearts when she told us she wanted us to be her "real" Mom and Dad and that she wanted to be our 'real' kid. We found out that this meant having the same name as the people with whom she lived, a luxury that children living in foster homes did not possess."

Liz and Len were appalled to discover how much Carla had been abused in her few short years of life. She had never been hugged, complimented, been made to feel wanted. She had never had a birthday party or participated in any sort of celebration, been given a cake or a present. She had never seen a picture of herself and didn't believe she had ever been a baby ("I was a big kid when I was born"). She had been so mentally and physically abused and deprived that the Nottos wondered sometimes if it weren't too late to try and save her.

"Now Carla is fifteen. A beautiful young lady who is as warm and loving and outgoing as any child born into a caring home. She has truly been a gift from God. We have received far more from Carla than we ever gave. And it looks as if she has accepted us as her 'real' Mom and Dad."

Pointing to a banner by the door (IF YOU WERE ACCUSED OF BEING A CHRISTIAN, WOULD THERE BE ENOUGH EVIDENCE TO CONVICT YOU?), Gordy and Lynn discussed the commitment they hoped the couples would leave with. The

107

commitment of a Christian, they said, implies an obligation to rank temporal matters according to God's plan. It implies a commitment to competence in one's professional field, a loyalty to Christ and the Gospels, a life inspired by the Beatitudes. The Christian marriage commitment includes three areas: 1. a commitment between husband and wife to become a new entity or covenant reality; 2. a commitment to complete the act of procreation by providing their children with an integrated education which develops them as persons, Christians, and servants to their fellow human beings; and 3. a commitment to the world—to give witness to the unity and indissolubility of marriage.

Beth and Bob stressed the need to build on the weekend, not to let the achievements dissipate through lack of dialogue. They urged the couples to try and continue the P.R./C.D. for ten minutes each daily: the 10/10 Plan. They said the questions could be picked up from the Marriage Evaluation sheets, from a passage in scripture or any book. It could be anything that was troubling one of the couples, from the trivial to the serious—from "What is my favorite dish you cook?" to "How do I feel about jealousy?" *(Agape* magazine, to which the couples would receive a year's subscription, carries a monthly calendar with topic suggestions for each day.)

Along with an envelope to enclose a donation to cover the weekend's cost, the team couples passed out several sheets to be filled in. One was to provide feedback about how the weekend had been run. Another was to list the commitment the couple was prepared to make to improve their marriage. Then there were some 23 topic questions for Continuing Dialogue, which included reflections about the weekend, and which the couples were urged to work on at home. Finally, there were various optional forms for the Renewal of Marriage Vows (see end of chapter).

The Demarests went to the lake for the last time to work together on their final statements. On their Commitment Sheet they wrote:

HE: To include Betty more in everything that's important to me, to exclude her from nothing. To help set up the routine chores in a way that we can share them (including one surprise meal a week cooked by each), to try and include God in our whole life, and to work toward this first of all through the cursillo, being faithful to our weekly group meeting and attending the monthly Ultreya. To work together to make the kids feel a part of our new unity and fuller life—and to be sure they know they are especially and individually loved and appreciated. To work more for our church and neighborhood community.

SHE: I want to be more completely in Donald's writing life. I will try to read his work with love first. I will put self-pity in the cellar and hang Christian martyrdom from the balcony. I will try not to get too tired on routine chores to enjoy my Donald and my children.

COUPLE: We will be unafraid about exploring the future and each other with absolute openness, confidence and trust. We will try to share this renewed love and faith in each other with our children, our friends, co-workers and everyone we meet. We will try to fulfill the Prayer of St. Francis as "instruments of God's peace," so that everyone with whom we come in contact will be happier for it and recognize the One who sent us.

We will try to do the 10/10 at least weekly, after Friday dinner, and as often more as seems necessary. We will say one decade, at least, of the rosary nightly with any of the children who want to participate. We will read the Bible aloud as a family celebration.

Dusk was falling as the hand bell summoned them to their last meeting with the group and the team couples. As they entered the conference room they were given another packet of materials (some suggestions about dialogue, a history of M.E., poems and prayers, a Marriage Creed on parchment, a copy of *Agape)*. They placed the love letters they had written earlier, their notebooks and Commitment Sheets on the altar, as Lynn tuned her guitar for a closing paraliturgy.

Couples had moved off the stiff chairs and were sitting on the floor, grouped around the central table, huddled close to each other, conspiratorial islands in the sea of togetherness. Most were smiling, grinning, laughing, touching, fondling. Only two couples sat apart on the chairs. (Betty Demarest, who picked up such things, had heard from two wives in the washroom that they were on the verge of divorce; that their husbands had come on sufferance, made the Encounter as a final gesture.) One of the wives, a pretty, dark-skinned girl with a Mexican name, was crying and scooping Kleenex from a box beside her as if they were peanuts. Her young, beefy, busdriver

109

husband looked sullen. The other wife, a tall, striking blond was looking at her husband interrogatively, challengingly.

When Father John joined them, he was wearing simple white vestments. He explained that the closing "Covenant Service" was based on God's Presence in the Scriptures. He reminded them that Jesus had said that "where two or three are gathered in my name, I am there."

The theme of the service was introduced by Gordy's reading of a passage from Thornton Wilder's *The Skin of Our Teeth:*

> *Mrs. Antrobus says calmly, almost dreamily: I didn't marry you because you were perfect. I didn't even marry you because I loved you. I married you because you gave me a promise. (She takes off her ring and looks at it.) That promise made up for your faults. And the promise I gave you made up for mine. Two imperfect people got married and it was the promise that made the marriage.*

Father commented, "Our married lives are a continual call to listen to God's presence to us as a faithful lover, as one who embraces us even as a husband his wife, even as our finger bears the imprint of our uniqueness carried forever through life as our own. Now let us listen to a song by the Dameans, 'Rainbow,' from their album, *Beginning Today.*"

When this had finished, he asked the couples to pray, with husbands and wives taking alternate verses from Isaiah 49:14-16 and 51:16.

M: But Zion said, 'The Lord has forsaken me,
   my Lord has forgotten me.'
W: Can a woman forget her suckling child,
   that she have no compassion on the son of her womb?
M: Behold, I have graven you on the palm of my hands...
   And I have put my words in your mouth, and hid you
   in the shadow of my hand . . .

Next, Bob and Beth took turns reading from Jeremiah 31:31-34 and John 15:1-17. Instead of a homily, the couples were invited to share their reflections about the readings, about the weekend. Almost all participated in bearing witness to how much closer they had become, how much they hoped to continue to build a better marriage on the good beginnings they had achieved. The Boston Irishman, who had started the weekend so confident that he was merely going through some motions, brought a round of laughter when he exclaimed: "I didn't even know who my wife was before this weekend. Holy

Moses, I've been entertaining an angel unaware. Now I realize I've discovered how much she's put up with. And I hope she'll go on, because I've found out I can't live without her."

After almost half an hour of shared reflections, Father John began to summarize briefly the key ideas discovered by the couples and how they had been reflected in the scripture readings. He then invited the couples to renew their marriage vows as a couple and thus complete their part of the Covenant Service. He began by renewing his own covenant with God in his priesthood and religious life—especially his pledge to be of service to the people of God. Bob and Beth renewed their marriage vows in their own words, and this seemed to encourage the others to come up to the altar with the phrases they had worked out for themselves. Most used variations of the suggested formulas: "I love you and in Christ's name I ask you to share my life forever . . . ." "To be my helpmate always and to be my special friend and for the love of God . . . ." "To love, dialogue with and honor you all the days of my life . . . ."

The Demarests read out what they had written together: "Thirty-one years ago we promised to love each other and to share our lives. I renew this promise with even more wide-open eyes and a deeper commitment, and ask you to share in my continuing growth and increasing love to the very end."

The Boston Irishman said, "The first forty years are the hardest. I ask you to share my golden years as my cherished better half, Mary, my darlng."

At the last moment, the tall blond ran to the altar with her husband. "We'll make it," she vowed. "It's been a struggle, but we'll make it this time, dammit." Half-crying, she pledged to "honor and obey, to love and cherish you till death do us part." Sheepishly her mate promised to try and be a "more understanding husband."

Father John, after leading the couples in a prayer for marriages and families all over the world, for their own families and friends, and for themselves to have courage to remain true to their weekend commitment, led them in the *Our Father.*

There was a final chorus of "They'll Know We are Christians by Our Love," with the couples arm-linked around the room, swaying and shouting the familiar verses:

We will walk with each other, we will walk hand in hand.
We will walk with each other, we will walk hand in hand,
And together we'll spread the news that God is in our land . . .

Father John and the team couples blessed each couple individually.

Then it was all over in a rush. Couples embraced other couples and exchanged addresses. They hugged and thanked the team couples, who stood by the door with going-away presents for each: a tiny bell to ring when dialogue was needed, a huge match to keep the fires of love alive.

"Goodbye," they said, "Love each other. Goodbye. God love you."

As Don carried their suitcase out, Betty Demarest paused at the entrance and patted the brick. "You've been a pretty nice school after all," she said. Their oldest son honked at them from where he had parked his jalopy beside the tennis courts.

POSTSCRIPT

Don: I think it was St. Augustine who said, "Love and do what you want." Presumably because if you love someone (God or your spouse), you'll do what they want. How does this apply to the Marriage Commitment and to Open and Apostolic Marriages?

Jerry: Giving, you receive, is another way of saying that. In the Old Testament we have an image of God as a parent. God becomes believable when you think in terms of your children and what you want for them. The image of God as the husband, which we get in Hosea, becomes stronger in the New Testament. This is easier to understand. Perhaps Christ isn't believable until people have experienced what love of one's spouse means. The M.E. "faith experience" comes through experiencing the love of the spouse.

Marilyn: If you love someone, you will encourage them to be free, as God does. The mother who can't let her child go doesn't really love him.

Jerry: And it's the making up for mutual deficiencies. I couldn't give a weekend without Marilyn. It would be just a head trip. Marilyn internalizes and personalizes what I have to say.

Don: If you were asked, 'What is the most important thing about the Encounter weekend?' what would you say?

Jerry: To see it whole, not in bits and pieces. To feel the flow of the whole 44 hours. We found this out when we were working

112

on the new translation of Calvo's Manual. It all fits together, so much that if anything is left out the flow is broken.

Marilyn: If team couples don't see this, if they do the weekend mechanically, we call them 'technicians.' You have to understand why Calvo puts each element where he does. The whole pattern is so sound.

Jerry: We have a one-page sheet now called the "Overview" to help team couples see the pattern. First there's the Encounter With Self. Nothing can take place unless this works. You have to accept yourself as you really are, recognizing that God made you in his image. Calvo is a profound psychologist in what he has to say here. It's material all the popular books are trying to catch up with, *I'm O.K., You're O.K.,* and the like.

Marilyn: But Calvo doesn't stop with the Encounter With Self. The purpose is to know what you're sharing and to be convinced that it's worth sharing.

Jerry: Then we move on to relationship. Marriage in the World Today sets the individual couple in the larger context. The Law of Growth zeroes in again on your own situation. Symptoms of Spiritual Divorce and Subjects for Understanding break this down into manageable chunks. Worldwide M.E. calls this "Areas for Reaching Out" (AFRO), which is perhaps a better phrase.

Marilyn: Once you have had a chance to examine your own life, you are given a look at the Scripture framework. The Parable of the Sower introduces God's plan. It asks if you are open to hear God's plan.

Tom: God's "Plan" is not a good translation of the Spanish. The American idea of a Plan or Program is not what Calvo meant. In Spanish it has implications of a dream, of being adaptable, rather than of a blueprint or being fixed in concrete, and it includes a future in which your children will play their part.

Jerry: God has something to say about marriage. Community: Image: Unity. This involves the idea of bringing out what is best in others. God's love is a visible sign in the Trinity, say, or the Garden of Eden. The Mystical Body, with the hands and the feet being as important as the head is another sign.

Marilyn: Confidence and Dialogue introduce ways by which we can achieve God's Plan. At my wedding I have made a commitment, to my spouse, before God and the community. But this commitment brings me certain rights. I have a right to intimacy and to complete sharing in all my spouse has and does.

Jerry: This is why, in Minnesota, we add Human Sexuality here. Because Cana is a tremendous mystery. As Calvo says, no human being can achieve complete unity. Dialogue isn't enough. The couple can't hack it alone. They need God to change the water of their ordinary lives into the sacramental wine of his community love.

Tom: Calvo calls Saturday night, "the night of pain." It involves the recognition of Christ's healing grace, and the process of putting the past behind us.

Marilyn: Then comes Sunday morning and Sacrament and Its Graces. This is right out of the French theologian, Henri Caffarel.

Jerry: At this stage, when the couple is open to God and each other, aware of Christ's presence, Calvo gives us the Marriage Evaluation—which he calls "The Grand Dialogue." The first question is "Why do I want to go on living?" Unless you can answer this completely and honestly, Calvo says, you shouldn't go on.

Marilyn: The next question is "Why do I want to go on living with you?" This is "The Great Encounter," the key question of the whole weekend.

Jerry: When you put this Overview on the blackboard, it's like turning on a light. The whole weekend falls into focus.

Marilyn: The team couples see the whole instead of the bits and pieces.

Jerry: The next step is Marriage spirituality. We have to realize that it's not the same thing as monastic spirituality, but how we live as married couples. We have to realize that God is present and has a plan for the two of us. We have to recognize Christ's presence in our marriage, the strength and mystery and pain of being fully human. When couples give their talks each is so unique, much more than couple prayer. Marriage spirituality is reality with God inside it.

Marilyn: I have a mental block about 'spirituality.'

Jerry: The people on the National M.E. Board are in the process of exploring all this. As Tom said, there isn't too much on the theology of marriage.

Marilyn: I guess what this stage is about is 'what is the purpose of married life?' You can use the mountain climbing example. You help each other up. If one falls, you don't cut the rope.

114

Jerry: The next step was erroneously translated. It shouldn't be Open and Apostolic Marriage or even The Open and Apostolic Family (although that's better). The proper translation is The Commitment of Christian Marriage.

Marilyn: First of all to each other, then to the family and the community. It's not an idolatry of the couple relationship.

Jerry: The concept here is sharing. If there is love, it will flow out to the community.

Marilyn: Don Thorman, publisher of *The National Catholic Reporter,* has a marvelous expression, "attractively holy," to express the outgoing apostolic aspect of this phase. Actually, he was describing Pat Crowley in an editorial.

Jerry: But Calvo doesn't make a point of the couple going out and taking on this project, that good work. He says that if there is awareness it will flow out and be creative. Couples will be open and caring because their love for each other urges them to be this way.

Marilyn: We have a saying, 'To Make Love, is to Make Life.' The significance is that couples not only create children; they are life-bearers. Our job is to give life to others.

Jerry: There are still many ways the Encounter experience can be used beyond the weekend, beyond the marriage and the family. It's like a new form of energy, as Calvo says, that will apply to all aspects of life and all sorts of needs.

Don: Like the sun. The sun has been here since the beginning. But now that we are running out of fossil fuels, we're going to have to harness the sun for new energy. The M.E. principle, the M.E. experience, can be applied to almost every area of life.

M.E. Materials
MATRIMONIAL EVALUATION

1. What are my reasons for wanting to go on living?
2. What are my reasons for wanting to go on living with you?
3. What is my main defect as a husband (wife)?
4. What is my main defect as a father (mother)?
5. What is my main defect as a Christian?
6. What is my principal quality as a man (woman)?

WE TWO

1. What are the things I like most about you?
2. What are the things I like least about you?
3. What is it that most unites us?

115

4. What is it that most separates us?
5. What is superficial between us?
6. How can we increase our mutual confidence?
7. Do I see you and accept you as you really are?
8. Do you see me and accept me as I really am?
9. What do you put up with in me?
10. What do I put up with in you?
11. Am I satisfied with our sexual relations?
12. Do I make you happy in our sexual relations?
13. Am I happy in our sexual relations?
14. I feel I need your help specifically in _____
    _____
15. I think I should help you specifically in _____
    _____
16. What can and should we improve in our marriage?

GOD

1. Are we helping each other to know and fulfill His will?
2. What is drawing us closer to Him and to each other?
3. What is separating us from Him?
4. Have we discussed confessing to each other? Do we want to work toward this goal?
5. What graces or helps do we need most urgently?
6. What does God expect from us at this period in our lives?

CHILDREN

1. Do we have all and only those that God wants us to have? (responsible parenthood)
2. What do we think about each one of them?
3. In what are we in agreement and where are we not, about them?
4. In what areas are we giving bad examples to them?
5. In what do they lack in confidence in us?
6. Are they trained in freedom and in love?
7. Do we know how to communicate with them? Do we listen?
8. Are we educating them to material well-being or to be ready to make great sacrifices for needy people?

FOR THOSE WITHOUT CHILDREN

1. Have we discovered how our marriage is to be fruitful? How?
2. How can we use maternal and paternal graces?

116

3. What specifically must we do to realize our mission in the world and in the church?
4. Have we discussed honestly and completely our reasons for not having children of our own? Have I helped you accept these reasons? How?
5. Have you helped me? How?

RELATIVES

1. Are we striving to be at peace with them all?
2. Do any of them interfere with our married life or family?
3. What should we do about it? Let's help each other to see clearly.
4. Should we be doing something for certain ones? Who? What?

NEIGHBORS

1. Are other people really persons to us? How do we know specifically?
2. Is our house open and warm? How much true hospitality?
3. What are we doing to help other couples and families, especially the needy ones?
4. From now on what can and must we do?
5. What is our contribution to the life of our church?
6. Can we increase or deepen this contribution?

OUR HOME

1. What is the main failure in our home as such?
2. What is our chief asset or talent?
3. How can we improve our family spirit? (let every member propose ways).
4. How can we increase our family joy, love, unity, apostolicity?
5. How can we communicate these gifts to others?
6. Does our family as such worship God?
7. What is our goal as a Christian home?

SOCIAL

1. How can we foster peace and understanding in our family and spread it to the world?
2. How can we "live" the proper sense of authority and obedience?

3. Do we ever visit cloistered religious communities to inform them of the social evils and problems in the world and ask for their prayers and meditations on possible solutions to specific problems, injustices?
4. How can we answer the demand of the hierarchy and of God to carry the message of families to all married couples?
5. In the spirit of poverty, how can we simplify our family expenditures so we have time and money to extend the kingdom of God?
6. How can our family open itself to the community, the diocese, and the nation and the world?
7. Are we aware of the fact that we need the poor just as much as they need us, and maybe even more? In what way do we need the poor? What can we do to fulfill this need?

THE DEMAREST'S MATRIMONIAL EVALUATION

I. **SELF**

1. *What are my reasons for wanting to go on living?*

B: I guess because I'm not ready to die. I have so much to get done. I have so much to teach the children, still. My feelings are a mixture of fear and hope.

D: To get my writing done. To communicate with others some of what I've discovered and felt and seen and heard and what it means to me—in a way that might help them to appreciate the world God has made, to find themselves and their place in it. But even more, to be with you as long as God allows—to watch our children grow up and then their children. I feel happy about this.

2. *What are my reasons or wanting to go on living with you?*

B: I have faced the fact of not living with you—of your dying or just not coming home one day—and I've found that I'd be living as only one third of a person: one arm, one leg and a piece of a heart. This scares me.

D: Without you I can't do any of the above things. A writer, especially, needs a secure base, a place he can come back to when he has plunged into the dark depths of his soul or relived the traumatic moments of his life. Otherwise (without this lifeline), he can't make it. Without you there'd be no children. Utter emptiness all around.

3. *What are my main defects as a husband (wife)?*

B: Pin me down to one. I think the worst are seeing my own faults in you, in not taking the beam out of my own eye before judging your motes. I feel guilty about this.

D: Selfishness. Preoccupation with my own concerns, without recognizing your contribution to them, or your own equally important concerns. This stems from more serious sins of pride and anger. I tend to feel helpless about this.

118

4. *What are my main defects as a parent?*

B: As a mother I've often been too busy for the kids—too busy trying to find us. Thinking back I feel sorry and conscience-stricken.

D: As above. Impatience with the children. Lack of interest in their concerns often. Fear of making a fool of myself in front of them—or playing the heavy father the way mine did—has shut me off from them.

5. *What is my main defect as a Christian?*

B: I believe I haven't tried hard enough to see my God in me. I feel like a child who, out of pique, cannot express gratitude to his parents for a lovely present.

D: As above. Preoccupation with myself interferes with my being open and receptive to God and neighbor. Pride keeps me from acknowledging my dependence on Him and them. This makes me feel very small, like a boastful small boy who's run away from home and is too embarrassed to call home or go to the police station. Color me red, blue and purple.

6. *What is my principal quality as a man (woman)?*

B: I guess it's a fault and a virtue—a facility to experience the joys and sadness of others more easily than my own.

D: Sensitivity. Awareness. Interest in other people, ability to identify with them. *When* I can burst out of my cocoon. This quality gives me a feeling of freedom.

II.   **WE TWO**

1. *What are the things I like most about you?*

B: I like the intensity with which you listen to each of us. I like your openness. It makes me warm all over.

D: Your patience, your cheerfulness, your willingness to submit to my (our) needs, interests, moods. Your gaiety, your trust and faith—in me, the children, life, God. Your sensuality and sexuality. The many ways you renew me save me from despair.

2. *What are the things I like least about you?*

B: I am afraid of your anger.

D: Your occasional tendency to play the martyr, to expect other people to anticipate your needs. This is terribly frustrating.

3. *What is it that most unites us?*

B: Our need for each other unites us more than sex or kids or our similar backgrounds.

D: Our children. Our faith. The security in sharing these things.

4. *What is it that most separates us?*

B: Our own insecurities. Our conflicting moods. Feelings of loneliness.

D: Lack of understanding of the things that are important to the other. Feeling shut out.

5. *What is superficial between us?*

B: Our pride.

D: Our tendency to let things ride, not rock the boat. And so not discuss some of the deep concerns that have emerged this weekend. Uneasiness.

6. *How can we increase our mutual confidence?*
    B: Trusting each other. Accepting the fact that we don't want or need to hurt.
    D: Taking time to share more with each other, even if it means getting away together more often. My trying harder to make you realize how much you count, how much you contribute, so that you'll realize your feelings of martyrdom have no basis.

7. *Do I see you and accept you as you really are?*
    B: No, I don't think I really do, because there are many times I see you through the eyes of someone else. I feel ashamed about this.
    D: I try to. Perhaps I see and accept the real you, better than you do.

8. *Do you see and accept me as I really am?*
    B: I think you give me credit for more than I really am, but I like that.
    D: I think you idealize me on the one hand and fail to completely understand me on the other. I am neither as good or as bad as you sometimes think I am. Perplexed.

9. *What do you put up with in me?*
    B: My horror of mess and confusion; my flightiness and moods (at least they are getting better, aren't they?).
    D: My selfishness, my secretiveness. Mixed feelings. You shouldn't let me get away with it.

10. *What do I put up with in you?*
    B: Your love of clutter and complete unawareness of time and place. You see distant things beautifully but often you don't notice the ground under your feet. I yearn over the times you walk in a mud puddle and don't even realize you're getting your poor feet soaked.
    D: Your flightiness, your silliness, which I usually find endearing. Not always.

11. *Am I satisfied with our sexual relations?*
    B: I am very satisfied.
    D: Always, but more and more. I appreciate it's an area in which you have never tried to put me down, or make me feel inadequate, or unwanted.

12. *Do I make you happy in our sexual relations?*
    B: You say I do. You look happy.
    D: I hope so. I try. I would like you to tell me more about what you like and dislike here.

13. *Am I happy in our sexual relations?*
    B: Always.
    D: Yes, yes!

120

14. *I feel I need your help specifically in . . .*
    B: Understanding myself, getting over my moods, being patient with our children, getting out of the house more often to do things with and for others.
    D: I need your help with my novel, to keep me honest and not just show off. I need your help in sharing myself with others, because if you hold back I am only sharing half of myself. I need your leadership in going toward God, because you have always been my spiritual guide and director.

15. *I think I should help you specifically in . . .*
    B: Getting rid of the clutter in your life (emotional as well as material). Helping you see the ground under your feet. Being your seeing-eye dog in unimportant things.
    D: Getting over your feelings of insecurity, jealousy, not being needed or loved enough.

16. *What can and should we improve in our marriage?*
    B: Communicate more. Accept each other as we have this weekend.
    D: I think this has been covered. We are learning to take off masks, tear down walls. Let's try to keep it up. Let's begin with the fact that I love you more than anybody in the world, more than I've ever loved anybody else (warts and all). And for such a hypercritical, judging, evaluating person as myself this means you must be pretty great. I don't think I'm capable of sustained love for a shallow or mean or selfish person.

III. GOD

1. *Are we helping each other to know and fulfill His will?*
   B: Not as much as we should.
   D: Somewhere we have gotten off the track. Perhaps because a sense of community has been missing. Getting back into the cursillo should help.

2. *What is drawing us closer to Him and to each other?*
   B: Finding Him in each other and getting involved in the cursillo again.
   D: The children and getting older.

3. *What is separating us from Him?*
   B: Selfishness.
   D: Pride, selfish concerns, vanity, sloth. When we exclude each other we exclude Him.

4. *Have we discussed confessing to each other? Do we want to work toward this goal?*
   B: The cursillo group reunion will take care of this.
   D: I'm scared of this. I'd rather have you tell what I've done to hurt you and I'll try to make up for it. Old wounds don't have to be opened unless they still fester.

5. *What graces or helps do we need most urgently?*
   B: Praying together. This always makes me feel so close to you and Him.

> D: Patience, an awareness of the needs of other people, a willingness to share our abundance of emotional and material things.

6. *What does God expect from us at this period in our lives?*
> B: An example to the kids and our co-workers.
> D: To become closer to each other so that we can offer ourselves to Him as a complete package, an unbroken gift. Then, through Him, to others.

IV. CHILDREN

1. *Do we have all and only those God wants us to have? (Responsible parenthood.)*
> B: Yes. I'm so grateful to Him.
> D: I think God realized that five is all we can handle.

2. *What do we think about each of them?*
> B: (Goes at length into appreciation of and pride in each of the children.)
> D: I think they have finally realized that we love them equally but in different ways; that we appreciate their differences and respect their individuality and have not tried to mold them into what we want. That we have tried hard not to interfere too much or control their lives.

3. *In what are we in agreement, and where are we not, about them?*
> B: I think we usually agree and have worked together.
> D: Not trying to run their lives. I think, because of my domineering father, this has been more of a concern of mine than yours. Perhaps we've been too permissive but they seem to have turned out pretty well. I admire you for the efforts you've made to cut the apron strings, sever the umbilical, even when it's been painful.

4. *In what areas are we giving bad examples to them?*
> B: Not always presenting a united front, letting them see our disunity.
> D: Fighting, sarcasm, not always letting them see our love for each other.

5. *In what do they lack confidence in us?*
> B: Perhaps they don't really realize how much we love each other.
> D: Our fights have left scars on them as well as on ourselves. Perhaps they lack confidence in my being able to put food on the table for them.

6. *Are they trained in freedom and love?*
> B: I think so. I hope so. I have a deep feeling this is true.
> D: In spite of bad moments, I think we've busted our guts trying (and occasionally almost broken our hearts).

7. *Do we know how to communicate with them? Do we listen?*
> B: At the best of times and in crisis. Perhaps not enough.
> D: More than most parents, I think. M. feels we haven't, I suppose. And we haven't done all we might for D.

8. *Are we educating them to material well-being or to be ready to make sacrifices for needy people?*

B: Perhaps we've been too austere with them, materially, without giving an example of sharing with others worse off.

D: It's worked with most of them, I think. A few have reacted in the opposite way, trying to get more creature comforts. On the whole, I think they show a concern for others. More than we do. I give us a B- here.

V. RELATIVES

1. *Are we striving to be at peace with them all?*

B: We tend to be too wrapped up in ourselves. In spite of our efforts I wonder how much the sons-in-law feel welcome for themselves.

D: I feel badly about the way I treated your mother and the way I treat J.

2. *Do any of them interfere with our married life or family?*

B: Our relatives are so scattered. I wish they were closer so that they could interfere.

D: Those days are over.

(3. & 4. The Demarests had no comments.)

VI. NEIGHBORS

1. *Are other people really persons to us? How do we know specifically?*

B: You have more real friends than I do. But I think I have a better relationship with our neighbors. You're too busy for sharing small things.

D: I give us low points here. Perhaps because we've moved about so much that we haven't struck roots in our church or local community. The East Side was better, when we were more involved in the parish and I edited the community paper. But we moved to the West Side to establish relationships with people we could help. I think we are beginning to be accepted.

2. *Is our home open and warm? How much true hospitality?*

B: I think so. I don't like to invite people too often because of your need for time to write.

D: You certainly make it so. Our hospitality is mostly confined to the clan. They seem to feel at home and welcome. Hospitality in Dorothy Day's sense is lacking.

3. *What are we doing to help other couples and families, especially the needy ones?*

B: Not enough. I feel badly about this.

D: Not as much as we used to. Perhaps when I finish the novel...

4. *From now on what can and must we do?*
   (B & D both wrote: Let's discuss this. It's a real failure.)

5. *What is our contribution to the life of our church?*

6. *Can we increase or deepen this contribution?*
   (same answers as to 4. above.)

VII.   OUR HOME

1.   *What is the main failure in our home as such?*
B: I feel no one else cares if it's clean or not. It's OUR home. You and the boys should care and share more in the house-work.
D: Perhaps that we don't invite enough other people into it, make our children's friends feel more welcome. I feel we use it as a refuge.

2.   *What is our chief asset or talent?*
B: Neither of us wants to keep up with the Joneses. (I need help in keeping up with me!)
D: Not putting on a front, having a house that is lived in, making people who drop in feel at home. We're good at entertaining. We should do more.

3.   *How can we improve our family spirit?*
B: Have a little more relaxed time after dinner to share the day. I feel rushed to clear the table for the typewriter. At least we could drink our coffee together.
D: Carry on with the sharing and communication we learned this weekend. Involve the children in it. I'll try to overcome my feelings of being in a hurry.

4.   *How can we increase our family joy, love, apostolicity?*
B: This is getting repetitious and time must be running out.
D: Taken care of already.

5.   *How can we communicate these gifts to others?*
B: Practice on our children.
D: By communicating with each other first, then going out, hand-in-hand.

6.   *Does our family as such worship God?*
B: Not enough together. I'd like to revive the family rosary.
D: This is too individual. Each to his private mass or preferred church. In our terror about imposing on the kids, we shut them out.

7.   *What is our goal as a Christian home?*
B: To center it around the portrait of Our Lady of Guadalupe. To make family meals a communion table. To share our joy.
D: Liturgy means the day-to-day work around the house. We should get this sense of the liturgical into our family life. Remember that God is present, invite Him, recognize Him, thank Him more often.

VIII.   SOCIAL

1.   *How can we foster peace and understanding in our family and spread it to the world?*
B: First by convincing J. and others that being a Christian doesn't mean being a hypocrite or a pharisee. By making our children more aware of our dependence on God.
D: The chief way I can do this is in my writing, and to some extent my work (with the State Dept. of Education) and teaching. Although I should like to become more involved with the

124

lay apostolate, I'm jealous of my writing time (I've wasted so much of it, frittered it away in penny-ante journalism).

2. *How can we "live" the proper sense of authority and obedience?*
   B: You could exercise more authority and I could practice more obedience. Then change roles. I'm really a Woman's Libber.
   D: By giving God His place, these fall into line.

3. *Do we ever visit cloistered religious communities, etc.?*
   B: There are too many questions to think about and answer properly. I'm sorry we've lost contact with the Trappists in Oregon.
   D: Funny question, perhaps presumptuous. Perhaps I can do this through my writing without taking this role too seriously.

4. *How can we answer the demand of the hierarchy and of God to carry the message of families to all married couples?*
   (B. didn't answer. D. wrote "See above.")

5. *In the spirit of poverty, how can we justify our family expenditures so we have time and money to extend the kingdom of God?*
   B: Time has run out. I have writer's cramp.
   D: I can't think of any luxuries, apart from smoking. The books and magazines are tools of my trade. If my royalties ever amount to anything, I could use them for apostolates like the Catholic Worker, Guadalupe Area Project, and such. But we could be more generous with our time.

6. *How can our family open itself to the community, the diocese, the nation and the world?*
   B: No answer.
   D: Through my writing, your prayers, Pepe's painting and acting, John's concern for animals, Dana's nursing, Ruth's marvelous concern for her children, Marie's teaching. And sharing these and letting each other know we believe in the other's work, and helping each other when we can. I'm feeling repetitious and written out. Hurray for the bell!

125

RENEWAL OF MARRIAGE VOWS
Optional Forms

I take you to be my _____ . I promise to be true to you in good times and in bad, in sickness and in health. I will love you and honor you all the days of my life.

* * * * * * * *

H. _____(name)_____ years ago I circled your finger with this ring as a sign of unbroken love and as a promise of care and concern without end. Today, I repeat that promise and take you again to myself as God's gift.

(Placing the ring on her finger:) We are one body and one life in Christ, come what may, now and forever.

W. _____(name)_____ years ago, I accepted a ring from you, a sign of my willingness to live within the circle of your love. Today, I repeat that promise and take you to myself as God's gift. And in my turn, I give you this ring as a sign of my faithfulness and as a promise of my love.

(Placing the ring on his finger:) We are one body and one life in Christ, come what may, now and forever.

* * * * * * * *

H. _____(name)_____ I love you, and I dedicate myself to you again. I want you to know me as I want to know you. In Christ I want to share with you and with our children all the good that He has given me. I ask you to help me grow and overcome what is not good. I will provide for you and with this Eucharist pray that our love will last forever.

W. _____(name)_____ I love you, too, and I rededicate myself to you. I want you to know me as I want to know you. In Christ I want to share with you and our children all the good He has given me. I ask you to help me grow and overcome what is not good. I will cherish you and with this Eucharist pray that our love will last forever.

> TOGETHER: And the two of us will share our love, first with our children and then with all we meet. In this way we will bear witness to the Kingdom of God we share.

> * * * * * * * *

_____ I love you and, by sharing this bread and cup, I ask you once again to share my life. On my part, I promise you my Love.

> * * * * * * * *

_____ I love you and, in Christ's name, I ask you to be my helpmate forever.

> * * * * * * * *

_____ I promise and ask you to be my special friend in and for the love of God.

> * * * * * * * *

_____ I thank you and God for all that we've shared and I now ask you again to be a part of my life.

QUESTIONS FOR CONTINUING DIALOGUE

1. How do I feel about a weekend spent with you away from the children?
2. What do I feel was the most fun thing we did this weekend and how did it affect our unity?
3. How do I feel my feelings about what happened today affect our unity?
4. What do I feel you love most about me?
5. How do I feel when we receive the Body of Christ as a couple?
6. How do I feel after rereading your Encounter weekend notebook?
7. How do I feel about the growth of our nonverbal communication since the Encounter?
8. How do I feel I could reach out to you more to strengthen our unity?
9. How do I feel I have loved you today and how has this affected us?
10. How do I feel when I observe one of your traits in our son-daughter?
11. How free am I of you and how does this affect us as a couple?
12. How do our individual friendships affect our unity?
13. How do I feel our relationship with God has become more personal?
14. How do I feel my achievements affect our relationship?
15. What would you like best if you could have one favor from me?
16. What are some things I would like you to do for me in a day to make us feel closer?
17. How do I feel our being more open and loving towards our friends can affect our unity?
18. How have we stimulated growth in one another?
19. Where do I need your help more?
20. Where do I think I have to help you most?
21. How are we doing on our confidence and dialogue?
22. Do we show affection for each other?
23. How are we progressing in our mutual prayer?

QUESTIONS FOR CONTINUING DIALOGUE

(Answers written by Demarests in week after Encounter)

2. What do I feel was the most fun thing we did this weekend and how did it affect our unity?

Betty: Hard to say ONE thing. Perhaps us really talking. Getting your undivided attention. I *like* talking to you, especially about us—not in relation to . . . (is that where 'relations' comes from?) So many of my guilt twinges which I was afraid would emerge from their grave now have big rocks on top of them.

Don: The most moving thing was getting closer to you, learning to understand you and feel part of you so that even the love-making was fresh and new and a deeper way of getting to know you and express my love for you.

6. How do I feel after rereading your Encounter weekend notebook?

Betty: So much of it makes me feel tender and good (parts make me feel quivery all over). I'm not afraid that we'll lose our Encounter. I think many of our rough spots have been exposed and faced, not smoothed over. But time and *our* patience will smooth them so they won't bother us.

All day at work I've been surprised at the feeling of *how* much you love me. I like to be loved. I feel tall and straight and young and warm.

Don: A warm glow of recollection, a feeling of joy like an electric buzz in the pit of my stomach, gratitude for the honesty and loving kindness of the words you wrote. Appreciation for the struggle you have with words and yet how well you expressed yourself and helped me to understand the real you.

Determination to take care of the needs you expressed, to help you with your insecurities, to try and overcome the faults that bug you. Hope that we can keep and build on the closeness we achieved this weekend and not let it gradually seep away like old bath water. Faith that God will help us grow in unity and loving kindness, if we ask Him to do so.

Such overwhelming tip-to-toe love for you as my partner, mate, fulfillment, means of wholeness (and holiness)!

9. How do I feel I have loved you today and how has this affected us?

Betty: I feel I have loved you most in trying to let you alone to do your writing and not asking you to help with "things" just so that we could share them. I'm glad I'm married to you today because I know I would have deteriorated into a 'Keep-Up-with-the-Joneses.'

Our children have become more like you. I'm glad you are you because you like dogs and put up with cats, because you will eat burned omelette and store-bought pie. You are so patient with your frustrations (except when playing tennis or bridge!). You are so uncritical of us. That makes our relationship bloom.

Don: I've been pretty tied up in my novel but I've been grateful for your letting me do it. Your quiet loving presence in the background really helped. I thought of you and our early courtship days when I described how Johnny felt about being separated from Haidee. Thank you for the haircut, the delicious dinner and for helping Pepe get ready for his trip.

129

19. Where do I need your help more?

Betty: I need not so much more help as continuous help ... to catch me when even the keel starts rocking. You are so wonderful about seeing the whole picture, while I focus on some small point. I need help most of all, I guess, in organizing the necessities.

Don: In finding things, in managing THINGS, in not getting too frustrated when things get misplaced or go wrong.

In finding my way to God; in being honest and open with Him and with each other; with our children and friends. In being honest as a writer.

In being less selfish, aware of what other people (our children and in-laws especially) need and hope for from me.

Reassurance of your faith in me as a person, as a husband, father, friend, writer.

20. Where do I think I have to help you most?

Betty: I need to help you in the small points. (Or do I only think I should?) I guess I feel I have to help you find things (I hate that!) I do feel I have to try and make some order (but maybe it's just for me).

I guess I can help you so we never get back to the terrible days of the drinking and fights.

Don: To overcome your lack of faith in yourself, your lack of respect for your mind and intuition. To help you to an awareness of how lovable and exciting you are as a person.

To help you cheer up when you get overcome by duties, things, inconvenience, people.

To share your moments of disappointment and uncertainty; to help you turn them into feelings of satisfaction and certainty—because between us, with God, everything is not only possible but wonderful.

To help you see even the worst moments of the past as learning experiences and signposts to future growth.

130

Chapter

Six

CHAPTER SIX
Follow Up: After the Weekend What?

Coming down from Cloud Nine is always a jolt. The tremendous discoveries about each other and the new feeling of union which followed are often dissipated by the exigencies of the real world. The M.E. universe of roses, daisies, butterflies, songs and liturgy, love and freedom from mundane concerns, quickly gives way to the need to make a living, wash dishes and diapers, adjudicate children's quarrels, pay bills. In fact, all the misunderstandings the weekend was supposed to solve have returned, twice as vehemently.

For a while, most couples try sincerely to follow their written Marriage Commitment. They strive to dialogue faithfully. But gradually the daily 10/10 becomes every other day, or weekly, or intermittently. Or, worse, it becomes routine and mechanical. Judgments creep in. The notebooks become a receptacle for what the team couples had called "garbage." It is the Parable of the Sower all over again. Weeds and thorns spring up to choke out the hard-won trust.

And then, about a month after the weekend, the love letters arrive. Sometimes couples read them with a sense of Paradise Lost. They read them and fasten their hands upon their hearts.

It was to take care of this that the various M.E. follow-up programs were devised. They vary in the different expressions. In Worldwide Marriage Encounter, the follow-up techniques are highly structured. The team couples and encountered couples come together for a "Rookie Renewal" or "Initial Reunion" two or three weeks after their weekend. They are immediately enrolled in Neighborhood Circles for regular

133

meetings. Sometimes "Rap" sessions are suggested, which are comparatively informal; but these are structured to lead to the almost monthly "Image"[1] Circles, which follow a strict pattern according to the guidelines set up by the central organization. Reportedly there is tremendous pressure exerted on couples to attend these Image groups regularly. According to Antoinette Bosco[2] reluctant participants are told "Isn't it a shame, you were away for a weekend, but never *made* the Encounter." Then there are annual Rallies, which have been held in the New York area since 1970 and in which many thousands of Encountered Couples take part. Father Gallagher promoted this as a "Stand Up for Christian Marriage" demonstration and couples were urged to come out in full force to bear witness that "they would no longer sit silently by while all sorts of assaults were made against marriage as an institution." However, for the Worldwide expression, the "absolutely non-negotiable" aspect of the Marriage Encounter (a conviction they have raised almost to a dogma) is the daily written 10/10.

National Marriage Encounter, which follows the Calvo Manual and is a loosely structured association of autonomous local groups, has also accepted the need for some sort of follow-up to the weekend. According to Barbara and Armando Carlo, former National Executive Couple, the momentum of the weekend should be continued by some sort of support-group activity: "Follow-up programs should foster a growing aware-ness of the couple's responsibility within the context of their marriage . . . (as well as) an opportunity to share in the experience of Christian community."

Most National M.E. groups offer various forms of Post-Encounter follow-up which are voluntary and organized around locally felt needs. A Chicago couple, Rose and Don Killip, who have worked with the Carlos, are quoted as saying:[3]

---

1. An acronym for "I—Marriage—And—God."

2. *Marriage Encounter,* op. cit., pp. 114 ff. This approach is, of course, well-intentioned. The zeal of almost all Encountered Couples is channeled by Worldwide for a purpose which approaches the messianic. 'Couple Power,' according to founder, Father Gallagher, is to be harnessed to change the world as part of the Catholic Church's missionary purpose ("In, through and for the Church"—see his book, *The Marriage Encounter: As I Have Loved You,* especially the last chapter). Father Calvo also looks on Encountered Couples as agents of change, forerunners in his expected worldwide Revolution of Love. But he is less concerned with movements and organizations than with the individual family (rather than just the couple) and he is definitely committed to the ecumenical, especially interfaith, approach.

3. Bosco, op. cit., p. 105.

"We feel that imposed rules or regulations hinder growth ... We prefer to offer many suggestions for dialogue, including the 10/10, but realize that any *one* suggestion limits dialogue."

Father Calvo, who started M.E. with the help of MFC couples, has always suggested that the best follow-up to the weekend would be participation in the Christian Family Movement. In his Manual, under "Post Encounter," it is stated that "the couples who have attended a Marriage Encounter can continue and strengthen new ideas and conjugal values through the *Retorno,* through Family Encounter and through the Christian Family Movement."

Consequently the first Manual for a Follow-Up program was put together by members of the National M.E., including the Sextons, and the Carlos, and Father Tom Hill, and representatives of CFM, in collaboration. The introduction to *The Encountering Couple* (first published in 1971) states: "It is one among several follow-up programs that can be used after the M.E. weekend. The weekend gives couples the experiences, the tools and the direction. *The Encountering Couple* seeks to build on this foundation .... Ideally, the program should lead to all the couples forming a sense of community between themselves. Then the whole group will become a support group for each of the individual couples. This, after all, is Father Calvo's aim for the Marriage Encounter movement. He wanted couples to deepen their unique relationship through dialogue and to spread the Word of God to others."

The Encountering Couple provides for 11 meetings based on the Weekend Topics (e.g., "Encounter with Self," "Marriage Spirituality" and the "Open and Apostolic Couple"). It is suggested that the meetings start with a prayer, continue with a sharing of how the couples have been carrying out their commitment and then center on a special topic, built around a witness talk, readings from the Bible and other sources (such as the Documents of Vatican II), and group discussion. A time is allowed for Personal Reflection and Couple Dialogue on some suggested questions. After a closing prayer, there is a wine and punch social.

To follow Father Calvo's lead, there are two Evenings of Reflection (which resemble a mini-Retorno) programmed, and questionnaires which focus on the Family Relationship. (For a typical session see the end of this chapter.)

In 1976 National Marriage Encounter published another follow-up booklet: *Image: A Continuing Dialogue Group*

Manual. Developed by three Milwaukee team couples and Father John Furtmann, it provides for twenty monthly sessions over a two year period, and includes two Dialogue Workshops. "Image" is here described as "a reflection of the M.E. weekend . . . It can also be said to reflect the unity and beauty that we found at our encounter weekend . . . or the image of God in our marriage."

Again it is built around themes from the weekend, includes suggested scripture readings and contains Talk Outlines to be followed by the Presenting Couple, a different one for each evening. A series of questions about the theme topic are phoned to the group a week in advance.

The meeting begins with a twenty minute presentation on the selected theme. At the end of the talk, the techniques of dialogue (P.R. and C.D.) are reviewed and the group couples are given a series of questions, including the ones that were already phoned in, to answer in their notebooks. After a set period (usually 10/10), the host couple shares some of their reflections. Other couples are invited to participate on a strictly volunteer basis.

This is followed by a song, and a scripture reading (or, if a priest or minister is available, a paraliturgy). It is suggested that the couples dialogue about how these experiences make them feel. ("What does this song say to me?" or "How do I live this passage from the Gospel?") It is also suggested that any readings be done twice (once by a husband, once by a wife), slowly and clearly.

The final stage, the Agape, is signaled by the serving of refreshments and is an informal sharing of experience. "As the group spirit develops with time, couples may wish to share where their relationship has been since the last meeting—sharing their crises, joys, challenges and growth. It is a means of clueing everyone in, so that support can be given to each couple by the group if it is appropriate. (Example—health problems, loss of job.) This sharing builds a sense of community."

Although *Image* is more structured than *The Encountering Couple,* it carries the following disclaimer: "The outline included with each presentation is suggested only. If you want to change or create your own, be free to do that; or use part of outline applicable. From personal experience we've discovered that the most difficult topics and questions have brought us the greatest growth." (For a typical session see the end of this chapter.)

In the National expression the Anniversary Weekend is usually a special occasion, rather than an annual event. In Memphis, Tennessee, they waited four years before staging one. According to Ken and Shari Lee, the Tennessee team couples had for some time felt a need "not only for follow-up and community building, but also for 'something' between the M.E. weekend and the *Retorno.*" They decided, after attending an Anniversary Weekend seminar at the national convention, that their special celebration should be different from the regular Encounter in three ways: 1. the pace of the weekend would be more relaxed, with "more time to play and pray"; 2. the emphasis would be on attitudes and values rather than feelings; and 3. that it would include group sharing. The special rhythm they developed involved Presentation, Personal Reflection, Couple Dialogue, Group Sharing and Prayer Reflection.

This Anniversary Encounter prompted a letter from one of the participating couples who said: "It did for our heads what the first weekend did for our hearts."

In contrast, the 1975 Anniversary Encounter in South Bend emphasized feelings and dialogue. Shorter talks allowed the couples more time for P.R. and C.D. Because they found that on the regular weekends the two most neglected subjects were feelings about death and sex, they limited the Subjects for Understanding questionnaire to two: 1. *"What feelings do I have about death that I haven't shared with you?" and 2. "How do I feel when I want to make love and you don't?"* They also used the Feelings Inventory (see Chapter Two). According to Lois and Jim Martin, area representatives, they played down the need for the written 10/10, since this was an occasion of guilt for some couples. "We also cautioned the couples not to expect the same sort of high they experienced on their first weekend. We did hope that they would experience new growth and perhaps find a 'high' in depth."

The Sextons have experienced many kinds of renewing weekends, especially as part of National Board meetings and get-togethers of Minnesota area directors and team couples. Such an Anniversary Encounter, according to Jerry, can be a special occasion for sharing and growth. After five years of encountering, he feels that he and Marilyn and many of their close associates know and accept each other's faults and so can risk revealing weakness. "For instance," Jerry says, "these people know that I am a compulsive, competitive person. They accept me as such and love me for what I am."

Of course, one of the most valuable means of building community and encouraging growth is the various M.E. publications which range from a four-page mimeographed sheet to the large, glossy publications of the two expressions (Worldwide's monthly *Spirit* and National's *Marriage Encounter*—which changed its name from *Agape* with the May, 1977 issue, and which is most professionally edited by Robert Genovese). National's affiliates publish some 80 newsletters, including Long Island's *Sharing,* the New Jersey *Encounter-Recounter* and the first-rate *En-Rich-Ment* from Virginia. Local outlets are serviced by *A Letter from St. Paul,* a leadership newsletter and materials packet from National M.E. headquarters, edited by Sister Kay Leuschner, C.S.J.

In June, 1976, Father Calvo wrote answers to "Twelve Vital Questions" posed by Father Tom Hill which were published in the September, '76, issue of *Agape.* In reply to *"What do you expect to happen on or after a weekend?"* M.E.'s founder wrote:

> First, that during the weekend each couple experience an intimate, loving, profound, communication *in* the Lord. And then, after the weekend, that the couple become integrated into the community. First of all in the basic community, their family. Then the community of the Church, in which they can offer the gift of the relationship they have discovered during the weekend. So, first they will offer it to their children and then open it up to the local community, spreading out from their immediate neighborhood—thus creating other independent circles like ripples in a pond.

THE FAMILY ENCOUNTER AND THE RETORNO

Father Calvo has written and spoken frequently (and increasingly of late) of the danger that the Marriage Encounter weekend, because of its very power and success, can lead the couples to turn in on themselves, to the exclusion of their family and their community. He calls it the sin of "conjugalism," whereby what had been selfish, self-centered singles become selfish, self-centered couples.

More and more Father Calvo is looking to the family, rather than to what Worldwide calls "couple power," to bring about the changes that are necessary for a better world. He is quoted in the *National Catholic Reporter* (July 1, 1977) as saying:

"The family is the key to the revolution. The energy of the family is not dying; until now families have been in the stone age . . . Revolution is necessary. If we don't bring it about, someone else will. The M.E. couples are the ones who are building the reality of the 'new family.' If you do not succeed, your children will find other ways."

The Family Encounter, which builds on the experiences of the Marriage Encounter and adapts many of its methods to achieve intergeneration dialogue, has only recently begun to catch on in the U.S. Begun in Murcia, Spain, in 1969, as a natural outgrowth of Father Calvo's insights, it was spread to other countries by the *Movimiento Familiar Cristiano* (the Spanish-speaking CFM), especially in Guatemala and Costa Rica. The first Family Encounter in the U.S. was conducted in San Antonio, Texas, in March 1975 by a leader family from Guatemala for Spanish-speaking families who belonged to MFC.

The first Calvo-directed English language Family Encounter was held in Minnesota the weekend of August 27-29, 1976. With the help of Father Calvo and his translator and assistant, Jose Hernandez, the Rollin Glewwe family of South St. Paul put the weekend together. Nine families from Minnesota, Iowa, Nebraska, Ohio, Wisconsin, and Michigan attended.

According to the Glewwes (who have been commissioned by Father Calvo as the National Family Encounter Coordinators), the program builds on the need and desire of Encountered Couples to extend a similar experience to other members of their family. "Family Encounter," Joan Glewwe says, "really does the same thing as Marriage Encounter in that it helps you discover your children—and they you—as intimately as you did your spouse."

Although the Family Encounter weekend (which took place in the same Mendota dormitory that the Demarests had made their M.E.) follows a similar rhythm, there is more emphasis on developing a feeling of self-worth. ("Junior and senior high school kids often have a very negative self-image," Mrs. Glewwe says. "The weekend is designed to make children aware of self-worth within their own family.")

Although Family Encounter weekends vary there is usually Personal Reflection and writing in the notebooks. Instead of Couple Dialogue there is Family Dialogue in which subjects for Family Understanding are discussed (drugs, drinking, dating, discipline and authority have their share but *'Where does God fit into our family?'* also, perhaps not surprisingly, has a prominent place).

On Saturday morning there is a session devoted to the techniques of listening. Then the families break up into two groups. One consists of all the parents except the team couples and four kids. The other has the team couples working with the remaining children. On Saturday afternoon there is a talk on feelings, followed by a game called "S.I.S. and S.O.S." For the first each family member writes in its notebook the "Strengths I See" in myself. For the second each writes about the "Strengths Others See" in you. These are shared among the family members.

Although twelve year old children can effectively participate, the Crippens had brought their ten-year-old, and the average age was probably 14. Because of these there were a lot of games,, and as many sessions devoted to drawing and collages as individual writing.

The Demarests and Sextons attended the closing session and were impressed by the feelings of closeness and accomplishment the group exhibited—a different sort of high from that of a Marriage Encounter closing, but perhaps more exuberant. The families had worked together on a Family Coat of Arms, a drawing-collage which represented their consensus about the family's greatest achievements.

After a paraliturgy, the members participated in a session of witness reflections about what the weekend had meant to them, individually and as a family. They explained their Family Coat of Arms or read from their notebooks.

Brian (age 10) said that at first he thought there would be a lot of crying, but instead it was fun. "The thing I liked best was when Father Tom wanted us to write down something bad or unfriendly we did to someone else but never apologized. After that we burned the paper up. It was just like you go back and take it away."

Colleen (age 15), "I learned more about my family and how I felt about them and they about me."

Andy (age 14), "We got to express our feelings without having to worry about being yelled at, or being grounded."

Dan (age 15), "At first I thought 'Tah'dah' we're going to end up in a big revival meeting. But it was fun. Then I was worried

140

about the notebooks. I thought I'd get writer's cramp. But the notebooks are the best thing, because I really learned how my family feels about me and each other. I think the team was really responsible for the success of the weekend. When they talked about their family, I could kind of relate to them. They spoke in a way that wasn't over the heads of the smaller kids and it wasn't kid stuff for the adults. I'd have to say I'm glad I went."

In a letter published in *Agape* in September, 1975, Father Calvo made a plea that American families try the Family Encounter:

Let's not lose any more time talking about the generation gap. Let's stop talking about the necessity for communication between parents and children and start dialoguing, building together with hope. Family Encounter, which was born in Spain, like M.E., offers a means of encountering, reconciliation and profound communication between parents and children, between brothers and sisters. Let's extend the Family Encounter to the other nations of the world. The new life of the family can become the new life of history. Then mankind will again believe in love.

Although the Family Encounter is aimed at families with children aged 12 to 21, the same methods with even younger children can be used at home successfully. How one family has accomplished this has been demonstrated in an article "How Our Family Uses the Dialogue to Encounter," by the O'Hay family from Memphis, which was published in *Agape* in March, 1975, and reprinted in the July, 1977, issue. Father Calvo is also developing a home study course for the Family Encounter.

Although the *Retorno* evolved a year later than the Family Encounter, Father Calvo now sees it as the second step, the reconciliation stage, in a couple's development. In answer to another question from Father Tom Hill ("Where do you see the Marriage Encounter leading?"), he wrote:

I now believe that the Marriage Encounter leads serenely, inevitably toward the *Retorno* and that the *Retorno* leads serenely and inevitably toward the Family Encounter. So that the family, whose parents have discovered each other in the Marriage Encounter and dedicated themselves profoundly to God, have, in fact, returned to the altar and become reconciled to God. Then, right after that, immediately, they should sit down on the ground and become reconciled with their children, admitting their faults, recognizing their errors. This family is taking an important and transcendental step which is leading it toward the community.

The *Retorno,* then, is a return to God, a reinforcement of the third stage of the weekend, the We-God stage, a balance between couple dialogue and couple spirituality. Rather simply, it could also be called an Encounter with God, with the emphasis on discovering Him within the relationship.

The first *Retorno* was put together by Father Calvo to help the original M.E. couples grow in their spiritual prayer life. The first English language *Retorno* was held in Ireland a year later. It came to the U.S. in 1972. But it has only been within the last year, under the inspired direction of Gene and Mary Lou Ott and Father Gerry Koob, S.J., that it has begun to develop and spread in this country in a way which resembles the early days of M.E. As of May, 1977, it was active in 31 states (plus Canada, Ireland and Taiwan) and 62 cities.

According to Mary Lou Ott, the *Retorno* is the second step in Father Calvo's vision of Christian Marriage. It is a weekend that balances couple prayer and couple dialogue under the direction of one team couple and a priest or religious. The weekend is geared to provide couples with an opportunity to turn to God for a renewal of their relationship in light of their relationship to God Himself.

She explains that the weekend is divided into four stages: a period of reconciliation between the husband and wife, in which through P.R. and C.D. the couple investigate the level of trust and openness in their relationship and the barriers to deeper union; then three phases in which God is encountered through Scripture as Father, Son and Holy Spirit. Each of these phases follows a definite rhythm: presentation by the team; private P.R. and C.D.; orientation to selected passages of scripture; period of prayer alone; period of prayer as a couple; period of review as husband and wife; and, lastly, a period of faith-sharing with the other couples.

"The phases," Father Koob adds, "deal with God's working and presence in the couple, as Father, as Lord and Brother, in His Spirit as the One who covenants the couple with Himself. The focus is on God's gifting them to be witnesses of His love and unity to the world around them."

142

Gene Ott points out that the *Retorno* is not a movement or organization, but rather a ministry. It is not restricted to Catholics, but is based on a Trinitarian theology and Sacramental understanding of marriage. And, since Father Koob made his Encounter with Worldwide, it attempts a reconciliation between the two expressions. "Although it is not absolutely necessary for the couple to have made a Marriage Encounter," he adds, "the M.E. experience does open them to sharing and dialogue, and provides the impetus for a couple's search for a relationship with God."

Perhaps Father Calvo has best summed up the true meaning and purpose of the *Retorno:*

> *I am convinced that a Marriage Encounter without God at its center, without spirituality as the atmosphere and climate of the whole weekend, is converted into a technical set-up which is more or less obvious and more or less powerful, but which does not bear fruit. I have often said and written that the secret of M.E. is not a technique (or its technique) but God, the Holy Spirit. The same thing may be said of the Post Encounter. Again God must be the center. This is how the Retorno* came about. I am so pleased to discover how many couples in this country are tired of technique and thirsting for God. They give testimony to how unique the *Retorno* truly is . . . impelling them more and more toward God and toward their children and the community. Because a couple could never achieve God's Plan just as a pair. Two cannot be the image of God shut up in themselves. Love needs Three. That is God's image: One in Three.

Among other follow-up programs which Father Calvo has been developing are the Priest's Encounter and the Encounter for Sons and Daughters.

M.E. Materials

MEETING 2 — The Many Faces of Me
ENCOUNTER WITH SELF*

PURPOSE:
To strip away my masks and come to a deeper awareness of who I am and can become.

Reprinted from the Encountering Couple

OPENING PRAYER:

SHARING OF COMMITMENT:
Have each couple let the group know how they lived up to their commitment from Meeting One. If any couple cares to pass when it's their turn, don't pressure them. They may choose to share after the others finish—or sometimes, not at all. If we respect our spouse's feelings as important, how much more must we respect the feelings of another couple.

THEME:
Personal Witness: ask for a volunteer to share his/her thoughts and feelings about—

1. The difficulties I've had in discovering my real, true self.
2. The masks, games and other obstacles I use to keep others from knowing me.
3. The good, likable qualities I've discovered about my real, true self.

Readings:
1. Galatians 4:21-31 and 5:13-15 (Paul's words on freedom).
2. **Cure of Mind and Cure of Soul,** J. Goldbrunner, p. 29
3. **Religious Values in Counseling and Psychotherapy,** C. Curran, p. 350

PERSONAL REFLECTION AND COUPLE DIALOGUE:
(Suggested time limit—15 and 15 minutes.)

1. What masks, games and other obstacles have I found especially difficult to overcome? Why do I have this difficulty?
2. How do I feel about sharing my good qualities with you?
3. Am I easily threatened? Why?
4. How do I feel when threatened? (Cite some examples.)

GROUP DISCUSSION:
1. Review your list of likable qualities about three people you know. Are these qualities real? Put on? How do you know the difference?
2. How can we, as a group, support each other
   —in breaking out of the boxes into which we put each other?
   —in removing masks?
   —in being more honest in our relationships?

144

3. How can we do this with our children?

COMMITMENT:
I will personally commit myself to _____

_____

_____

_____

_____

so that I can get to know myself better.

PREPARATION:
The time and place of Meeting Three: _____

_____

_____

Glance ahead to the worksheets. Clarify any misunderstandings about what's expected before the next meeting.

CLOSING PRAYER:

SOCIAL:

Preparation for Meeting Three:
1. Watch a TV program that portrays family life and marriage. Does this program "show it like it is"? What influence do such programs have on you? On your children?
2. What influences do *Playboy/Playgirl* and other media have on our notions of the image of man and woman?
3. What do these modern means of communication tell us about marriage and family life? Do these ideas fit in with our Christian ideas of love, marriage and family? How do they agree or disagree with the Christian idea?
4. How many divorced people do you know? What are some current statistics regarding the divorce rate?

Personal Reflection and Couple Dialogue:
1. How has our relationship grown in the past month?
2. How has encountering (discovering) myself helped our relationship to grow?

MARRIAGE SPIRITUALITY*
Personal Liberation

Purpose of Presentation: Marriage Spirituality is the quality or state in marriage where the relationship provides an animating or vitalizing force to give life to each partner. Society has defined roles which limit us in becoming a whole person. Every human has male and female components. The more both components are awakened and developed in any given individual, the more fully alive that person will be. "The glory of God is man fully alive." (St. Irenaeus) Reference: "The Secret of Staying in Love" by John Powell, Pages 10 and 62.

Preparation for Meeting by Presenting Couple

Method: A. Write personal reflections and then dialog on the following questions:

1. What do I consider feminine traits and how do I feel when I act in a traditionally feminine way? How do I feel when I don't act in a traditionally feminine way?
2. What do I consider masculine traits and how do I feel when I act in a traditionally masculine way? How do I feel when I do not act in a traditionally masculine way?
3. How do I feel our traits complement each other?

Telephone these questions to your contact and host couples in advance, so they can phone them to the other couples in your Image group to dialog on before the meeting.

B. Use the following outline to organize the feelings and experiences you have discovered in your dialog.

Limit your talk to 20 minutes.

The Meeting

Dialog Question: What potentials have you helped me develop and how does this make me feel?
Sharing: Ask couples to share experiences and feelings on this subject and questions they reflected and dialogued on.
Suggested Scripture Reading: Genesis 1:26-27 and Genesis 2:7.

---

*Reprinted from *Image: A National Marriage Encounter Continuing Dialog Group Manual.*

Outline of Talk

I. **Introduction** (Suggested time: 1 min. for each spouse)

A. See "Purpose" above.

B. We are each sharing on our own "masculine" and "feminine" traits, our feelings about them, and especially on how my spouse is helping me to develop my potential in becoming a whole person.

II. **Body** (Suggested time: 5 min. for each spouse)

A. Society and family have stated what is proper as far as being a male and being a female. A set role limits a person's development because we expect ourself and each other to behave and feel in a certain manner.

   What did my family and friends expect of me, as to what was proper behavior and appropriate feelings for the sex I am?

   Example: Expressing feelings, talents and skills, expressing sexual needs. How did I feel when I didn't fit the mold? How do I feel now?

B. In what ways do I continue to break the traditional role for my sex? How did I feel about this at first? How do I feel now?

C. The attitude of looking at myself as a **total** person with all sorts of potentials liberates me to become freer in exploring who I am and what I can become.

III. **Conclusion** (Suggested time: 4 min. for each spouse)

A. Marriage can be a search together. What potential/potentials have/has my spouse helped me develop? How does this make me feel? How does this affect our unity?

B. What potentials do I want to develop? What do I need from you, my partner, to help me in this process?

   Example: Praise, encouragement, patience, other. What fears do I need help to overcome?

147

Chapter Seven

CHAPTER SEVEN
OFFSHOOTS: Bringing the Encounter to Those Who Need It Most

Father Calvo is worried that the Marriage Encounter movement in the U.S. is chiefly a middle-class movement, taken up by comparatively affluent, comparatively liberal couples. He is quoted by *National Catholic Reporter* as replying to a statement at a board meeting in Houston in 1975 that 'We are changing the world:' "But where are your black people? There wasn't one. And in three days there wasn't a word of Spanish."

Father Calvo is probably unaware that it is the suburban middle class in the U.S. who are chiefly responsible for promoting new movements. Especially in the Catholic Church it is they who have been the vanguard in such lay apostolates as the cursillo and the Charismatic movement, as well as M.E. and CFM, and earlier organizations devoted to interracial justice and ecumenism.

It is typical of such people that they have brought the Encounter approach to areas not considered by Calvo in his targeting on the family. Encountered couples have developed variations of M.E. for engaged couples, the widowed and divorced, alcoholics, gamblers, prisoners, mixed marriages and as an ecumenical bridge to Jews as well as Protestants.[1]

---

1. In this and subsequent chapters, unless specifically mentioned, programs referred to have been developed within the National expression.

THE ENGAGED ENCOUNTER

The Engaged Encounter was developed by a Detroit couple, Betsy and Jim Carr, in 1968. Active in the CFM, they had made a Marriage Encounter for the same reasons the Sextons had, seeking a new direction for the CFM Third Phase. "We sensed," Betsy reports, "what a tremendous good Marriage Encounter would have been if we had made an Encounter prior to our own marriage." Using material from their weekend, with adaptations for those who were not yet married, the Carrs, together with John and Kay Devine and Father Ed Haggerty, presented the first Engaged Encounter in February, 1969, at Gesu Parish in Detroit. With the help of Father Ruben Tanseco, a Spanish-speaking Jesuit from the Philippines with experience as a clinical psychologist in marriage counseling, they translated and adapted material from Father Calvo's Manual that would be pertinent for those contemplating marriage.

In 1970, Detroit began a series of Engaged Encounters. Teams were trained—consisting usually of a couple married for a number of years, preferably with children, and a newly married couple. By 1972 they were giving an encounter a month and the news was spreading across the country. It is impossible to estimate how many Engaged Encounters have now been given, but in Minnesota alone, there have been over 40.

In September, 1976, the *Engaged Encounter Manual* was published. A group of Minnesota couples and priests took the Detroit experience and adapted it for several situations. One option allows for a weekend at a retreat house or similar facility; the two day program (aimed at college students) provides for Saturday and Sunday sessions, as does the two day program for a Parish Engaged Encounter.

The weekend E.E. follows the Calvo Manual pretty closely, except that the presentation talks and questions are focused on exploring what the couples expect from marriage and each other, rather than what is happening in a marriage. For instance, after the introductions, the couples are asked: *1. Why did I come?, 2. What do I hope to gain?, 3. How did we meet?* After the "State of Marriage in the Modern World" presentation (which emphasizes the need for preparation for a marriage and not just a wedding: "Years are spent in preparing for jobs in our society but little time is spent in preparation for one of the most lasting commitments the couples will make in their lives"), the questions for personal reflection are: *1. What have been the two happiest times that I have shared with you?, 2. What do I like best about you?*

In "Symptoms of Spiritual Divorce," the couples are asked to look at ways they are dissatisfied with each other, weaknesses (such as jealousy) already present in their relationship and possible areas of conflict. In "Subjects for Understanding" such topics as "Should the husband be the head of the house?" and "Will both of us work?" are explored. A question box labeled "Topics for Additional Discussion" is suggested, with questions to be answered by team couples.

On Sunday, the couples together draw up a "Plan for the Future" and plan their wedding liturgy. The final liturgy usually resembles a wedding and includes some of the ideas the couples have decided on for their own. (For further topic suggestions and questionnaires from the E.E. Manual, see the back of this chapter.)

Even more than on the M.E., the right sort of witness from the team couples is vital. According to the Manual:

> The married couples open their marriage experience so that the young couple can see a marriage from the 'inside.' By the team's sharing, another model is presented to the young couples besides their own parent's marriage. Because of the openness of the team, cross-identification takes place since they see that they are not alone in working at marriage. They see that other couples have the same fulfillments and obstacles.[2]

According to Barb and Greg Morneau, Minnesota veterans of Engaged Encounters, the chief benefit of an E.E. is the modeling which enables young couples to establish good communications from the very beginning. Greg adds, "E.E. is also designed to help prevent marriages that shouldn't happen. The weekend gives the couple an out, the chance to cancel or postpone a marriage if there are any doubts."

"We've been involved in a lot of weddings," Barb says, "as a result of the weekend. But we also usually lose one or two couples."

2. "We now see clearly that the way most of us learn the art of living is not through instruction, but through observation of how others act. Our marital taboos have closed off this whole area of learning to couples, and this is a major explanation of our high rates of marital failure today. The learning that goes on in couple groups is dynamic and powerfully effective."
—David and Vera Mace, "What Happens in Couple Groups," *Faith at Work*, Feb., 1976.

One couple who decided to go ahead with their marriage wrote: "We've been made aware of how little people plan beforehand. We now have a better understanding of the importance of communication in marriage and a new technique for better communication. We have learned that we really have to work hard if we are going to grow together."

Another Minnesota team couple, Norm and Mary McGraw, say: "We were married for eight-and-a-half years before we learned the benefits of dialoguing. Now we wish we could have made something like E.E. before we were married. Engaged couples now have an opportunity to learn an effective tool for communication right from the start."

The Engaged Encounter is being used increasingly by U.S. dioceses to take the place of the often hurried, haphazard or lecturing Pre-Cana Conference.

THE BEGINNING EXPERIENCE

The Beginning Experience (originally it was called the "Beginning Encounter" but the title didn't seem appropriate) was developed by Sister Josephine Stewart, SSMN, of the Catholic Renewal Center of North Texas as a result of pastoral work done with divorced Catholics. It was aimed at those who had been married and are now single either because of divorce or death.

The flow of the weekend has some similarity to M.E. and the style is the same. Most presentations are done by two people, a man and a woman who are divorced or widowed. There is a period of written reflection on specific questions and then dialogue in small groups in place of couple dialogue. It begins, as does M.E., with an introduction to feelings and Encounter with Self. The talk on "Symptoms of Spiritual Death" explains the five stages of grief as defined by Elizabeth Kubler-Ross in *Death and Dying:*[3] disbelief, anger, bargaining, depression and, finally, acceptance. The M.E. stage which is called "Confidence and Dialogue," where there is a build-up of trust in the marriage partner, is replaced by "Trusting Ourselves and Others," and "Trusting God" substitutes for the Marriage Commitment.

A major difference in emphasis is on reconciliation and sorting out what is "realistic guilt" and what is psychological

3. Macmillan, N.Y., 1969.

guilt. Saturday night has talks on Reconciliation, and Realistic and Unrealistic Guilt, followed by opportunities for the Sacrament of Reconciliation or counseling.

The high point of the weekend comes on Sunday morning. The participants are encouraged to write a letter of closure to the former spouse—which is not always mailed. Instead of the M.E. question at this stage, *"Why* do I want to go on living?" (which, it is felt, may pose problems for people in a state of depression), the P.R. question is *"How* do I want to go on living?"

According to Sister Josephine, the program was aimed originally at divorced Catholics. "In addition to the normal grief accompanying any separation or divorce, many separated or divorced Catholics see themselves as standing on the periphery of the Church like unwanted or unloved naughty children. The Beginning Experience aims at providing an atmosphere of acceptance by the Church for such Catholics."

The weekend has been opened up to widows and widowers, because, although the circumstances of their loss were different, the grief process is very similar.

It was also opened to non-Catholics, especially single parents. "It goes without saying," Sister remarks, "that there are millions of Catholics and people of all denominations throughout the U.S. who are single parents, something that was not looked at within the Church. Unlike the M.E. where the husband and wife go home together to a loving atmosphere, the single person goes home to an empty apartment or to the responsibilities of single parenthood and sole support of the family. The weekend program initiates a renewal of life for the separated or divorced and hopefully creates a space where these persons can come together for a weekend and re-evaluate themselves and their lives and move on to the future with hope."

The two parallel themes, she explains, which run through the Beginning Experience are the personal "passing through" the stages of grief to acceptance and the theme of Jesus' "passage from death to resurrection." The program provides for an experience of death and life. This includes trusting oneself and others as created and loved by God, trusting that God is present in the circumstances of one's life, forgiving oneself and accepting God's forgiveness, closing the door on one's symptoms of death, experiencing new life and reaching through love to others.

"The purpose of the Beginning Experience is to close the door gently on the former marriage (and this is true even for the widowed). It is my experience as a counselor that what keeps people in a state of depression or in a state of bitterness and anger (so that they no longer have a positive approach to life and to themselves) is that they carry around a heavy bag of depression because they are holding on to what they have lost. Our objective for the weekend is to come to the point on Sunday morning of closing the door gently on the marriage, not slamming it shut so that it is done in anger or bitterness and will fall open again, but trying to finish the business of putting the past behind and getting on with the future. In this respect it is the opposite of M.E., which is a bonding and a closeness. The purpose of the B.E. weekend is to close off the past, especially the negative past, and get on with living."

A divorcee who made the first weekend wrote: "I went prepared for a weekend away from four children. I found myself unable to give or receive love, shut off from all my feelings. I think the biggest effect of the weekend was in letting myself feel the pain, because it was only in feeling the pain that I was able to turn away from it and feel the love of others, both from my children and my friends."

Grace Ross, who works in the Minnesota M.E. office and who was an early team member, says: "It is not magic but rather an instrument, a very good tool. I have seen it work. It provides a place for a grieving individual to be heard and understood. It focuses God's healing power into bruised and hurting lives . . . I am healed as I give—out of my own pain— and see the resulting growth in others. Some describe us as 'wounded healers.' It's exciting and rewarding."

The first correspondent wrote: "The thing that I personally came away with was a feeling of being somebody, being accepted again. The family's attitude was very bad; the Church's was even more curt. I found myself in a place where nobody had time for me. I wasn't being a good Catholic . . . Now I have become again the person I was when I was younger. I feel very good, part of a fantastic family . . . I even feel that there is unity between me and the Church."

A 51-year-old woman, widowed seven years with four children, two still at home, says: "I wanted to be released from my overwhelming love for my deceased partner. I wanted to be set free with my great love. I couldn't believe it when I finally said it out loud. During the weekend I experienced tears of sorrow and they helped me wash away the past, but something new was the experience of sharing with my small group who had tears of joy when I found my answer."

"I went into the weekend unable to love," another divorced person wrote, "only hating and hurting. It has taken a lot of work, but I've finally decided that hating isn't worthwhile. I can really say, 'Thank you, God, for my divorce;' because without it, I'd never have grown into the person I am today!"

ENCOUNTERS FOR OTHER NEEDS

It was during a regular Marriage Encounter that Charlie D. found the inspiration to help other alcoholics like himself. "By Saturday noon," he says, "I'd had it up to here. I wanted to leave, no question about it. But then one of the team couples revealed a family drinking problem during one of the presentations and that made all the difference."

Charlie discovered that he wasn't alone in that room full of people 'with good marriages seeking to make them better.' At least one other couple, a team couple at that, knew from direct experience the pain and alienation which alcoholism brings to a family. Shortly after the weekend he went to a hospital which specializes in treating the chemically dependent. And he has been dry ever since. "M.E. had opened my eyes to the possibilities in myself and my marriage and I knew I had to do something about it." The something involved helping others as well. Charlie and his wife, Bette, began looking for ways to put on weekends directed especially at marriages which were in trouble because of the drinking of one or both spouses.

They found Father Doug Fiola, who was administering a program for the chemically dependent in Rochester, Minnesota. He had also worked on weekends and had been considering the possibility of adapting M.E. for his program. In fact, he had already arranged for M.E. team couples to speak before AA and Al-Anon groups.

Together they set up the first weekend Encounter for Alcoholics in Rochester in the spring of 1975. Their weekend makes use of some of the material from AA and Al-Anon, which is rich in spiritual tradition, including the Twelve Steps, the Twelve Traditions and the Serenity Prayer. But otherwise it follows the Calvo Manual. They recognized that alcoholics are in special need of the communication tools that the M.E. provides. "Often a recovering alcoholic," Father Fiola says, "finds it easier to dialogue with others suffering from the same disease at AA meetings than with his spouse."

From the beginning they have used a team made up of non-alcoholics as well as one with a chemical dependency problem. "I think that is the ideal arrangement," Charlie says. "By listening to two other 'straight' couples the participants discover that, apart from drinking, their marriage problems are no different from anyone else's."

In addition to the weekend, the D.'s feel that follow-up is essential. "The weekly group atmosphere with other couples is vitally important. It provides both feedback and discussion, plus the assurance that the group will furnish social support as it is needed."

Jerry H. wrote after his weekend:

> Although I am now what is referred to as an 'arrested' or 'recovering' alcoholic, my marriage was very sick until recently. Now I believe that my marriage can be called a 'recovering' marriage. My active alcoholism raised havoc with the communication, trust and intimacy which had once existed in my marriage. Even after I got into what's called the 'recovery process,' my marriage relationship didn't change much. I learned to share and remove some masks outside my home with groups of other recovering alcoholics. I learned I could even use these groups as an escape. Needless to say, our marriage got to the point that it looked like a 'terminal case.' I went into the weekend with mixed feelings of hope and terror. I didn't really know what was going to happen, but I felt it had the potential of either helping or ending my marriage.
>
> At one point during the encounter when they were presenting 'Symptoms of Spiritual Divorce' I felt both guilt and sorrow. I felt my marriage was dead and I was responsible. By the time the weekend was nearing its end, I was shedding tears again, but this time of joy. It wasn't hopeless. My wife loved me. She was as frightened as I was, but we were sharing again and planning the future together.

The Catholic Renewal Center of North Texas—the people who were responsible for the Beginning Experience—were also the first to put on a Marriage Encounter in prison. The Federal Correctional Institution in Fort Worth is exceptional in its determination to make the rehabilitation process work. It devotes special efforts to making its "residents," as the prisoners are called, involved in programs which help them relate to themselves and the community in a positive way. Married prisoners are allowed to live together. It seemed to provide a challenge to M.E.

According to Terry and Sue Goddard, whose letter was published in *Agape,* January, 1975:

> When we arrived at F.C.I. we were approached by fellow residents who asked if we were interested in Marriage Encounter. We questioned in our minds what kind of marriage program could be offered to a man and wife who were Federal prisoners . . .
>
> (But) we found the M.E. to be a total inner enrichment that strengthened our marriage relationship, regardless of external conditions. Several staff members have made the Encounter and seem to feel that the experience is worthwhile for both them and the residents. From a correctional point of view, it's interesting to note that discipline irregularities have dropped sharply for residents who have encountered. We believe that M.E. influenced and led these residents toward more positive lifestyles . . .
>
> Throughout the years of penology it has been established that the destruction of the family is not conducive to effective and successful rehabilitation. F.C.I. residents involved in M.E. indicate that it is a sturdy program and can be used positively toward achieving our constant goal of being productive citizens.

What has been discovered in these various experiments is that ordinary sharing and hurting couples can help others in the same situation in a way that is often beyond the reach of professional counselors. Another discovery has been that Marriage Encounter which was intended, in the U.S. at least, (and continues to be so considered by Worldwide) for good marriages only, can help people who are in trouble.

Sometimes, however, problems surface during an Encounter which call for professional treatment and these are referred to an appropriate agency when the couples request it. It is this situation which prompted Father John Higgins, who is attached to the National office, to initiate his Marriage and Family Ministry.

This is a training program for M.E. couples who are willing to help marriages that are in trouble, either by offering support and listening skills or by referral.

"We chose the name Marriage and Family Ministry," Father Higgins says, "because we were unhappy with the term 'counselor' or 'paraprofessional' (we decided we did not wish to be, nor could we be, either). What we did want to do was to continue to be people who could reach out with understanding, love and care as Father Calvo suggests team couples should in his Manual. Also Vatican II invited married couples to 'minister to and care for' other married couples and those engaged to be married. We wanted to say, 'Hey, it's o.k.; we have been there. There are problems and we care about them.' We also began to recognize that with some professional help we could develop talents and gifts to put to the service of others. This was very much the way it was and should be in Christian and Jewish communities."

The response from the Twin Cities professional community was extremely supportive. People such as Dr. Richard Hey of the University of Minnesota Department of Family Science, Dr. Sherrod Miller of Interpersonal Communications, Inc., and Tom Hubler of the Gestalt Institute, helped develop a training program which involved group facilitation, crisis intervention, methods of referral and advice about chemical dependency and marital sexuality.

According to Father John, "It was the feeling of the local professional community that there are many people who need help but who either don't go to professionals or who just don't know what to do. There are already a good number of non-professional people who are already volunteering their time and gifts to reach out to people who need help. The AA movement is the oldest, but there are lay volunteers for drug problems and many others. While recognizing that we aren't professional marriage or family counselors or therapists, the professionals felt we could provide a real service."

So far about 20 M.E. couples have completed the 40-hour course.

PARISH ENRICHMENT AND HOME STUDY COURSES

One way to reach Father Calvo's "poorest and neediest families"—or the many more thousands who will never make an Encounter for financial or other reasons— has been to present the M.E. in a parish setting. To distinguish this from the regular weekend encounter, it is usually known as 'Parish Marriage Enrichment.'

160

In an article in *Agape* (October, 1975), Steve and Kathi Smith of West Orange, New Jersey, report that in Rhode Island and New Jersey there has been a concerted effort on the part of M.E. leadership to bring the Encounter to those who are least likely to seek it out—the lower income or inner-city couples—through their parishes.

John and Kay Devine of Detroit in another article *(Agape,* January, 1976), point out that there is a tremendous need and hunger for help with their marriages within the parishes that is largely unacknowledged and unexpressed:

> A marriage enrichment program should be put on at a parish level to reach more couples, to expose whole parishes and the community to the fact that there is something for marriages. That there is something that will help your relationship to grow. We must reach couples that may never be able to get away on a Marriage Encounter weekend.

Father John Gilbert, pastor of the Nativity of the Blessed Virgin Mary in Bloomington, Minnesota, discovered that with very little advance publicity a marriage enrichment program in his parish received a tremendous response. "It was the biggest turnout for any adult program in our parish. An announcement in the parish bulletin, one announcement from the pulpit and posters in the church lobby drew ninety couples. In terms of my ministry this type of program fulfills a real need."

The main problem has been to adapt the M.E. format with its retreat house facilities and its concentrated (and uninterrupted) time span of 44 hours to a parish setting. The most successful and often-used approaches have been a telescoping of the Calvo Manual's Four Stages into a one day, a one-and-a-half day and a four session approach—which in Detroit is spread over four weeks.

Father Gilbert's parish used the one-and-a-half day program, which runs about twelve hours. The program mostly used in Rhode Island lasts about fifteen hours, almost two days. The Detroit program is presented one night a week from 8:00-10:30 p.m. for four consecutive weeks. According to the Devines, four sessions were chosen because ten hours seemed to be the minimum in which the material could be adequately presented and "because people will commit themselves to four sessions. That doesn't seem too long. If you make it six, they will think, 'Do I really want to go six times?' " The Devines call their program "Happiness is Being Married." One evening is devoted to "Communicating our Sexuality" and includes a pretty explicit one-hour film put out by the Ortho Pharmaceutical Co. of Toronto.

There are problems involved with Parish Enrichment that don't come up on the regular weekend. One is how much to charge. In some parishes the program is free, paid for from funds set aside for adult education, with the food and materials often contributed by volunteers. But, as the Smiths point out, this is especially touchy in an inner-city parish: "It puts us in conflict with those people's legitimate pride. People in the inner city will not accept something for nothing." So in Rhode Island and New Jersey the suggested donation is usually $10 per couple.

Another difficulty is the space factor. Most encounters are held in retreat houses or special accommodations reserved and set up for the weekend, where there are bedrooms and ample facilities, not only for the conferences but also for private reflection and couple dialogue. In a parish there are usually a library, a hall and classrooms which can be put to use. It is suggested that the team couple in charge survey the lay of the land and plan logistics well beforehand.

Then there is the problem of how to get participation from the couples, who are often not as relaxed as they would be on an Encounter—where they are more likely to be strangers instead of neighbors, or people who at least see each other frequently in church. For this reason group discussion is often included, as well as the use of a discussion box (which may have to be stuffed initially). The Devines explain this: "In a parish some may be a little afraid if they raise their hand and ask a question, because they will expect that other people may think something is wrong with our marriage."

Follow-up is handled differently in different parishes. In Detroit the system to accommodate this is to establish parish activities: discussion groups run by the original participants on the Presentations in the Calvo Manual; often there is a family-centered liturgy, plus group discussion, as an anniversary celebration. In Rhode Island, the Smiths explain: "We try to steer couples away from the follow-up groups for a couple of reasons. First of all, we believe that it is better to get them involved in a parish CFM group, which can then carry on the parish involvement which we've stressed." Their other concern is that involvement of the parish participants with those who have made a regular Encounter can lead to a put-down by those who consider the weekend the only way to go. Here we have the problem of elitism again.

The parish program has certain definite advantages. One is that there is already a built-in community. It also leads more easily and inevitably to the Fourth Stage of the weekend ("We-God-World"), to the third year of the CFM program and to Father Calvo's hope that an encounter will open couples to the world so that they will "pass from being a couple-dominated and nuclear family to becoming a thermonuclear family—that is intercommunicating, united and radiating out to the community."

The Smiths emphasize the need to stress the parish apostolate—"so that everything in the program is centered on parish involvement, parish activities, the people in the parish getting to know each other, with these couples making all that possible."

They describe an experience which took place at a parish follow-up meeting. Everyone was quite articulate about how much they had obtained from the program, except one couple who had remained strangely silent. When challenged, the husband explained that he had been searching for words to describe how he felt. "I've known these people most of my life," he said. "But I've never loved them before. We've worked together and played together—but not like this. I now have a real feeling of love and concern for them as people and as families."

Because of his concern to reach the poorest and neediest families, Father Calvo, in 1976, initiated a program of home correspondence courses which he calls F.I.R.E.S. (Family Intercommunications Relationships Services).

"F.I.R.E.S.," he says, "is my last dream. It isn't a movement. It's not an organization. It's simply a dream." Included in the program are a series of booklets which are a sort of do-it-yourself guide to Encounter basics. They include "Home Encounter" (in three manuals: *Self Encounter, Marriage Encounter At Home* and *Family Encounter At Home),* "Home Retorno" *(Personal Retorno, Marriage Retorno At Home* and *Family Retorno At Home)* and "Engaged Encounter." As we went to press, these were still in preparation. In an Open Letter to Encountered Couples, Father Calvo wrote:

163

F.I.R.E.S. is a desire to reach all the homes of the earth without any sort of discrimination . . . to give each family, complete or incomplete, the opportunity to encounter itself, to discover its vocation and its mission and to launch out as a family to build new communities which will renew the face of the earth . . . F.I.R.E.S. proposes to serve the individuals, married couples and families inside their own homes and in the natural environment of their own neighborhoods—with the profound conviction that each family can and should be a Household of God.

From his modest office in Washington, D.C. (1425 Otis Street, N.E., Washington, D.C. 20017), Father Calvo offers workshops for the people who have taken his home correspondence course and would like to share it with other families. He also continues to develop variations of the Encounter experience to meet other needs.

He has put on "Fraternal Encounters" in several cities for the leaders of diocesan apostolates which have reached a point of conflict, or who feel the need for better cooperation. In San Antonio, Texas, these included Spanish-speaking members of Marriage Encounter, CFM, cursillo and charismatic groups.

Above all, he strives to reach out to the poorest and neediest with Encounters for members of the ghetto, especially those "incomplete" families in which a parent is missing. In early 1977, in collaboration with Father Ed Hogan, CFM chaplain, Father Calvo held a Family Encounter for fifteen black families from the parishes of St. Ann's, St. Peter Claver's and St. Gregory's in Brooklyn. There were 23 children, aged 14 and up, and, of the fifteen families, eleven had single parents. After individual family members had made an Encounter with Self, there was intra- and inter-family dialogue—"which," according to Father Hogan, "prompted some pain and some joy."

Recently Father Calvo headed an Encounter for 50 Spanish-speaking teenagers from 14 to 21 years old at Mt. Alverno Retreat House in Warwick, New York. To emphasize their family relationship, it was called an "Encounter of Sons and Daughters." As reported by Father Hogan in *Marriage Encounter* (June, 1977), Father Calvo greeted the participants on Friday with a welcome song in Spanish and then explained that the purpose of the weekend was for each to "encounter oneself first as a person, second as a child of God, third as a member of their own family and fourth as a founder of a future family."

The weekend ended with a fiesta and a Mass attended by parents, grandparents and siblings. Among the closing testimonials, according to Father Hogan, Abel Rivera said that the weekend had helped him learn more about himself and to be more compassionate to others. Demaris Caceres spoke of her commitment to try hard to change her attitude about her family. And Fernando Pimentel chimed in, "I feel happy. I want to be more of a Christian in my home."

Meanwhile, back in the northwest, Father Tom Hill put on a Marriage Encounter for residents of the Cheyenne Indian Reservation at St. Labre' Mission in Ashland, Montana. He says that he learned more from them than they did from him— "about the sacred and about stability" which are the mainstays of Indian culture. And there are M.E. couples currently working out an Encounter using sign language for the deaf and mute.

As Gabriel Calvo says: "It is our hope that the poorest families, which are the ones God loves the most, will have the opportunity so far denied them to discover their interior energy and enroll actively in the march of history toward a future full of hope."

M.E. Materials
ENGAGED ENCOUNTER*

Symptoms of Spiritual Divorce
DISSATISFACTION
1. Am I dissatisfied in any way? Explain.
   e.g. Manners   Education
          Dress   Family
          Income   Friends
          Speech   Habits
          Job   Other

ESCAPE
1. What diversions or escapes do I use in my life? Why?
2. Could they be harmful to our relationship?

WEAKNESS IN RELATIONSHIP
1. What weaknesses do I think already exist in our relationship? Explain.

*Reprinted from the *Engaged Encounter Manual*

e.g. Quarreling	Misplaced trust
Jealousy	Avoiding subjects
Nagging	Ridicule
Rudeness	Indifference
Role expectations	Lack of tenderness
Other?	

2. Am I going into this marriage thinking that it is possible it might be a failure? Why?

CONFLICT

1. Do we have serious disagreement about anything? Explain.

e.g. Family	In-laws
Politics	Religion
Race	Death
Money	Others . . .

Subjects for Understanding

RELATIONSHIP TO EACH OTHER

1. How do I feel we should settle conflicts?
2. Should the husband be the head of the house?
3. Can our present income support my standard of living?
4. Should our budget include charity, church support, insurance, savings or investments?
5. What health problems do I have?
6. What minimal health practices should we follow?
7. How will we spend our weekends?
8. Should we share a mutual interest in each other's work?
9. Will both of us work? For how long? Why or why not?
10. What will I be responsible for around home?
11. What do I feel our vacation needs are now? In the future? Alone? Together?
12. What are my needs for privacy?

RELATIONSHIP TO OTHERS

1. Would I like to have children? How many? When?
2. What are my feelings on birth control? Should we practice it? How?
3. What do I feel our relationship should be to our families?
4. What place should friendships have in our marriage?

RELATIONSHIP TO GOD

1. What religion will we follow? How actively?
2. What relationship do I feel to God right now?

Chapter

Eight

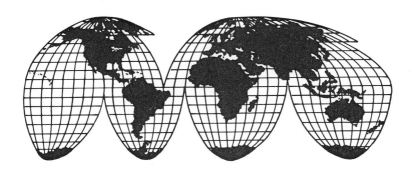

CHAPTER EIGHT
THE ECUMENICAL THRUST: "That All May Be One"

As we have seen, the "Worldwide Expression" of Marriage Encounter views its mission as the renewal of the Catholic Church. Although it has been open to non-Catholic couples to attend a weekend, once they have made their Encounter, they are encouraged to return to their own faith community. Only Catholics are allowed to be on the team, which always includes a Catholic priest, or on local boards. Worldwide has been extremely generous (with both money and training) in helping other faiths set up their denominational Encounter. Apart from the Jewish Marriage Encounter, which Father Gallagher helped initiate, there are Protestant Encounter groups which range from the Episcopalian to the Seventh Day Adventists, and which are affiliated with Worldwide. According to Father Gallagher, it is hoped that exposure to the Catholic experience will help them become "more Methodist, more Lutheran, more Jewish, etc."

Typical of Worldwide's pre-Vatican II ecclesiology is its emphasis on the "Four Marks of the Church," that is, "one, holy, catholic and apostolic." Evidently for Father Gallagher, "that all may be one" implies a reunion with Rome.

National Marriage Encounter, with its roots in CFM (which for some years has stressed ecumenism), has welcomed couples of all faiths almost from its beginnings. Strongly influenced by Vatican II in its theology of Church, and at the urging of Father Calvo, it has seen its mission as "promoting the

169

restoration of unity among all Christian and Jewish couples."[1]

In "A Statement of Philosophy and Purpose of the National Marriage Encounter"[2] adopted by its board in February, 1975, there is a significant paragraph:

We believe there is a need and desire by married couples to examine truly the meaning and presence of God in their individual and married lives. We see a response to this need and desire as an essential aspect of National Marriage Encounter. The National Marriage Encounter's philosophy and structure, based on Judaeo-Christian concepts, beliefs, and morality enables couples to appreciate more fully the presence of God in their lives. *We invite and encourage couples of all faiths or of no religious affiliation* to bring the experience and the many benefits of the Encounter into their lives and to become an integral part of the local group.

1. Father Tom Hill offers this explanation of the ecclesiology of the National Expression: "The difference between the two major expressions of M.E. is based on the answer to the question, 'What is Church?' Worldwide normally follows the model of the Roman Catholic Church as a centralized power or structure with the 'primacy of jurisdiction.' The Church is understood as singular ('there is one church'). The primacy of Rome is a highly efficient model to accomplish the mission of the Church.

National, on the other hand, focuses on the local church. The local church, or the people of God, is responsible for the mission of the Gospel. The pattern is taken from *Lumen Gentium* #18 which stresses the primacy of Rome but also adds the dimension that the divine mission was given to the twelve apostles and not only to Peter. The diocese, or the local church or community, is a valid Church. National M.E. communities are based on this model, which has four main elements:

1. Consciousness: We are the Church (or the People of God) and we are responsible for the Gospel, prayer worship and support of Christian marriage.

2. *Koinonia,* or Sharing: The local responsible groups must live in union with others. Together we are the church.

3. Ecclesial Commitment: (a) Vertical: The Church, which is an event and an experience is guided by the hierarchy. The community is guided in its vocation, or call, to share their relationship with each other and God; (b) Horizontal: The local churches or communities interchange resources and the ministry of communities.

4. Responsibility: Responsibility for faith and gospel lies with each member of the Church, not only with the priests and the hierarchy. The Church is not a pyramid but rather a circle, the mystery of the People of God.

There are five elements by which the Church may be recognized: (a) The Holy Spirit: God's presence, especially in human life and history; (b) Jesus Christ: Present in the Gospels and the Eucharist; (c) The People of God: The laity is the nucleus of the Church and part of the authentic meaning of 'Church'; (d) Charisms, or Gifts with the Church: These involve the religious orders and the various lay apostolates, including Marriage Encounter; (e) The Hierarchy: the leadership of the Church, defined by Vatican II in terms of service rather than dominion.

2. "National Marriage Encounter has tried to pattern itself after the local church concept. And its goal must remain with the enrichment of marriages and with helping couples discover their marriage within God's Plan or revelation.

The difference between the two expressions lies essentially in their starting point. The ecumenical approach begins with the idea of the local Church or community, and that is 'relationship in and with the Lord.' This is a call and vocation from God. And it is the unifying fulcrum of marriage, family and brotherhood." Father Tom Hill

If the daily 10/10 dialogue is the one non-negotiable tenet of Worldwide, the ecumenical and interfaith aspect of National is, according to Jerry Sexton, its major non-negotiable concern. As a case in point, the Family '77 Conference, co-sponsored by the Family Ministries Staff Conference of the National Council of Churches, the Christian Family Movement and the National Marriage Encounter, was originally billed as a celebration for "Christian families." At the Sextons' insistence it was opened to Jewish families.

They see Marriage Encounter as being one of the few strong and viable expressions of ecumenism and interfaith action in which Catholic lay people are involved with people of good will of other faiths.

Father Gerry Koob, S.J., has said, "I'm concerned about the issue of Ecumenism, about what we mean and what we experience by 'Church.' I'm also convinced that Catholics have far too narrow an understanding of the scope of the reality we call 'sacrament.' I'm also quite convinced that every marriage is a 'mixed' marriage, that some other than Catholic marriages are more deeply sacramental than some Catholic marriages, that is, the people involved in them are more alive to God's presence in their relationship and more responsive to that presence."

In another article in *Agape,*[3] he quotes the Jesuit theologian Avery Dulles as maintaining that "a loyal Catholic if he were not somewhat ecumenical could hardly be at home in his own church. At least since Vatican II it should be clear that a Catholic not only may, but must, esteem the heritage of other Christian communities. He not only may, but must, desire to overcome the present division in the Christian family ... (It is no longer proper for Catholics) to think and act as though the Roman Catholic Church, and it alone, was the one, holy, catholic and apostolic Church of Christ. Protestant and Orthodox Christians, by virtue of their Christian faith and baptism, belong to the Church of Christ and, as such, deserve the highest respect."

Father Koob goes on:

> The division of Marriage Encounter into various expressions based on the differences between Christian denominations is directly contradictory to this principle.

3. "Ecumenism—Danger or Opportunity," December, 1976.

If it had been left up to the laity in the early days of M.E., I do not think that this would have ever happened. I'm referring to distinctions based on 'differences' among Christians, because, for the moment, a distinct Jewish expression makes sense to me. Separate Christian expressions of Marriage Encounter strike me as yet another instance of fostering a mentality which holds that our differences are more important than those things which unite us . . . I am convinced that the motivating force which brought about an 'Episcopal' Marriage Encounter and other denominational Encounters was a combination of fear of the loss of integrity and an unconscious mentality of perfectionism in Catholic leadership . . .

That is what troubles me about dividing the world into 'Encountered' and 'non-Encountered.' Even more to the point, Marriage Encounter is really asking for trouble if it refers to itself as 'the major force of renewal in the Church.' Such a position equates M.E. with the Holy Spirit and fosters a misplaced perception of what M.E. can really be.

I think these dangers can be avoided by a very positive step forward. Let Marriage Encounter be in service equally to Christians of all denominations, a service involving Christians of many denominations. Let it foster sharing among people of all denominations. And, at the same time, let it encourage everyone to take what they learn back into their own faith communities. If Marriage Encounter could become a servant to all, it would not be a threat to any.

Jerry Sexton believes that M.E. has been of special help to "mixed"[4] marriages, especially when these involve Catholics

4. The term 'mixed marriages' is one which National M.E. now tries to avoid. In an editorial in the April, 1977, *Marriage Encounter,* Robert Genovese explains why: "The term is one that, in itself, poses problems. It's a 'leftover' term, one that comes from the times when Christians scarcely spoke to each other. It's also a term that carries connotations of wrong-doing on the part of those who have entered such marriages. 'Mixed marriage' carries with it a certain stigma. And for that reason, I'd prefer to call such marriages 'inter-Christian' or 'inter-faith' marriages." The same issue carries an article on the ecumenical guidelines that the Catholic Church in Canada—following the lead of the French hierarchy—has laid down for 'mixed marriages.' Its preamble states: "The basic principle of such an ecumenical approach is that representatives of both religious communities should be equally involved in the preparation, celebration and after-care of Christian mixed marriages. Every sociological study in this field shows that the great danger in such marriages is not the 'conversion' of one spouse to the faith of the other, but a general indifference to all religious influence by both parents, and eventually, by their children as well." As can be seen, even with the best will, the term dies hard.

and Protestants. "For the first time, perhaps," he says, "the non-Catholic spouse is accepted without feeling threatened or being made to feel that he is a second-class citizen. As Beth and Bob Barnes discovered, marriage spirituality can be shared without conversion. Recognition of the treasures of the other faith can enrich a marriage and lead to greater unity."

He quotes figures that demonstrate that in 1975 37% of marriages in the Catholic Church were between Catholics and those of another faith. "These do not include marriages involving Catholics performed in another church or before civil authority. If you were to include these, the figures might reach 50%, and they are growing."

"It is a problem that the Church is not really facing. It is swept under the rug, although it is a major cause of division and separation in Christian marriages."

M.E. has found, especially in the South, that these marriages are one of its major issues. Tom and Kay Farrell, past Executive Couple of Marriage Encounter in Maryland, the District of Columbia and Virginia ("Mar-Va"), found that, in their two Catholic dioceses, two-thirds of the couples who had married in the last five years were of mixed religions. "From the very beginning," they write,[5] "we've had couples from all denominations. So we decided that there would be no restrictions on participation within the M.E. movement. All we wanted to do was help couples look at their marriages and afford them the opportunity to grow in their marriage and relationship with God. We did this regardless of their religious denomination."

Mar-Va has concentrated on the ecumenical approach, "the restoration of unity among Christians." ("We've chosen to limit our discussion to 'Christians,' because the Jewish M.E. is quite strong in our area. We send all Jewish couples to them for their weekends.")

There have been problems in Mar-Va. Some Catholic couples left the movement, claiming that the ecumenical approach was "watering down their faith." And since the Worldwide expression is strong in the area, "claiming to be *the* Roman Catholic M.E., Protestants wonder whether we only claim to be ecumenical, just for the opportunity to convert them when they come to the weekend."

---

5. *Agape*, February, 1976.

"We took a hard look at ourselves. And, again, we decided that we were sharing ourselves—not teaching. We do believe that the couple's relationship with God is important to their relationship with each other. But, there is no reason why any couple can't trigger another couple to look at their relationship with God—no matter what the religious affiliation of the team couple is.

"So now Mar-Va is a Catholic ecumenical movement in M.E. Protestant couples are a part of our teams and are in responsible organizational positions. The weekend is open to all and closes with a liturgy (based on the scriptures), in which all can participate . . . However, we believe that the whole evolution has been worth the effort. And the couples have benefited. On the one hand, Catholics have gained a respect for the religious convictions and depth of their Protestant neighbors. Protestants, on the other hand, have had an opportunity to get acquainted with Catholics, particularly with priests and sisters. So, in effect, we think we have eliminated the need for separate organizations for each religious denomination."

It is, perhaps, significant that Father Gerry Koob was active with this Mar-Va experiment for five years before accepting a position of leadership in the *Retorno*. He has been especially concerned about the two issues that have been most divisive in ecumenical and interfaith movements: the Sacraments, and, especially, the Eucharist. As regards the Sacrament of Marriage, an important part of the M.E. weekend, Father Koob takes exception to the attitude that 'Only Catholics have the sacrament. Therefore, only Catholics can present the talk on sacramentality.' ("Anyone who has ever had anything to do with seeking an annulment of marriage between two baptized persons has had first-rate experience of how deeply the Roman Catholic Church feels about the sacramentality of non-Catholic marriages.") He quotes the German theologian, Father Bernard Häring: "Marriages are sacramental everywhere in today's world where spouses love each other faithfully and respectfully, where they help each other come in closer contact with the God who is love . . . the uniqueness of Christian marriage lies in the belief that marriage is related to the unique manifestation of God's love in Jesus Christ."

Instead of M.E. couples using the term 'our sacrament,' Father Koob would like to hear them say 'Our love union is one of the unique ways the life of Jesus Christ is present and active

174

in the world today.' *"A sacrament,"* he says, *"is not what we have, but what we are—the channels of the presence and activity of Christ."*

"When it comes to celebration," he goes on, "we have problems. If we choose to close the weekend with a Roman Catholic Mass, one of two things is going to happen. Either we end the weekend on a divisive note, or we play around with Eucharist . . . (But) the door is open to many other forms of non-Eucharist celebrations. I believe that the situation in which M.E. finds itself in the country today is a fertile one for exploration in this area. Following Father Dulles' suggestion, I'm interested in seeing what we can do in the area of shared Scriptural prayer . . . "

"I submit that the Mass (which I dearly love) is a celebration of Roman Catholic identity and is meant for contexts in which we celebrate this identity . . . It is also quite exciting to experience a deeply meaningful moment of prayer together with all Christians. And, more to the point, nobody leaves such weekends feeling like second-class citizens."

Following the thinking of Father Koob and the recommendation of the Third World Conference on Faith and Order at Lund, Sweden, in 1952 ("We should do together all that can be done together, and to do separately only that which must be done separately"), the Mar-Va M.E. has developed a liturgy in which couples of all denominations can share meaningfully. ("As it happened, we still have Catholic Mass and Methodist services—but these are outside the normal course of the weekend.")

"We also changed the terminology," the Farrells say. "(Instead of) the talk on 'Marriage as a Sacrament,' we refer to marriage as a 'communicating sign.' We've found that we can talk about the same concepts and theories without getting involved in doctrinal differences—provided we use the terms we've evolved. In many ways, this has helped Catholics more than it has those of other denominations. Most Catholics, like us, were raised to think we knew all we needed about 'sacraments.' Once we hear the word, we almost automatically tune out everything that follows. Well, once we got away from the standard terms, Catholics began to realize what we were talking about."

The situation in Georgia presented similar problems. Rita and Jim Shomenta, former executive couple of Georgia

Marriage Encounter write:[6]

> The Catholic population in Atlanta is only three percent of over a million and a half people living in the area. Outside of the Atlanta area, the percentage falls to as low as one-half of one percent, and even to zero in some places. Another factor we took into consideration were the couples who first came to make the Encounter. They were either from mixed marriages or both were Protestants or Jewish. These couples wanted to be within the Encounter. We were also very lucky to have for our spiritual director Father Larry Hein. For a number of years he was involved in many ecumenical discussions with Protestants and Jews. He helped us develop a common terminology which would unite us into community of the Spirit. So now we have a weekend program that all couples can totally experience and participate in.

As a substitute for 'sacrament,' they use the term 'Covenant-Mystery'—which is from Ephesians 5:21-23 and which "is rooted in the whole relationship of God to his people, of spouse to spouse and of God to the spouses."

Georgia has come up with a paraliturgy, which is not unique to any given tradition within Christianity or Judaism, but which is built around the Covenant-Mystery. It includes readings from Isaiah (54:4-10), Jeremiah (31:31-44), the above-mentioned passages from Ephesians and selections from John, chapters 15 and 17, on the themes of covenant, friendship and unity. The liturgy ending the weekend concludes with a renewal of covenant vows first for religious celibates, then for the clergy, finally for married couples.

"We feel the philosophy of ecumenism," the Shomentas conclude, "must continue beyond the weekend experience. Our M.E. community brings the same spirit to its follow-up programs. We also maintain open lines of communication with Jewish, Episcopalian, Lutheran and Catholic religious denominations. Couples of all faiths are invited to participate on our teams. They act as board members, or anywhere in our organization that their talents fit."

An interesting ecumenical Anniversary Encounter was held in Scotch Plains, New Jersey, Sunday, June 8, 1975. It was discovered at a Fanwood-Scotch Plains Ministerial

---

6. *Agape*, December, 1975.

Association meeting that not only were three ministers and two priests encountered, but that there were four expressions of M.E. within the 8,000 family community: National, Worldwide, Episcopal and Presbyterian. "It was," according to Father Carl Arico, "like having the United Nations of Marriage Encounter."

The ecumenical service was held in the Immaculate Heart of Mary auditorium and was attended by 32 couples. The steering committee which planned and ran the celebration included a Catholic priest, an Episcopalian priest and his wife, a Presbyterian minister and his wife, and lay couples from National, Worldwide, Episcopal and Presbyterian expressions. It has since, apparently, become an annual event.

JEWISH MARRIAGE ENCOUNTER

According to Joe and Deanie Crane,[7] National Coordinators of Jewish Marriage Encounter (they serve on the National M.E. Board of Trustees along with Rabbi and Julia Kligfeld), during the latter part of 1970 and 1971 Jewish couples were attending Catholic (Worldwide) M.E. weekends in increasingly large numbers. "The vast majority of these couples found the weekend a meaningful, moving experience . . . But during the same time there was a growing desire among the Jewish couples for experiences in Encounter more geared to their backgrounds."

After a renewal and recruiting program, which drew crowds of 500 and 600, the first Jewish Marriage Encounter was held in October, 1972, in Cranford, New Jersey. In the three years that followed, the Jewish Encounter would train over 100 couples (including rabbinic couples), encounter over 10,000 couples and spread to some 18 states. J.M.E. operated as an affiliate of Worldwide until 1974. Then the Jewish couples looked into the philosophy and purpose of National M.E. They found these to be in agreement with practices already being carried out in J.M.E., especially since they were making considerable use of the Calvo Manual. "Since 1974," the Cranes say, "the National and Jewish Encounters have worked closely together in all phases of their activities, freely sharing information and ideas and experiences."

In 1975, the first national convention of J.M.E. was held in June at Syosset High School on Long Island. Several hundred

7. *Agape*, June, 1975.

Jewish couples from all over the country attended, along with members of the board of National M.E. Father Calvo was the featured speaker. Programs for teenagers and engaged couples were also initiated in 1975. Family Encounters and an adaptation of the *Retorno* are likewise being planned.

According to the Cranes, "Perhaps this marks the beginning of what many of us see as the true goal of the Encounter to involve not only the married couple, but all people; to bring this message of love and understanding to all created 'b'zelem Elohim' ('In the Image of God')."

Gabriel Calvo has been delighted by the progress and spirit of J.M.E. "It is tremendous," he said recently, "the extent to which Marriage Encounter has become an opening to our Jewish brothers and sisters. Thousands and thousands of Jewish couples are becoming encountered in God's marvelous plan and are renewing their covenant with the Lord, not only as couples but also as families."

Rabbi Bernie Kligfeld, a stocky man with a pepper-and-salt spade beard and some of Father Calvo's bounce and charisma, has put on workshops at National M.E. conventions—which he calls "A View from the Temple"; he writes a monthly column on "Spiritual Reflections" for *Marriage Encounter* Magazine and has contributed a chapter, "The Jewish Marriage Encounter," to Herbert Otto's anthology, *Marriage and Family Enrichment*.[8] He told Don Demarest that in 1971, as chairman of the Committee on Family Life of the Central Conference of American Rabbis, he decided to investigate Marriage Encounter to see if some of its techniques and methods could be adapted for Jewish use. "Father Gallagher invited us to attend a weekend. Although my wife and I had decided to go along as observers, we unexpectedly found ourselves caught up in the sweep of the Encounter. When the weekend was over, we found that our lives had been profoundly changed."

Julie Kligfeld, who is at least as ebullient as her husband, and a lot more outspoken, says, "I went along with a great deal of trepidation. There was all this talk about love, but I hadn't been the recipient of a great deal of it from Christians. Father Bill Gaffney, however, did so much to make us feel welcome and respected that he completely broke through any walls I'd tried to erect. If anybody had ever told me that I'd be

8. Abingdon, Nashville, 1976.

participating in a Catholic Mass and thoroughly enjoying it, I'd have told him to get his head examined. But this weekend we made so many friends, so many beautiful people who seemed to really care about us, that we felt we should join in the service with them as a sign of friendship."

According to the rabbi, apart from the theological differences, there are some practical problems that make the weekend impossible for many Jews, Conservative as well as Orthodox. "It begins on the Sabbath and many Jews cannot by tradition do any writing on the Sabbath. The Encounter is pretty impossible without writing."

Consequently, the Jewish Encounter begins Saturday night and ends late Monday afternoon. And kosher food is served.

"Apart from that, our weekend follows the flow of the Calvo Manual pretty closely. Our Encounter begins with a worship service, 'Havdala,' which separates the Sabbath from the rest of the week. Then we use the Encounter with Self and Areas for Reaching Out—since Martin Buber's notion of the dialogic relationship between the 'I' and the 'Thou' has obviously played an important role in Father Calvo's thinking. The whole question of 'openness' is also part of the Jewish tradition. The question was once asked: 'Where does God live?' and the answer was given, 'God lives where man lets him in.' When we are open to each other we are also open to God.

"Instead of the 'Sacrament of Marriage' we have what we call 'Sanctification and the Couple.' The Jewish word, *Kiddushin,* applies to the ritual of marriage, but it also has a cosmic significance, an expression of the basic holiness of life. The relationship is ordained by God and the degree to which the couple fulfill the *mitzvah,* the commandment to love each other (not as an emotion, but an act of the will), is the degree to which their marriage is sanctified.

"The home is known in Judaism as a *Mikdash M'at*—a small sanctuary, a place where God is sought and his presence can be felt. In a true marriage we create the *Mikdash M'at* whereby the relationship between the husband and wife is raised to the highest value in our lives."

Although most Jews find an Encounter which draws upon the rich traditions and scriptural wealth of their own faith the most rewarding, the Kligfelds, the Cranes and many other Jewish couples participate actively in many National anniversaries and other Fraternal Encounters. There are some groups—most notably in the New York Catskills, in Houston

179

(where weekends are held alternately at a Christian church and a Jewish synagogue) and in Los Angeles—where the predominantly Jewish leadership feel that the interfaith sharing is of major value and in which Christian couples of various denominations play an active role.

Increasingly in recent years, other denominational expressions have found a closer rapport with National M.E. than with Worldwide, and have become affiliated with the original association. Most maintain their independence and faith autonomy.

In his speech to the National Board at Dayton in 1976, Gabriel Calvo said: "We need a very large vision. The ecumenical movement is in need of this vision. You represent more and more the pluralism of this country. We need a large mentality, because we are dealing with so many people who are different. Each community, no matter how small, has its own charisms."

Chapter

Nine

CHAPTER NINE
"THE ODD COUPLE": The Contribution of
Priests, Religious, Ministers and Rabbis

Because quite often on Encounters there are two priests, a priest and a sister, a brother and sister—either among the team couples or those encountering—they have been facetiously called "the odd couple." Sister Gertrude Brown, O.S.F., says she received strange looks and questions when she told lay friends that she was going to make a Marriage Encounter. People said, "A nun making a Marriage Encounter! Are you planning to leave the convent?" And, often during the weekend, "What's a gal like you doing in a place like this?"

"Actually," she says, "I feel that M.E. is a valid and important kind of ministry for Sisters. From my limited experience I have found that there was real witness value because of the love and unity and mutual support shown by members of our team. As a team member who is willing to share my feelings, my human relationships, my problems and myself as a person, I have helped those making the weekend and the other team members begin to see Sisters as really human, extremely feminine, very vulnerable, and, hopefully, lovable individuals.

"Many of the longstanding misconceptions and stereotyped impressions are discarded. It is good for married couples to see that problems are human, rather than marital, and no one is exempt from coping with them. I like being one of God's People—loving, working, feeling, supporting, helping, suffering, sharing together with my brothers and sisters in Christ. Isn't that what *agape* is all about?"

Sister Judith Tate, O.S.B., of Oklahoma writes: "Marriage Encounter doesn't really need ministers, rabbis, priests or religious, only couples. However, ministers (Sisters included) can do much to complete the experience and refine the basic theology. If the Encounter is a microcosm of the Church, all elements should be included. As members of a community, as nurturers, Sisters stand with the couples. Representing both the world of work and the world of prayer, Sisters can make a unique and unifying contribution to the weekend."

According to Brother Don Byrne, FSC:

> I am not a cleric. I am a layman, attempting to live a different but similarly religious life style, like married persons. I choose to be alone with others. I do not wish to be married. Because of all this I grow with and share my changing seasons with married friends. I reach out a hand to broaden the community of married love, to remind us of the kingdom and its incompleteness . . . Commitment, fidelity to person-commitment, are important to me because I have made such commitments to other Christian Brothers and to members of my communities. I bring to the team the experiences of my caring and sharing in life—the daily being in love out of love of love, the daily pasch of my own personal love affair with the Mystery laid down among the poor . . . I bring the spirituality of my life: friendships, love-creating with men and women, the daily leaven of sharing a home with people and being committed to stand with them in their personal growth. In short, to make unity common again, to be where you go, to believe in life more than death. I laugh in the midst of waiting and listening. I cry in the aloneness of holiness with God and of a single bed. More lately I am silent and humbled. We have encountered and now I am more than I was, more me with you.[1]

On a weekend priests and religious do their P.R. and C.D. together. They share in elements of the liturgy. Religious often provide the guitar music and lead the songs. They show the way in taking off masks and breaking down walls.

In Jewish Marriage Encounter there is always a rabbinical couple on the team. Since rabbis and cantors must marry to fulfill the commandment "be fruitful and multiply," a rabbi

---

1. *Agape*, April, 1976.

stands for the marital commitment as well as the priestly one.

Rabbi Bernard Kligfeld, writes of "Jewish Marriage Encounter" in Herbert Otto's *Marriage and Family Enrichment: New Perspectives and Programs:*[2]

> The team couples and rabbinic couples who give the presentations on the weekend seek not only to share their experience with other couples and in so doing to strengthen their own sense of the value of the Encounter experience, but also to spread the impact of Encounter as a force to strengthen Jewish marriage and family life ... (Couples are urged) to reach out to their rabbi, their temple, their community to make a loving temple and a loving community.

Catholic priests have repeatedly testified to the extent that Marriage Encounter has helped them to grow both as a person and a priest and, especially, how it has helped them to reach out to their parishioners and to build community. Father John Gilbert, pastor of the Nativity of the Blessed Virgin Mary, says of the marriage enrichment program in his church (see chapter seven): "I didn't know what to expect. I was anxious. I never did anything like this before. But the couples met their pastor in a special way and saw his growth in prayer and Christian life. The experience reinforced and encouraged me to continue to grow in my religious life."

Father Joseph M. Champlin, pastor of Holy Family Church, Fulton, New York, has written a book about how much Marriage Encounter has changed his life. In *Alone No Longer*[3] he writes: "The enormous growth I saw in the prayer life, charity, generosity and spiritual wisdom of these encountered couples—persons moving rapidly past and beyond me in many instances—led me to the realization of how much they and other lay persons have to teach me."

It was this awareness that recently led thirty-one Crosier priests and brothers to put on a 44-hour renewal program based on the Calvo Manual in Hastings, Nebraska. It was conducted by two priests and a brother and three married couples. Reportedly, one of the major benefits the participants received was inspiration from the "deep spirituality" of the lay couples.

2. Abingdon, Nashville, 1976.

3. Ave Maria Press, Notre Dame, 1977.

In most such accounts, by brothers and sisters, ministers, rabbis and priests, the emphasis is on the interaction and balance between the two callings. The ministers become more human and learn to respect the spiritual growth of the lay people. Father Champlin says: "Priests and married couples, in the Marriage Encounter view, consequently bear a responsibility to each other. They have a stake in each other's relationships. My love as a priest for you and others can help you grow as a couple. Your love for each other and for me helps me grow as a priest."

Ed and Sandy Dufresne, who apart from being married, are ordained ministers of different denominations, see theirs as a double vocation and a different sort of service. They spoke of this at the National M.E. Conference at Dayton and Ed has written about it in *Partnership: Marriage and the Committed Life:*[4]

> Today, partnership between a man and a woman can be something more than a cultural necessity. As marriage becomes less the handservant of the prevailing culture, the possibility it holds for a life of full Christian commitment becomes more apparent.
>
> Now we are free to choose marriage as an alternative life-style for commitment. And, once married, we continue to see alternatives for commitment *within* this way of life. This enables marriage to take its place beside other life-styles which traditionally have been vehicles for a radical assertion of faith. One important reason why the celibate and the monastic life-styles proved such effective channels for Christian commitment was that they almost always involved a person in making a conscious choice for one life-style over all others out of a commitment to Christ. Of course, there was nothing fundamentally Christian about the single or communitarian ways of life any more than there was about the married way of life. But because, among other things, they were exceptional and unexpected ways of ordering one's life, they were able to meet the challenge to leave all behind and follow in a way that was hardly possible for marriage.
>
> Significantly, the very threats to marriage as a social institution in today's culture—the increased freedom of

4. Paulist Press, N.Y., 1975.

choice, the acceptance of rival life-styles, the new options available within partnership—are, in fact, blessings of genuine liberation for the committed Christian. The age-old rivalry between the affairs of God and the business of marriage has been considerably weakened. Partnership takes its place with other ways of life as a context for a full-blown spirituality of commitment.

The ministry of Christian couples, ordained or not, has been recognized by Vatican II *(The Church in the Modern World* #48 and *Decree on the Apostolate of the Laity,* #11). Father Tom Hill writes in *Marriage Encounter* ("What's My Role?" May, 1977) of the enlightenment he received from a couple who are working in the Marriage and Family Ministry (see chapter seven). Speaking of a couple who had come to them for help with a problem, the husband said: "All I could tell them was that I could not solve their problem, but I could listen and care and pray. My presence through listening, caring and praying, gave the other couple the power and strength and courage to work through their own problem . . . Being present to them as they struggled honestly and courageously, I began to trust a little more in the power and presence of God working through and in my own life."

"Once or twice," Father Tom writes, "at the close of an M.E. weekend, I walked away with the feeling that my importance and role on the specific weekend was that of a 'liturgical functionary.' I was present mainly because of the power to consecrate and celebrate the Eucharist. In other words, my function was important but not the reality of the person who was invested with this power. I was asked neither to share as a human being nor as someone who has received a specific call. The feelings come from frustration at not being able to blend the two realities of my life . . .

> *These two main ideas together—the couples' awareness of their power to listen, heal and share their life experience; and my own realization that the priesthood and mission is a central part of my life—point up the direction that Father Calvo has emphasized many times. The process of Marriage Encounter is the discovering of the couples' own reality in the light of God's plan of salvation. My role in Marriage Encounter is similar but also adds the dimension of clarifying that discovery in my own life and the lives of the couples who make a weekend."*

187

Father Gerry Koob, in writing about the ecumenical role of the priest in Marriage Encounter *(Agape,* December, 1976), has this to say:

"Is the ministry of the Roman Catholic priest one that is for Catholics only?" Some even go further and say that "Because saying Mass is 'my thing,' if you remove it, what have I to offer M.E.?" But, if the ministry of the priest is to build up the Body of Christ and to be a bearer of the mystery of God's presence in the world, then the argument is false, because M.E. affords many opportunities for priestly ministry.

I also believe that any priest carries within his attitudes and behavior the mentality of the Roman Catholic Church. The question here is his fidelity toward the implementation of a relatively new mentality of the Roman Catholic Church. The fact remains, any priest who fosters shoulder-to-shoulder work with other Christians in enriching Christian marriages is doing great priestly work.

Gabriel Calvo in an address to the Board of National Marriage Encounter in July, 1976, said, "What happens between you and me is reality. The kind of marriage that exists between spouses is reality. So we have to touch our reality. That's what the weekend is all about. Couples may not know this—they may not even believe it. But the leaders must know that this is the direction. M.E. is not praying or having a liturgy like the Mass. These are not essential to Marriage Encounter. The purpose is to bring about a deep dialogue in the Lord. We must rediscover this direction, this mystery, this reality."

But then, he went right on to say that "We also need a priest in Marriage Encounter. We need him because, as I've noticed in the U.S., there is a hunger for the spiritual, for essential values. The young people say they are searching for 'something more.' Many do not know that their search is for God. We need this kind of reality, too."

This seems to need further exploration. Just what is the role of the priest in Marriage Encounter? Since there didn't seem to be a complete explanation in Father Champlin's book, or even in Father Tom Hill's article, Don Demarest brought it up in the discussions about the weekend which took place at the Sexton's cottage beside a lake in Wisconsin.

Don: What is the contribution of the priest or religious on the weekend? What is his or her role?

Father Tom: I can only answer negatively. The weekend is different if there is no clergyman or religious.

Jerry: On the lowest level the priest reveals himself as a human being. When he drops his mask and comes on as a person, he introduces scripture into the weekend reality.

Marilyn: Protestants and Jews participate more fully when a priest is there for some reason. It's a sort of electricity.

Don: Could it be that he is the symbol of God's presence? Even in the Old Testament the priest was someone special. The anointed one.

Father Tom: The scapegoat. The person set aside. That's all part of it. The fact that we aren't married, that we have a different commitment—that we take vows of poverty (in the orders) and chastity—provides another element.

Betty: During the weekend I met Don's God and he met mine. Perhaps the priest helps bring the two together.

Jerry: Of course there aren't different Gods. The priest may help to bring the different perceptions into focus.

Don: Perhaps the priest balances couple dialogue and couple spirituality. But what is the difference between couple spirituality and individual spirituality?

Father Tom: I really can't answer that. It's something I've been wrestling with the five years I've been working in M.E.. But I do know everything is based on the individual spirituality or returning to God.

Jerry: It's a new element in marriage enrichment that Calvo introduced. The original church groups, Methodists and Quakers, even the Maces, concentrated on dialogue and communication without the prayer element.

Don: But even then it is mostly lay prayer. I'm still trying to get at the role of the priest. Is it leadership?

Father Tom: I prefer to say that my role is to witness to my relationship with God. My reality includes two aspects—the sharing in the Priesthood of Jesus Christ and my own humanity. Actually both depend on that relationship.

Jerry: It's more than just reading the scripture, a layman can do this. It's more even than providing the Eucharist.

Don: And it's more than the theology. There are first-rate lay theologians.

Father Tom: Perhaps we have to go back to the old word, "pontifex." The priest is a bridge builder. Between the spouses,

189

between the team couples, between the community and God. That is what he has been set aside for.

Jerry: For many couples the weekend is a conversion experience. Often when the husband or wife haven't been to church for years, they become active again.

Betty: When you realize you are loved ...

Marilyn: That this is what God is like. That He has touched you.

Jerry: People need that experience. They are hungry for it. What is it the charismatics ask, "Have you met Jesus?"

Marilyn: Take the Parable of the Sower. Ask yourself, "What sort of soil am I? Am I vulnerable? Can God touch me? And can I touch others?" If I am fruitful soil, I bloom for my spouse and for my family and for my community.

Father Tom: The three elements have to be brought together. The community is formed when unity is achieved: priest, team couples, encountering couples become one. We become a family, as Calvo demonstrates. Each of us plays our part. The contribution of the other vow, the unmarried vow, is extremely important.

Don: But this still doesn't explain that extra element a priest contributes to the weekend, which is something different from what a minister or a brother or sister contributes.

Betty: Marilyn mentioned the electricity that even Protestants and Jews notice.

Don: When I was in California I published a book by a Spanish priest—*A Priest Confesses* by José Luis Martin Descalzo. It's quite emotional but very moving for a layman. He goes into the mystery of the priesthood: the "alter Cristus," the "Other Christ" element.

Father Tom: According to Caffarel a mystery in theology isn't something that's just mysterious or unfathomable. It is precisely the operation of God in the world. There is the mystery of the Incarnation and the mystery of the Redemption, etc. The mystery of marriage, he says, is the work of Christ interacting with His Church, whose symbol it is and which stands for the unity of the Redeemer with Redeemed Humanity.

Don: What does the Sacrament of Marriage have in common with the Sacrament of Holy Orders?

Father Tom: In the same book, *Marriage is Holy,* the sacraments are described as "acts—Christ touching us personally, person to person." A sacrament is described as a ritual, an act of Christian cult, through which Christ's power acts on a specific human situation. Caffarel says that by the sacrament of marriage the couple is not only sanctified but consecrated, "rendered apt for divine cult" like the sacred vessels used in the Eucharist. Holy Orders, he says, brings us into closer communion with the Holy of Holies, and empowers us to speak to God in the name of humanity. In the same way the Christian married couple offers God not only its love but all love—including profane love and even the mating instinct of animals.

Don: So perhaps the electricity is the meeting or fusion of the two sacraments, the priestly and the connubial.

Tom: These are still words, inadequate representations of the "mystery" which is Christ's contribution. But until we have a deeper theology of marriage, it's probably the best we can come up with.[5]

---

5. Later, Father Tom Hill wrote: The key element for the priest is that his humanity affects his priesthood and vice versa. He is still 'set aside' from the community for the things of God, but still very much part of the community. Otherwise he could not build bridges.

Chapter
Ten

CHAPTER TEN
"THE REVOLUTION OF LOVE":
The Founder of Marriage Encounter Looks to the Future

In June, 1976, the Sextons took time from their busy schedule to sit down for an honest look at where Marriage Encounter had been and where it might be headed. "A Look at the Future of M.E." was included in a pamphlet distributed at The International Eucharistic Congress in Philadelphia in 1976.

"Where is Marriage Encounter going as a movement? Is it just a good weekend experience for couples, giving them some help in the area of husband-wife communication or is it something more? Is it one of the vehicles God is using at this time in history? We believe it is.

"Among the good fruit we can find are the following: 1. An estimated 400,000 couples in this country have already made an M.E. weekend. Marriages and families have been reunited. Many couples have had a faith experience and have returned to active participation in their church. An estimated 15% of M.E. couples have been 'turned on' to an active leadership apostolate in the area of marriage and the family.

"2. The Engaged Encounter. Thousands of married couples are helping to prepare young couples for marriage. These pre-marriage programs may soon include larger numbers than M.E. itself.

"3. The Marriage Retorno is truly a return to God. Weekends are now being offered in many states, with over 2,000 couples already involved. There is also a proposal for training couples to give spiritual direction to other couples and that is indeed an exciting prospect.

"4. Family Encounter. Many M.E. couples are now involved in parent-teen programs, teenage encounters, Christian Family weekends and similar activities.

"5. Marriage Enrichment programs for couples in the setting of their own parishes. These programs will potentially reach many more couples than those willing to make a weekend in a retreat house.

"6. Other special ministries to date include the Marriage and Family Ministry to train non-professionals in diagnosis and referral, the Beginning Experience for the divorced and widowed, Marriage Encounters for alcoholics, gamblers, prisoners, and others with special needs, the Priest Encounter and the Fraternal Encounter for leaders of organizations.

"What directions will the movement take during the next few years? Here are our predictions:

Weekends are now being offered by an estimated 250 M.E. groups and chapters in the U.S. We believe that this number will continue to grow and could double within three years.

More and more we will see the Marriage Encounter weekend as the 'turning on' or 'initial training' for couples who will then actively respond to the needs in their families, churches and local communities. The initiation of new types of programs to help these needs will continue.

We see Marriage Encounter graduates participating in pre-marriage preparation, marriage enrichment and renewal, family education and counseling in high schools and colleges, industry, vocational schools, adult education programs and the like. We predict that some Encounter graduates will become activists in politics, government and church, helping to bring much-needed attention to the problems affecting the health and stability of marriage and the family.

With the exception of some Spanish-speaking groups, Marriage Encounter in this country has been primarily a white, middle- and upper-middle suburban movement. There are now efforts to bring the benefits of M.E. to lower income and minority groups. We believe new forms of the basic weekend will be adapted to reach these groups. We see couples moving out of the Encounter and back into local churches—where they will unite with others from Cursillo, Charismatic, Christian Family Movement,

Teams of Our Lady, etc., to help renew local church communities. This process is already underway in many parts of the country.

We don't know exactly how, or in what form, but we do believe that, as much of the above takes place (and we are confident it will), people in this affluent society of ours will be more and more willing to share the gifts they have with the poor of the world.

We believe that this is God's plan and that it will come about as Father Calvo envisioned it, if we just allow God's love to flourish through our relationships in marriage and the family.

Father Gabriel Calvo first mentioned his dream of a future worldwide "Revolution of Love" in a letter to the editors of *Agape* early in 1975.

We believe that working to help a married couple form a true community of love, a community open to the love of their children, and to the love of the whole society around them, that is really working at the root of things—that is, doing a fundamental job for the whole world.

There is within each couple a divine energy of love, and, if it can be brought alive, it can loose a true revolution of love over the whole earth. But, in order for this energy to produce a human 'thermonuclear explosion,' it has to be released by a deep sharing between husband and wife, through the communication of their feelings and of their whole life together. It cannot be done in just one moment. It is done rather through the sharing and dialogue of many hours and many days. This is where the true revolution of love begins.

But it does not end there. Starting with the transformation of the couple through their deep communication of feelings, it moves on to the revolution of love when parents and children start to listen to each other: when they reconcile by admitting their respective mistakes and faults; when they communicate to each other in depth their feelings, their hierarchy of values and their whole life, so that they join together around one table in the name of the Lord and become a leaven deep in society. Then they give to society, which is confused by so much having—they give society instead an image of being, of family life, the basic and fundamental community of human living.

And family love shown to the world, through a deep and sincere love of parents and children, is dynamic and 'thermonuclear' in its energy. This love must be liberated, must be freed. It is freed from two energy sources, as they say in modern science: the energy source of parents and the energy source of children. And it results in a chain reaction, releasing the most potent and tremendous energy that can be released in the world, beginning when the couple share their love of husband and wife, as we've said before—and that's the part that is indispensable. Then their love can cause a fire of love to break out all around them, to the very ends of the earth, transforming the whole world.

So we believe that to work for deep communication between husband and wife is really to begin the revolution of love in the world. But we can't stop there—we have to be working in other areas . . . in the dimension of the whole family and the whole of society, so that the revolution of love will be total. Complete.

And here we see the image of the 'little churches,' the small communities of parents and children, the same example that the first Christians gave. When people can look at these families scattered throughout society, but in communion with one another, and say: "Look at how they love one another," then they have the example of parents and children searching and struggling together, in the twentieth century, for a new kind of family—the communitarian family—that creates a 'new man' for our new society.

Father Calvo wrote another letter for the Tenth Anniversary issue of *Marriage Encounter* (August, 1977). In it he expressed some reflections on what has been happening to Marriage Encounter in this country and some of his hopes for its future. Exerpts from this letter follow:

After two years of living and traveling constantly across this immense land, I think I can affirm the following:

1. The U.S. is the Number One Nation as far as assimilation, promotion and expansion of Marriage Encounter in the past ten years. 2. M.E. in its diverse expressions is one of the most dynamic and influential movements in North America today. 3. Monthly,

thousands and thousands of U.S. married couples are discovering and initiating a new style of living—as individuals, as couples, as families. 4. Another quite common characteristic of these couples is their religious renewal. Christians who seldom went to church before M.E. and seldom participated in parish activities, now feel that they *are* the Church and are becoming integrated into ecclesial communities.

This is, of course, a tremendous challenge to those who have discovered God's Plan for Marriage and the Family. It's an urgent call from God to all those who are now reading this letter. That is to pass on from being a couple-dominated and nuclear family to becoming a 'thermonuclear' family—that is, intercommunicating, united and radiating out to the world.

This is a call and a challenge to those families who are today building the families of the future throughout the world.

What will the families of the future be like? We don't know. But we are convinced that we have the essential and eternal secret: family love, God's fire.

Just like those generations which built the foundations of the wonderful medieval cathedrals, we know that we shall die without seeing these formidable new families of the future. But with faith, hope and love, we are marching toward them. And history will show that the families of the future will give thanks to the Most High for all that you have done, you pioneering families of 1977.

But perhaps the best statement of the way Father Calvo views the problems and pitfalls, as well as the hope and the promise, of Marriage Encounter in the United States rests in some of the answers he provided to Father Tom Hill's "Twelve Vital Questions":

"What do you see as some of the pitfalls of Marriage Encounter?"

I'd prefer to speak of the mistakes rather than the pitfalls—to emphasize the positive rather than the negative. There are things that go wrong in everything that happens in this life. The trouble is not that there are wrongs—that we make mistakes—but that we fail to recognize them and fail to correct them if we do recognize them. God is continuously calling on us to correct our faults. It is human to have faults. However, it is not truly human, not in the Spirit of the Lord, to remain in one's faults, to be content with one's mistakes, to deny their existence, to mask or hide them.

One of these faults—and I have often written about it— is that Marriage Encounter has converted itself into a movement that grows on itself and lives only for Encountered couples. It offers its services to the movement only and does not encourage couples to move out into the family and local community. It makes them too dependent on the movement's norms and directives.

This movement's major fault, then, is that it is in conflict with other movements dedicated to the same ends, at a time when we are faced with a common front of materialism and atheism whose aims are the destruction of the family. We must all unite against these evils. We must avoid making M.E. a contradiction which encourages conflicting movements.

That is why I believe this fault has only one solution— that Marriage Encounter leaders undertake a profound communication and come to a complete communion with the leaders of all movements which work for the renovation of the family, especially the Christian Family Movement and Family Life.

Let's get over this idea of looking at the movement as an end in itself, one that wants God to serve it. Let's move on to the idea of a movement which is an instrument of the Lord, that is a servant to the needs of the community—one that lives and dies with the community. What we need is not a movement which enriches itself more and more for its own ends—but a movement which impoverishes itself more and more for the community. The order I see is this: first the community of the family, then the ecclesial community and, finally, the local community, or neighborhood. If we do this, I believe we shall be following the Spirit of the Lord, who said, "If I am the master and I serve you, then you should do the same, each of you serving the other." But we must beware of another spirit, the evil spirit that descends on us—the spirit of possession, the spirit of domination, the spirit of manipulation. This, most certainly, is not the Spirit of the Lord, which is peace, love, clarity, sincerity, service and a love of works that help those most in need.

Jesus told us that we will be examined on what we do, not our intentions. He will not ask us about our participation in this or that movement, but will say, "I was hungry, I was thirsty, I was in prison, I was in need, and you gave me succor ... or you didn't." We can't escape this examination. It is our personal responsibility. The movements must be reunited to serve the community, not the other way around. The community should not be torn asunder in its attempts to serve various movements. Married couples should be working for the community through the movements—not vice versa. The movement is not an ends but a means. That's what the Lord inspired it for.

"Why is Marriage Encounter effective?"

I believe that the efficacy or the essence (if you will, the mystique or the secret) of Marriage Encounter must be sought beyond its techniques, which are the human element. Certainly the efficacy, the secret, is in the personal communication between the couples, which is an essential element in God's plan. But, as I see it, this is interpersonal communication *in* the Lord, realized in the *Lord.*

In my opinion, this is why the dialogue is effective. If we try to portray Marriage Encounter's success as due to propaganda, communication techniques only, or money, it will collapse like the Tower of Babel, because it was not built on the Lord. Jesus told us never to build on sand—but only on hard rock. That's why I believe that the efficacy of Marriage Encounter cannot be attributed to the god of technique. Rather, its effectiveness is due to the God of Love. A true "encounter" is a gift of God.

Jesus also told us that we cannot serve two masters, God and money. Money and the "power of this world" are strong—but the power and strength of the Lord are much stronger, much more powerful and efficacious. Perhaps this temptation to serve several masters is the most powerful temptation for the children of our time. If so, it will repay all our efforts to try and understand and cope with it. Eventually we will realize that inside each couple, inside each family, there is a mysterious supernatural force which is the strength of God. And if we use this strength we can change the face of the earth. Then violence will disappear; love will come; peace will arrive;

justice will be done. This is what I believe to be the secret of Marriage Encounter. But we will not see its effect until the Encounter has become a truly supernatural force.

"What direction do you see Marriage Encounter taking in the next ten years?"

This is a very difficult question, because I have never considered myself a prophet or one adept at divining the future. I'm very fond of this country because of its concern for what happens next. I'm delighted by your countrymen's attitude of scanning the horizon—of going forward with hope instead of looking back in anger. However, I don't believe I can answer this question. If there is an answer it can be found only in the community of caring couples.

At any rate, I see distinct possibilities that within the next ten years, perhaps even sooner, Marriage Encounter as a movement will have changed radically. I believe that the future of Marriage Encounter in this country, as in all countries, will be in line with the direction the Church is taking—that is, moving toward the authenticity of persons and toward the formation of small basic communities and locales in which the commandments of the Lord are truly lived. These will be communities on the march, poor communities, which present the spectacle of unity—that unity which Jesus asked of His Father, that unity for which He died and rose from the dead. This is my conviction. This is my prayer and hope.

And this is the impulse, the direction that I am personally prepared to work for. In this evolution there are many movements toward unity, dedicated to serving the local community. The local communities are beginning to trust the home. And so the family, the parish, the neighborhood are in union. The movements, too, are one—each with its own inspiration. There is the Cursillo, the Charismatic Movement, the movements to form lay leadership, the movements to restore the family—Marriage Encounter, Family Life, the Christian Family Movement. So many beautiful apostolates that the Lord has called into being. All these are united to go out from the homes, to emerge from the families, to carry the revolution of love into the world.

They all begin with the renewal of the community, not forgetting that the basic and fundamental community is the family. It starts with the family as it now exists, even those that are incomplete. Surely, all have faults. But they *are* families. They thirst for the justice of the Lord. And they need our help.

So, perhaps, these movements will discover in our present confusion the rebirth that the Spirit brings. It's the Spirit which is leading them all toward a deeper sense of the vitality of the Gospel rather than the vitality of the movements themselves. I believe that this age will meet in the Spirit of the Lord.

Then we will all move together, marching under the direction of the Lord, with Him in our midst. For this is the way of the Lord. This is the meeting of God's people, for He said, "I am with you until the end of the world."

So thank you for giving me this opportunity to express a few of my anxieties and my convictions, because the questions you have posed are those which have been on my mind and in my preoccupations. I'm afraid I haven't been able to answer all your questions, because I don't have all the answers to any questions. But this has been a beginning, one which the leaders of Marriage Encounter can carry forward—not with words but with your lives. As the Sacred Scripture says, "What serves it to say 'Lord, Lord,' if at the same time we don't do the Father's will?"

Finally, I should like to pray with all of you. May thy Spirit work in us, Lord, even in our tiny communities, especially in our families. Knock loudly on the door of each of our homes so that the fire of Your love may invade every home and hearth and heart—all our communities and organizations and movements. So that we can serve You, Lord, as the docile instruments of Your Revolution of Love throughout the world.

Let hate be done with, let there be an end of rancor and envy. Let violence and materialism be no more. Then all creation will be at Your feet. Through Christ Our Lord, Amen. Alleluia!

APPENDIX A
Where It All Began and How It Grew

THE LITTLE CHURCHES

The Marriage Encounter movement springs from a dream and a conviction. It began in Barcelona—that city of rugged individualists, poets and revolutionaries. It was started by a Spanish priest who is all of these things and who has extraordinary humility, immense energy and palpable charisma, besides. Father Gabriel Calvo is a small black-haired, black-eyed man who exudes energy and affection, is irrepressible as a child, as bouncy as a rubber ball, as direct and unexpected as a summer hailstorm. And he is convinced that:

> Inside each marriage there is a mysterious supernatural force which is the strength of God. And if we use it we can change the face of the earth. Then violence will disappear; peace will arrive; justice will be done.

Father Calvo was among the more than 800 priests ordained during the Eucharistic Congress held in Barcelona in 1952. The early years of his priesthood were devoted to working with young people and families. One day he was approached by Mercedes and Jaime Ferrer, a young couple who were looking for a way to serve God and Man through their marriage. Father Calvo decided that before married couples could realize their potential as an apostolate they would need to understand their relationship in the profoundest sense and build on it, to achieve within their own families the qualities that St. John Chrysostom had in mind when he described Christian families as "these miniature churches." As the Counselor-Founder of the Marriage Teams of Pope Pius XII, Father Calvo worked for a period of years in building the program which he called the *Encuentro Conyugal* and which we call Marriage Encounter.

Finally in 1962, a team of priests and married couples presented the weekend to a group of 28 couples from poor, working class families. During the sixties the Marriage Encounter movement grew rapidly in Spain. It took on international dimensions when it was presented at the International Confederation of Christian Family Movements (ICCFM) in Caracas, Venezuela, in 1966. Father Calvo and the Ferrers next put on a weekend in Mexico and the movement spread to most parts of Latin America under the auspices of the *Movimiento Familiar Cristiano* (the Spanish title for CFM, the Christian Family Movement, which began in Chicago in the forties).

CFM BRINGS M.E. TO U.S.

Again through the efforts of CFM, *Encuentro Conyugal* was brought to the United States in 1967. And in August of that year, the first English-language version was presented at the National CFM Conference at Notre Dame University.

It was the beginning of Marriage Encounter in the United States.

Pat and Patty Crowley, founders of CFM, were responsible for bringing M.E. to this country. Through their efforts, 50 couples and 29 priests from Latin America and Spain, began giving Encounters throughout the U.S. in August, 1968. This was the beginning of a rapid growth period for M.E. in this country, and also the start of a national organization.

In January, 1969, a weekend meeting was held for couples and priests who had presented at least two M.E. weekends. Four couples and five priests attended, and they became the first National M.E. Executive Board. Jamie and Arline Whelan were elected the first Executive Couple.

M.E. BREAKS WITH CFM

This first organizational step for M.E. also constituted a break with the CFM structure. In other countries, Encounter *(Encuentro)* was a part of CFM rather than a separate entity. At the CFM National Conference in 1969, the National Executive Board of M.E. passed the following resolution:

"That CFM and Marriage Encounter are two separate and independent movements with different purposes but a common interest in families and the Church, and therefore a liaison team will meet with the Executive Board of CFM when necessary on matters of mutual concern."

This basic relationship continued throughout the early 70s.

By the end of 1969, 70 Marriage Encounters had been presented in the United States. It was at this same time that follow-up groups began to flourish. These groups encompass small numbers of couples who meet periodically as a follow-up to their weekend experience. Now called Image Groups, Dialogue Groups or Encountering Couple Groups, they have become an integral part of the M.E. movement.

NEW YORK SPLITS MOVEMENT

In the early seventies M.E. also experienced some rather difficult "growing pains." The root of this was an internal difference which eventually led to the formation of a splinter group called "New York (later changed to Worldwide) Marriage Encounter." The basic difference centered around the concept of dialogue, with the New York-Worldwide group taking a fundamentalist approach.

National Marriage Encounter, as it was named in 1973, is interdenominational. In addition, National M.E. is designed to provide assistance to its affiliates across the country but in no way exert any strong, doctrinaire control.

Armando and Barbara Carlo and Father Jake Buettner were elected Executive Secretary Team in 1973. In August of that year, the first National M.E. "coming together" was held in conjunction with the CFM National Conference. This marked the beginning of a period of cooperation between these two movements which exists to this day.

Marriage Encounter has held national conferences each summer since 1974. At the 1975 Conference, Jerry and Marilyn Sexton and Father Tom Hill, OFM, Cap, were elected as the third National M.E. Executive Secretary Team.

As of today National Marriage Encounter is a movement of many people and many programs and is affiliated with many other family apostolates. As it continues to reach out to engaged couples, to married couples and families, one goal remains constant: "That all may be one."

In this it follows the directives of Vatican II on *The Church in the Modern World* and *The Apostolate of The Laity,* and Pope Paul's recent Encyclical *On Evangelization.*

Note: *Much of this material has been digested from "A History of the Marriage Encounter in the United States," which appeared in* **Agape** *in February, 1976.*

A LOOK AT OUR ROOTS[1]
by Father Gerry Koob, S.J.
U.S. Coordinating Team, Marriage Retorno

There is something about a tenth anniversary that calls for getting out the wedding album. I think it is a matter of getting in touch with who we are. It always seems to help to get back in touch with where we started. A few months ago I was having similar thoughts about Marriage Encounter and Retorno. So I set up an appointment with Father Gabriel Calvo and sat down with him, asking questions and listening. My direct purpose was to search out the origin of some of the phrases and sentences in the manual for the Marriage Retorno. But I got more than I had set out to get. I got a look at some of the root moments of the tree we now call Marriage Encounter, Family Encounter, Marriage Retorno and several other programs we now associate with Father Gabriel Calvo.

In 1952, a few months before ordination, the future Father Calvo was studying in the periodical library in his seminary (from which no one is ever allowed to remove a book). He was reading a magazine which reports the various talks given by the Pope during the course of each month. The Pope was Pius XII and the report was about a talk he gave on the occasion of the feast of Our Lady of Lourdes in February of 1952. He was calling all men and women to make a change—to no longer evangelize salvation from outside the human situation. "No, now we must approach the divine through the human. We must begin to enter more fully into the human situation and discover the divine within it."

As Gabriel read, his heart was on fire. He was discovering something about himself. "Me, I'll be a priest in a few months. What can I do?" He sneaked the magazine out of the library, took it to his room, copied it and underlined it—and carefully returned the magazine. He told me that this moment was one of the most profound moments of personal revelation in his life.

After ordination, Gabriel was missioned to a Christian Brothers School in Barcelona to be a chaplain to the students.

1. Reprinted from *Marriage Encounter,* August, 1977.

208

We call it "campus ministry" now. One day his superior general came to visit him. "Gabriel, come to the parlor; there is someone I want you to meet." Enter Jaime and Mercedes Ferrer-Escola. The young priest was deeply impressed by their obvious trust and openness with each other. They had each recently made the *Spiritual Exercises* of Ignatius Loyola and now they were looking for a Spiritual Director. But they wanted someone who would be willing to direct them *as a couple.* Gabriel had been schooled in the *Exercises,* but the suggestion of directing a couple as a couple boggled his mind. "Spiritual Direction is one-on-one; what is this, directing a couple as a couple?" Jaime and Mercedes and his superior general won him over. He went upstairs and took out the quotation he had written down from Pius XII. The Pope was calling all men and women to make a change, to enter into the human. And so the young priest who knew little about marriage and couples went to meet the family. There he met several other couples as "crazy" as Jaime and Mercedes. And as he says now, "Jaime and Mercedes became my spiritual directors."

Gradually a small group of couples was formed and they began having meetings on a regular basis in homes! (This was a matter for suspicion which eventually led the bishop to insist that Gabriel's local superior go with him to the meetings. The latter was somewhat elderly and had a hard time keeping awake at the meetings!) And they were searching, not quite knowing where they were going.

The couples had heard of a new movement for young people beginning in Madrid, the Cursillo. Some people said they were feeding the kids pills; others said it was the Holy Spirit. Jaime and Mercedes urged Gabriel to go make a Cursillo. He did and then sent five of his students to Madrid to share the experience. They came back on fire, alive with two basic insights.

The young men were newly aware of their felt connection to the mystical body of Christ. They were "De Colores," in the grace of God, *alive to God's presence* within them and alive to Christ as the one who made them brothers and sisters in the Whole Body of Christ. And secondly, they were *alive to prayer:* very human, direct, warm, personal and out-loud prayer to Jesus. Gabriel invited the five young men to come to the next meeting of the couples. They came, they shared, they prayed, and the couples discovered something new in their lives. They took that alive prayer home to their children. Gabriel points to that night as *the beginning.* It all started from that night.

Over the course of the next couple of years, the group developed a rhythm or methodology for their meetings. Gabriel would compose a sheet for each meeting, listing a topic, some pertinent selections from Scripture and a few questions for reflection. For the first week, more or less, husband and wife would pray and write separately. Beginning from an encounter with God's Word, each would consider: "What is God telling me through His Word?" In the written reflection each would consider what God was revealing about his or her behavior, attitudes, motivation, etc., and what were the underlying causes. And what changes are called for, what action needs taking. In the second week, husband and wife would pray together, share their written reflections and compose a common written document, their "child," the fruit of their common sharing. At the end of the second week, the couple met with the other couples and Gabriel for sharing. At the meeting, "everyone feeds, everyone eats." If one member of a couple could not get to the meeting, the other went with the "fruit."

In 1954 Gabriel journeyed to Rome for an alumni gathering to meet a Jesuit priest named Father Ricardo Lombardi, then known as the *alter vox,* the other voice, of Pius XII. Lombardi is the founder of the *Movement for a Better World,* a retreat movement now well established all over the world. Lombardi's program was geared for religious, priests, professional people. Its focal point is prayer in the Trinity and the discovery of the Christian vocation to build community. In Gabriel, Lombardi met a man who began to call him to deal with married couples. Gabriel eventually succeeded. In Segovia, Spain, in 1956, his couples made a Better World Retreat, and began to call themselves "Couples for a Better World."

By 1958 Gabriel had made contact with several other movements for couples developing around the world, including CFM in the United States, Teams of Notre Dame (Our Lady) in France and Father Pedro Richard's MFC in Uruquay, Gabriel began to get very concerned that the couples were beginning to think of themselves as "special" and were beginning to turn in on themselves. He wanted them to refresh their vision and to see more clearly that although they were (in their families) little churches, still, they were only part of the Church. Thus he called them to make a pilgrimage to Rome. In August of 1958, 100 couples and eleven priests journeyed to Rocca di Papa, across the lake from the Pope's summer residence, to the headquarters of Father Lombardi's MBW. They made another MBW retreat, this time with a focus on the laity as leaders in the Church. At the conclusion of the retreat they were welcomed into a private audience with Pius XII.

They returned home renewed. Pius XII died two months later. The couples took a new name: "The Teams of Matrimony of Pius XII." The Bishops of Spain wanted this movement in their dioceses, and as it spread throughout Spain it began to breed several off-shoots, new insights for families, religious education, etc. In the early sixties, it was all pulled together under one umbrella. Movimiento Familiar Cristiano. Gabriel was named National Assistant.

A few years later, it became clear to Gabriel's friends that the richness these couples were experiencing must be shared. Not to share it would be a sin of injustice. And so, with the couples, Gabriel designed a program, *Encuentro Conyugal* (now Marriage Encounter). The Spanish word, *Encuentro,* Gabriel told me, means "surprise-discovery."

In 1964, Gabriel met a childless, wealthy couple, Diego and Fina Bertomeu. They made the Encuentro and offered themselves in service to help the spread of *Encuentro* throughout Spain. Their generosity proved very fruitful, and things began to grow. In the course of the next few years MFC developed the Family Encounter. But by 1969, the Bertomeu's were discovering a couple problem. Many couples were making the *Encuentro* but were not picking up the spiritual dimension: the starting point in prayer was not being learned. And "our leadership needs nourishment, for they are working very hard but growing weary."

And so began another search with several couples. Gabriel approached them with the questions. What is your spirituality? How can we introduce others to it? How can we deepen what you already have? A year of searching yielded the small outline we now refer to as "the Marriage Retorno" manual.

THE ROLE OF CFM IN THE ORIGINS OF M.E.[2]

by Patty Crowley
Chicago, Illinois

In March, 1965, Pat and I stopped over in Barcelona, Spain, on our way back from Rome. We had been there for ten days,

2. Reprinted from *Marriage Encounter,* August, 1977.

taking part in the discussions of the Special Study group of Population and Birth Control.

When we returned home, we wrote a report in our family newsletter. Pat wrote, "After Rome, we stopped in Barcelona to attend a family group meeting. We picked up some new ideas on the importance of husband and wife discussing all their inner thoughts. They put Pope Paul's injunction about the importance of dialogue (as expressed in his first encyclical) into reality within the family."

I remember how impressed we were on hearing of this idea of "sitting down and learning the technique of dialogue." As a couple, we had always done this. But, the group in Spain had put dialogue into focus. We brought the idea back as an action item of the Christian Family Movement of Spain and pondered about how to use it here.

There were many family movements in Spain at that time. But shortly thereafter, this whole movement became united under the leadership of Jose and Margarita Pich. Its name was Movimiento Familiar Cristiano (MFC). The Pichs were the couple we had met in 1965 and we are forever grateful to them.

Then came the CFM Convention in 1967. It was one of the best, if the roster of speakers is any standard: Harvey Cox, Father Bernard Haring, Father Gregory Baum, Bill Antonio, Sidney Callahan, Father John Thomas and Gordon Zahn. Father Clarence Rivers thrilled us with his liturgies. And, a young man by the name of Ray Repp introduced his music, first to the hundreds of children at the meeting and then to all of us in CFM.

There were also representatives from other countries. Among these were Alfonso and Mercedes Gomez, the representatives of CFM in Mexico. Throughout the Convention, they kept coming up to us asking if they could introduce this new idea of dialogue which they had just experienced and about which they were so thrilled. They kept bugging us. We found it very difficult to find a place for them, because the program had been planned months before. There really was no place for them on the regular program. But, they insisted. Finally, and perhaps just to get rid of them, I approached the administration at Notre Dame and asked if a few couples could stay over a few days and make an Encounter. Meanwhile the Gomezes went about talking so enthusiastically to people that ten couples decided to stay and make the Encounter. They were all very impressed.

At the same time, the International Confederation of Christian Family Movements (ICCFM) was holding its third meeting at Notre Dame's Center for Continuing Education. Father Calvo, the founder of M.E., attended that meeting as an observer. His efforts were cited in the minutes of that meeting: "Interchange of Apostolic Experience. In this sense, the most important step given was the propagation of 'Matrimonial Encounter' that started in Spain and which, afterwards, Father Calvo took to Mexico and from there to other Latin American countries. It has spread to Patterson and Newark (New Jersey), New York, Lansing, Erie, Detroit and Chicago. The purpose of such Encounters is to show an efficient way to the dialogue and unity of the couple. To this point, Father Hessler, Father Calvo and the Gomezes proposed that some of the leaders present it to the convention. Everybody agreed and there was great interest."

The following year, on August 4th, 1968, the fifth meeting of ICCFM took place in Newark, New Jersey. At this meeting, we greeted and hosted a plane full of Spanish couples of the MFC. They had come to the United States to give Marriage Encounters all across the country. It was quite a project for CFM. The Spanish couples had paid for their way over; but CFM couples in this country took care of them, their transportation, housing and all their plans for giving Encounters in about fifty cities in this country. Most of the Encounters were for the Spanish-speaking. But we did insist that one of the teams be English-speaking, so that those who spoke only English could also share the experience. Soon, accounts of enthusiasm began to pour in.

At the sixth ICCFM Executive Meeting in La Pree, France, a written report stated: "The Crowleys gave a report of the U.S./Spain Marriage Encounter program in August, 1968. The Conjugal Encounters appear to be one of the best services rendered to date through the Confederation ... Plans are being made for a Conjugal Encounter at Notre Dame in August, 1969, at the time of the annual Convention."

The minutes of that same meeting also give a full report of the development of Marriage Encounter in Spain. *"Barcelona was the first center,* and there are now Encounter teams in 60% of the dioceses in Spain. In 1966, the Encounter came out of Spain and was given for the first time in Mexico. The first Encounter in the U.S. was given by Father Calvo and the Gomezes in Miami. Following this, Father Calvo met Father

Hessler and Encounters were given in many places throughout the U.S. In 1968, fifty couples and priests came over to the U.S. (from Spain) to give Encounters in fifty cities . . ."

At this meeting, it was stated that the Encounter should remain part of the International Confederation. Also, Jamie Whelan and Father Kenny gave a brief report on the development of the Encounter in the U.S. during the past year. About 80 weekends had been given up to that time.

I remember well the wonderful couples from around the world at the meeting at Notre Dame in August, 1969—the Alcocers from Mexico, the Sisons from the Philippines, the D' Silvas from India, the Gascons and Pichs from Spain, the Nolans from New Zealand, the Thompsons from Scotland, the O'Siochains from Ireland, the Murphys from England and the Maldoons, Luceys and Weisserts from the U.S. All of them made the Marriage Encounter at Notre Dame that weekend.

Couples' lives were touched. From that time on, the Encounter was promoted as an action for the International Confederation. At this meeting, various committees were established by the Confederation. Marriage Encounter was one of these. Jose and Margarita Pich were the couple in charge of coordinating the Encounter as it developed in various countries. At each meeting thereafter, a report was given of the developments.

Ireland hosted the next Confederation meeting in October, 1971. All the countries and, in the main, the same representatives were present as had been at Notre Dame two years previously. The Pichs and Father Calvo gave the first international "Re-Encounter" (now called the Retorno). I remember how we all loved it. Two days were spent, as husband and wife, dwelling on Scripture and our married life. Couples from other countries were also there for the first time— Japan, Ghana, France, Belgium, Malta, Chile and Venezuela. A team composed of John and Kay Devine and Father Jerry Fraser of Detroit gave these couples their first Encounter.

The Sisons of the Philippines, who had made the Encounter at Notre Dame, reported that "they introduced the idea in the Philippines in October, 1969. This year (1971), there were 27 Encounters on five islands and 24 couples had been trained to give Encounters." Taiwan had two Encounters. The New Zealand CFM reported that the Encounter had started—eight given in 1970 and several more in 1971. It was a similar story from others who had attended the meeting at Notre Dame.

Ten years later, Marriage Encounter has grown. There are two types of Encounter—and maybe more. I feel saddened, in a way, about these developments, but happy that so many couples have experienced the Encounter. However, it is disturbing to hear reports like one that recently came in. Couples have gone to the Philippines very recently, that is, to a place where Marriage Encounter has been going on for almost ten years, and they do not recognize the efforts and accomplishments of the great couples who preceded them. I am also saddened over the very apparent fact that the Marriage Encounter is no longer a service or an action of CFM across the world. It is now several movements, even though ICCFM still holds the legal right to the name.

In closing, I would like to offer a prayer for all who have or ever will make a Marriage Encounter—no matter which type.

O Lord, help couples to see in the dialogue a beginning of opening themselves to the World. Help them to know themselves through dialogue and yet to realize that, as they think about themselves and understand themselves, they can be really happy in their married life only when they become aware of the social injustices in the world. Help them, dear Lord, not to become so taken up and content with their own world of Marriage Encounter couples that they forget to struggle each day actively to discover how they can feed the hungry, give drink to the thirsty, clothe the naked, harbor the harborless and visit those who are sick and in prison.

APPENDIX B
National and Worldwide Expressions: Why Are There Two?

Any account of Marriage Encounter and all the tremendous things it has accomplished in the ten years of its existence in the United States has to face up to the fact that there are two divergent and often bitterly conflicting organizations that go by the same name in this country—that both claim to present the authentic weekend and follow-up that has accomplished such apparent miracles.

Anybody who cares about Marriage Encounter, and whose own marriage has benefited from the experience, has to ask

"Why are there two expressions? Why can't they get together?" Of the four books[1] so far published about Marriage Encounter, one *(The Marriage Encounter: As I Have Loved You* by Father Chuck Gallagher) makes no mention of Father Calvo or the existence of any M.E. organization anywhere in the world apart from the one which the New York Jesuit heads. The other three by people who made their Encounter under the 'New York' (now Worldwide) auspices, temper their gratitude for the experience with criticism of what they see as dangerous tendencies on the part of that expression. The authors of the present volume—the first to be written from within and in terms of the National expression—have tried to suppress the feelings of envy and superiority associated with the poorer and snubbed, but older and more legitimate branch of a family.

We can trace our roots back to Father Calvo, whom we revere and try to follow. But we have to admit that much of M.E.'s founder's criticism of the U.S. tendency to exalt the organization at the expense of its mission—and to see our own apostolate as somehow different and more important than the other apostolates—applies to ourselves as well as Worldwide.

In answer to the question, *What do you see taking place in this country as opposed to other parts of the world?*, Father Calvo wrote:

> I will try to answer this with an open heart, while appealing to God's spirit to provide me with words that are both gentle and strong—words that will heal and give us direction, words, however, that could wound. Yet, when God speaks, it often hurts inside, even though this is good and useful pain.
>
> As a rule, I do not like to search out differences. I prefer to look for what unites us. And what unites us is more than what separates us. But, there is one big difference between the United States and other countries, even though these other countries are coming close to this practice. This difference involves a change in meaning, one that leads to confusion and disorientation.

---

1. Gallagher, Father Chuck, *The Marriage Encounter: As I Have Loved Yo*[cut off] Doubleday, N.Y., 1975; Bosco, Antoinette, *Marriage Encounter: The Rediscovery of Lo*[cut off] Abbey Press, St. Meinrad, Indiana, 1973; Durkin, Henry P., *Marriage Encounter: 44 Hou*[cut off] *to Change Your Life,* Paulist Press, N.Y., 1974; Champlin, Joseph M., *Alone No Long*[cut off] Ave Maria Press, Notre Dame, 1977.

Just what is this change? When I met with the first couples in Barcelona we thought of ourselves as members of a movement that came to call itself the *Movimiento Familiar Christiano* (MFC). It was within this movement that I planned, wrote, corrected, consulted and begged for cooperation. The first Encounter was not for members of the MFC—but for poor couples, 28 members of the working class. The weekend was an action, a service of the MFC, conducted by team couples and priests who were active in the MFC. And that's how I thought it would remain—under the auspices of the MFC.

In most countries M.E. is still under the auspices of the MFC, or the World Conference of the Christian Family Movements, an ecumenical conference with one purpose and one form of service. Marriage Encounter was like this at first in the United States. But then, something happened. It began to be a movement of its own. And at that moment conflict started, the conflict with other movements—especially those whose only purpose was to reinforce the couple and to anticipate the needs of the families—whether these were complete or incomplete, or even if it was a pre-family, i.e., an engaged couple.

It is this change which is causing so much suffering and confusion in the United States. It comes from having so many organizations within the Christian community, all appealing to the same people and thus making it difficult to reach the neediest families, who are the ones so often most confused by this conflict.

When the leaders of National Marriage Encounter first read these words they felt a little smug. They saw it at first as well-deserved rebuke to Worldwide. But then, when they read it more carefully, they took it to heart as applying to themselves as well.

Father Calvo, although he has remained close to National Marriage Encounter, and has provided enormous help and direction—not only in the retranslation of his Manual but in helping set up the U.S. versions of the *Retorno* and the *Family Encounter*—has never cut off communication with Worldwide. He has worked diligently and patiently to try to bring the two expressions together.

Father Gerry Koob is another peacemaker. Although he made his Encounter with Worldwide, he has worked for eight years with National, especially in its ecumenical program in

217

Virginia. He has been quick to acknowledge the contributions of Worldwide, as well as its shortcomings. He has been equally frank about the contributions and shortcomings of National. Currently, as one of the leaders (appointed by Father Calvo) of the U.S. *Retorno,* he is trying to make this program a bridge between the two expressions.

In *Agape* (December, 1976) he wrote: ". . . For Father Calvo Marriage Encounter is just one step in the process. Father Calvo is a family man and a man of prayer in the deepest sense of the words 'family' and 'prayer.' But the process of dialogue does not stop at M.E. Now when M.E. landed in Long Island, N.Y., in 1968 something else happened and, as I see it, that something was really good. The couples and the priests there discovered (true) 'dialogue.' And my hat goes off in salute, especially to Father Charles Gallagher. Father Calvo had his finger on the importance of sharing feelings—as did several other communications psychologists, especially Charles Rogers. But Father Gallagher and his community in Long Island developed a very valuable tool for self-disclosure. I find it a real sadness that many groups in National Marriage Encounter have not yet discovered this insight . . .

"But what about daily 'dialogue'? Should a couple dialogue daily? I think there are far too many people in the world who are willing to tell others what they should do. 'Shoulds' and 'ought to's' just keep reinforcing the old negative self-image. One of the most discouraging experiences I've ever had was being in the home of an M.E. presenting couple who claimed to 'dialogue' daily. But they consistently talked down to their children. I could not fathom how they could be so much in touch with their own feelings and be so oblivious to their own children's feelings.

"In a word, I really think 'dialogue' is a very worthwhile art to master. It is a very high level skill in self-disclosure and listening. But Marriage Encounter has a long way to go to really find the way to teach people how to do it and motivate couples to master this art . . . 'Dialogue,' even daily 'dialogue' or 10/10, is, at best, a stepping stone or door opener to (true) dialogue . . . The trap for a couple is to think that 'dialogue,' even daily 'dialogue,' is the absolute end . . ..

"All of my eight years in M.E. have been spent in National Marriage Encounter. I don't regret it for one second. I find it tragic that Worldwide slipped into what I see as certain attitudes and practices which put their gift under a bushel basket . . . Though I love them as I do, I cannot salute what I perceive as teaching people through an appeal to guilt motivation. I cannot salute what I see as a system which breeds 'programmed' people, whose behavior comes across to me as governed by what they are 'supposed to do.' (Please note: these are my problems, originating from my perception, my experience and my interpretation. I own them.)

"I cannot salute what I perceive as a system of leadership which breeds a parent-child relationship between the leaders and followers. I am also concerned about the issue of Ecumenism, about what we mean by 'Church' (see Chapter Eight). But I doubt that what I perceive as flaws in the Worldwide system were intended by anyone. People are too good for that. But I wanted you to know where I stand and what experiences got me here."

Although several reconciliation attempts have been made by the leadership of National and Worldwide—with the approach coming first from one side and then the other—these have foundered on the issues of the daily 10/10 dialogue, the tight structure and recruiting methods of the one and the insistence on the Calvo Manual, the autonomy of local groups and ecumenism of the other.

Quite recently, however, the new Executive Secretary Team of Worldwide—Father Paddy Colleran and Dick and Barbara McBride—approached the Sextons and Father Tom Hill with the suggestion of holding a series of weekends of discussion and prayer to try and iron out these mutual differences—to at least, and finally, reach a *modus vivendi,* some agreement on ground rules for recruiting and referral.

The National Executive Team has written a letter, of which these are the key points:

> *Scripture reveals that God has given each a special gift to be used for the good of the entire body. Unity would necessitate the recognition and sharing of gifts. This is unity in the sense of mission, rather than uniformity of style. We see Worldwide having the gifts of numbers, power, money, organization and apostolic zeal. Our common enemies are loneliness, divorce, materialism, disfunctioning marriages and families, and atheism. We need your gifts to strengthen us against these forces. What gifts do you see in National M.E. that would help you? We believe that reconciliation can take place only*

between equals, with not only an acceptance of the other but a recognition of the other's gifts.

It would be most helpful personally and a prerequisite for our meeting regarding reconciliation for us to be able to have an understanding of your thinking on the following points:

1. Why in the history on your calendar and in the 'history' talks on your weekends, as well as elsewhere, is there no recognition of Father Calvo as the founder of Marriage Encounter? It has been quite evident to us and others that Worldwide has never officially recognized Father Calvo. We would like to hear evidence to the contrary.

2. Why did Father Gallagher (or Worldwide) change the original purpose of Father Calvo's Marriage Encounter from the renewal of the couple to the renewal of the Catholic Church?

3. Could you give us the history and reasons for changing Calvo's weekend from one of an enriching experience that would help the couple move to the Retorno and the Family? As we see your weekend now, it is a teaching weekend where couples are to learn the written feeling dialogue technique.

4. Would you clarify these terms for us as there appears to be a divergence between National and Worldwide in how they are used: Church; Sacrament (and its relationship to a 'mixed' marriage); Ecumenism.

5. Please give the history and reasons for the decision to encourage the establishment of separate "Faith Expressions" and the exclusion of Protestant and 'mixed' marriages from your teams and leadership.

6. Please give the reasons for your focus on the institutional Roman Catholic Church rather than on Jesus Christ. (This is really a part of questions 3 and 5).

*7. Please explain the **process** of your weekend as compared to the process as outlined in Father Calvo's Manual. How does it flow from one presentation to the next?*

8. How do you view your breakaway groups now affiliated with National?

9. What is your definition of dialogue (again as compared to that in Father Calvo's Manual)?

10. What is your definition of Marriage spirituality? We presume this to be the original goal of Encounter.

At this particular time we are not concerned with the merits of your definitions or viewpoints versus ours or Father Gallagher's. We are simply trying to grasp how you view the Marriage Encounter weekend and, especially, in light of how it was given to us by Father Calvo and the Spanish couples who originated the program . . .

We believe that secrecy breeds suspicion, misunderstanding and mistrust. Evil can flourish in the darkness of rumors, half-truths and lack of communication. Scripture says that the truth shall make us free. If openness and sharing self works for couples, it should also work for the various Marriage Encounter groups. To help create an environment of openness and understanding we make several proposals; many of these were also made to your predecessors. We make them again to you. We need no further approval from our affiliates in this area of communication and are ready to implement immediately:

—an exchange of workshops and speakers at our National Conferences and at as many local and regional M.E. functions as possible;

*—an exchange of articles in our national publications. We will give you one page each issue in **Marriage Encounter** (formerly **Agape**) Magazine in exchange for one page each month in your **Spirit**;*

—an exchange of board minutes, budget, financial statements, etc., from 1975 through the present;

—and ongoing exchange of contact lists and leadership communications.

We, too, pray like you for reconciliation but with the realization that God acts through people (all of us). May your letter and this response be a new beginning to an open and honest effort toward unity. We eagerly await your reply so that as with this letter, we can publish and distribute it to all of the National affiliates, so that they might participate with us in this new reconciliation effort. Your brothers and sisters in His name,
(signed) Jerry and Marilyn Sexton, Father Tom Hill, OFM Cap., Executive Secretary Team, National Marriage Encounter.

Again, Father Calvo should have the last word. In answer to the question, *What can be done about the divisions within Marriage Encounter?,* he replied:

> *I've been concerned with this for over a year-and-a-half. I have tried to gather people of good will together by holding "Fraternal Encounters" with the leaders involved. Both they and I have prayed, communicated, renewed our hopes and planned meetings.*
>
> *More concretely, I think, the divisions will be healed when the leaders of Marriage Encounter form a community with the leaders of the Confederation of Christian Family Movements. Such profound communion with CFM and Family Life cannot help but bear fruit. This will lead to unity.*
>
> *Hopefully the day will come when unity will be a reality. When all those who are working to help married couples and their families will be within one strong movement dedicated to this proposition: that the fire of the Lord should take over every home. Only this flame can bring an end to the conflict and confusion. But we must pray, because this is the work of the Lord and not some human technique or method of manipulation.*
>
> *I truly believe that if we pray together and approach each other with open hearts, unity will become a reality. Then the Lord will help us triumph over the Spirit of Evil. Then His will (not ours) will be done.*

APPENDIX C
Recommended Reading

A: Books About Marriage Encounter

Bosco, Antoinette, *Marriage Encounter: The Rediscovery of Love,* St. Meinrad, Indiana, Abbey Press, 1973. (Also available in paperback.)

Champlin, Joseph M., *Alone No. Longer,* Notre Dame, Ave Maria Press, 1977, (paper).

Durkin, Henry P., *Marriage Encounter: 44 Hours to Change Your Life,* New York, Paulist Press, 1974, (paper).

Gallagher, Father Chuck, *The Marriage Encounter: As I Have Loved You,* New York, Doubleday, 1975.

B: Books About Love and Marriage

Barbeau, Clayton, *Creative Marriage: The Middle Years,* New York, Seabury Press, 1976, (also in paper).

Bird, Joseph and Lois, *Marriage Is for Grownups,* New York, Doubleday, 1971, (also paper).

Caffarel, Henri, ed., *Marriage Is Holy,* Notre Dame, Fides, 1957, (paper).

Capon, Robert F., *Bed and Board: Plain Talk About Marriage,* New York, Simon & Schuster, 1965, (also in paper).

Ciardi, John, *I Marry You: A Sheaf of Love Poems,* New Brunswick, N.J., Rutgers University Press, 1958.

De Rougement, Dennis, *Love in the Western World,* New York, Harper & Row, 1956, (paper).

Dufresne, Edward R., *Partnership: Marriage and the Committed Life,* New York, Paulist Press, 1975, (also in paper).

Fromm, Erich, *The Art of Loving,* New York, Harper & Row, 1956, (also in paper).

Fromme, Allan, *The Ability to Love,* New York, Pocket Books, 1966, (paper).

Lewis, C.S., *The Four Loves,* New York Harcourt, Brace, Javonich, 1960.

Mace, David and Vera, *How To Have a Happy Marriage,* Nashville, Abingdon, 1977.

Mace, David and Vera, *We Can Have Better Marriages,* Nashville, Abingdon, 1974.

Masters, William H., and Johnson, Virginia E., *The Pleasure Bond: A New Look at Sexuality and Commitment,* Boston, Little, Brown, 1975.

Ortega y Gasset, Jose, *On Love,* New York, Meridian, 1957, (also in Mentor paperback).

Otto, Herbert, ed., *Marriage and Family Enrichment: New Perspectives and Programs,* Nashville, Abingdon, 1976, (also in paper).

Powell, John, S.J., *The Secret of Staying in Love,* Niles, Ill., Argus, 1974, (paper).

Powell, John, S.J., *Why Am I Afraid to Love?,* Argus, 1967, (paper).

Powell, John, S.J., *Why Am I Afraid to Tell You Who I Am?,* Argus, 1969, (paper).

Rogers, Carl, *Becoming Partners: Marriage & Its Alternatives,* New York, Delacorte, 1972, (also Dell paperback).

Shedd, Charles, *Letters to Karen,* Nashville, Abingdon, 1965, (also in Avon, Spire paperbacks).

Shedd, Charles, *Letters to Philip,* New York, Doubleday, 1968, (also in Spire paperback).

C: Books About Family, Parenthood, Personhood

Barbeau, Clayton, *The Head of the Family,* Chicago, Regnery, 1961, (available in paper from Liturgical Press, Collegeville, Minn.)

Gordon, Thomas, *Parent Effectiveness Training,* New York, Wyden, 1970, (also in paper).

Rogers, Carl, *On Becoming a Person,* Boston, Houghton & Mifflin, 1961, (also in paper).

Satir, Virginia, *Peoplemaking,* Palo Alto, California, Science & Behavior Books, 1972.

Sheehy, Gail, *Passages: Predictable Crises of Adult Life,* New York, Dutton, 1976, (also in Bantam paperback).

D: Books on Communication, Prayer, etc.

Berne, Eric, *Games People Play: The Psychology of Human Relationships,* New York, Grove, 1964, (also Ballantine paperback).

Evely, Louis, *That Man is You,* Westminister, Md., Newman, 1964, (also in Deus paperback).

Hovda, Robert and Huck, Gabe, *There's No Place Like People: Planning Small Group Liturgies,* Niles, Ill., Argus, 1969.

Miller, Sherod; Nunally, Elam; Wackman, Daniel B.; with Ron Brazman, *Alive and Aware: Improving Communication in Relationships,* Minneapolis, Interpersonal Communication Programs, Inc., 300 Clifton Ave., 1975.

Quoist, Michel, *Prayers,* New York, Sheed & Ward, 1963 (new ed., 1974).

E: Other Relevant Books

Buber, Martin, *I and Thou,* New York, Scribner, 1970.

Walter M. Abbott, S.J., ed., *Documents of Vatican II,* New York, Association Press, 1966 (paper).

Dulles, Avery, S.J., *The Resilient Church: The Necessity and Limits of Adaptation,* New York, Doubleday, 1977.

Häring, Bernard, *Sin in a Secular Age,* New York, Doubleday, 1973.

Kennedy, Eugene, *Fashion Me a People: Men, Women and Church,* New York, Sheed & Ward.

Kierkegaard, Soren, *The Living Thoughts of Kierkegaard,* presented by W.H. Auden, Bloomington, Indiana, Indiana University Press, 1963, (paper).

224

Merton, Thomas, *The New Man,* New York, Farrar, Straus, 1961, (also in Mentor paperback).

Schillebeeckx, E., *Christ, the Sacrament of the Encounter With God,* New York, Sheed & Ward, 1963.

Teilhard de Chardin, Pierre, *The Divine Milieu,* New York, Harper, (also in paper).

Teilhard de Chardin, Pierre, *On Love,* 1973, New York, Harper, 1973.

Teilhard de Chardin, Pierre, *The Phenomenon of Man,* New York, Harper, 1959, (also in paper).

CASSETTES

Making Marriage Work, Sidney Callahan and Eugene Kennedy, includes discussion guide, Thomas More Association, 180 N. Wabash, Chicago, IL, 60601.

The Family, 14 talks by Urban G. Steinmetz, Family Enrichment Bureau, Escanaba, MI, 49829.

(Note: Cassettes and records in English and Spanish by Father Gabriel Calvo on Marriage Encounter, Family Encounter and the *Retorno,* are available from FIRES, Inc., 1425 Otis St., N.E., Washington, DC, 20017.)

FILM

Sexuality and Communication, Ortho Pharmaceutical Ltd., 19 Green Belt Dr., Don Mills, Ontario, Canada.

GAMES

The 'Now' Communication Game, Herbert Otto, for couples and families (children 6 and up), The Holistic Press, 8909 Olympic Blvd., Beverly Hills, CA, 90211.

The Ungame, stimulates exploration of attitudes, feelings, motives and values for couples, families (children 5 and up), The Ungame Co., Garden Grove, CA, 92642.

N.B.: The following invaluable materials can be obtained from National Marriage Encounter, 955 Lake Drive, St. Paul, MN 55120.

The Calvo Marriage Encounter Manual, Third Edition, $3.00.

The New Chicago Supplement to the Calvo Manual, $1.50.

The Encountering Couple, $2.50.

The Milwaukee Image: A National Marriage Encounter Continuing Dialogue Manual, $2.50.

The Engaged Encounter Manual, $3.00.

Marriage Encounter (formerly *Agape)* Magazine, monthly, $6 per year.

The Marriage Enrichment Manual for Parishes (in preparation).

APPENDIX D
Whom to Contact. Where to Go
for further information about Marriage Encounter

NATIONAL MARRIAGE ENCOUNTER BOARD—Aug., 1977

Jerry and Marilyn Sexton
263 Dessa Lane
South St. Paul, MN 55075
612-451-0571, 451-1559

Father Tom Hill, O.F.M. Cap.
2159 Marshall Avenue
St. Paul, MN 55104
612-646-7139

Bob and Marge Agnew
8851 Greenhill Lane
Greendale, WI 53129
414-425-2855

Armando and Barbara Carlo
8331 East Monterey Way
Scottsdale, AZ 85251
602-947-0565

Joe and Deanie Crane
199 Boston Avenue
Massapequa, NY 11758
516-798-4136

Tom and Kay Farrell
305 McDonough Road
Annapolis, MD 21401
301-269-1139

Tom and Marie Howard
302 McClellan Blvd.
Davenport, IA 52803
319-355-2834

Rabbi Bernie and Julie Kligfeld
457 Lido Blvd.
Lido Beach, NY 11561
516-432-7862

Al and Sandi Locke
20606 Susan Ruth St.
Saugus, CA 91350
805-251-0122

Father Frank McNamara, S.J.
53 E. 83rd St.
New York, NY 10028

Jim and Adel-Marie O'Regan
2264 Habersham Drive
Clearwater, FL 33516
813-535-2277

Al and Dee Rohrbacher
RFD #1, Box 1402
Chester, NH 03036
603-887-4762

Steve and Kathi Smith
7516 Burke N.E.
Albuquerque, NM 87109
505-821-9452

Sister Judith Tate, O.S.B.
P.O. Box 60155
Oklahoma City, OK 73106
405-843-7441—office
405-751-2145—home

Paul and Marge Tepper
3021 Runnymede Drive
Norristown, PA 19403
215-279-9879, 215-279-3921

CFM Liaison
Father Ed Hogan
345 Adams St.
Brooklyn, NY 11201
212-855-2534

226

NATIONAL MARRIAGE ENCOUNTER AFFILIATES—April 1, 1977

ALASKA
Fairbanks
Paul & Lucy McCarthy
Box 80687
College, AK 99701
907-479-2804

Father Bill Dibb, S.J.
Sacred Heart Cathedral
1316 Peger Road
Fairbanks, AK 99701
907-456-7868

Juneau
Ken & Joan Grieser
487 Douglas Highway
Juneau, AK 99801
907-586-1847

ARKANSAS
Little Rock
Dick & Pat Bausom
#11 Broadmoor Drive
Conway, AR 72032
501-327-0422

Father Richard Oswald
Our Lady of Good Counsel
1321 So. Van Buren St.
Little Rock, AR 72204
501-666-5073

Subiaco
Gus & Ann Buss
315 Sutton Street
Fayetteville, AR 72701
501-443-2273

Rev. Herbert Vogelpohl
New Subiaco Abbey
Coury House
Subiaco, AR 72865
501-934-2610

CALIFORNIA
Beale AFB
Major and Mrs. Lionel Boudreaux
3368 Laurel
Beale AFB, CA 95903

Central California
Marc & Pat Grimm
609 Ramona
Modesto, CA 95350
209-524-4592

Lafayette
Father Al Garrotto, O.M.I.
Mount Mary Immaculate
3254 Gloria Terrace
Lafayette, CA 94549
415-934-2411

Marin and Sonoma Counties
Paul & Cheryl Sartorio
417 San Carlos Way
Novato, CA 94947
415-897-3544

Modesto
Carl & Jan Schuetze
310 Leveland Lane
Modesto, CA 95350
209-522-0969

Sacramento
Dave & Romana Mitchell
4513 Argonaut Way
Sacramento, CA 95825
916-481-1607

Southern California
Al & Sandi Locke
20606 Susan Ruth St.
Saugus, CA 91350
805-251-0122

COLORADO
Denver
Mark & Nan Benecke
1423 South Ward St.
Lakewood, CO 80228
303-986-0735

CONNECTICUT
Errol & Marilyn Terrell
591 Three Mile Hill Road
Middlebury, CT 06762
203-758-2165

FLORIDA
Miami
Pat & Carol Farrell
20245 N.W. 3rd Court
Miami, FL 33169

Father Joe Carney
Little Flower Rectory
1270 Anastasia Avenue
Coral Gables, FL 33134
305-443-8389

227

Orlando
Mike & Mary Jo Nocero
103 Satsuma Drive
Altamonte Springs, FL 32701
305-862-0144

Father Ed McCarthy
St. Margaret Mary Church
P.O. Box 206
Winter Park, FL 32789
305-647-3392—home
305-425-3556—office

Lower Pinellas
Del & Mary Fisher
11195 Regal Lane
Largo, FL 33540
813-595-7223

Father Richard Colbert
St. Pete Catholic High School
6333 - 9th Ave. No.
St. Petersburg, FL 33710
813-344-4065—office
813-347-1773—home

Upper Pinellas
Jim & Adel-Marie O'Regan
2264 Habersham Drive
Clearwater, FL 33516
813-535-2277

GEORGIA
Atlanta
Kathy & Dale Harsh
1510 Garden Lane Circle
Marietta, Georgia 30062
404-971-2694

Valdosta
Bob & Lil Ellison
2314 Park Lane
Valdosta, GA 31601
912-242-3363

IDAHO
Idaho Falls
John & Terri McFee
737 Hansen
Idaho Falls, ID 83401
208-523-7634

ILLINOIS
Chicago
Steve & Nicole VanderVoort
1915 No. Cleveland, Unit A
Chicago, IL 60614
312-266-8133

Father James Friedel, O.S.A.
201 East Ohio Street
Chicago, IL 60611
312-821-8576
Peoria
Ed & Kay Schraith
807 So. Fell
Normal, IL 61761
309-452-9589

Father Robert Aaron, O.M.I.
King's House of Retreats
Box 165
Henry, IL 61537
309-364-3084

INDIANA
Evansville
Jeff & Linda Hayes
Sunnyside Road
Washington, IN 47501
812-254-6467

Father Jim Blessinger
Holy Redeemer Rectory
918 W. Mill Road
Evansville, IN 47710
812-424-8344

Hartford City
Karl & Sandy Benkeser
2315 West Jackson
Muncie, IN 47303
317-282-4795

Father Keith Hosey
John XXIII Center
407 W. McDonald St.
RR #2, Box 303
Hartford City, IN 47346
317-348-4008

Huntington
Donald & Mary Jane Bartrom
933 Cherry Street
Huntington, IN 46750
219-356-6626

Father John Holt, O.F.M. Cap.
St. Felix Friary
Huntington, IN 46750
219-356-8010

South Bend
John & Kathy Jakubowski
841 South 27th St.
South Bend, IN 46615
219-289-4569

Father James Trepanier, C.S.C.
Holy Cross Mission House
Notre Dame, IN 46556
219-234-1067

IOWA
Cedar Falls
Gary & Kay Aitchison
922 Ninth Street
Ames, IA 50010
515-232-0314

Father Mel Hemann
Highway 18 and Clark St.
Charles City, IA 50616
515-228-1071

Cedar Rapids
Joe & Kathy Connell
1932 - 4th Ave. S.E.
Cedar Rapids, IA 52403
319-362-6025

Father James Goedken
1st Ave. and Edgewood Rd. S.W.
Cedar Rapids, IA 52404
319-362-2135

Davenport
Marriage Encounter
Diocesan Office
2706 Gaines Street
Davenport, IA 52804

Davenport - Western
(Iowa City Area)
Dick & Sis Vogel
1601 Prairie
Grinnell, IA 50112
515-236-6923

Davenport - Eastern
George & Barb Balunis
P.O. Box 198
Pleasant Valley, IA 52767
319-355-4033

Father Bill Kaska
St. Mary Magdalen Church
Bloomfield, IA 52537
515-664-2553

Des Moines
Bob & Sharon Holz
4253 Foster Drive
Des Moines, IA 50312
515-255-6954

Father Frank S. Palmer
700 3rd Street
Des Moines, IA 50309
515-244-3761

Dubuque
Dan & Barb Nicholson
889 Walker
Dubuque, IA 52001
319-556-5797

Father George Karnik
408 Clara Avenue
Manchester, IA 52057
319-927-4710

Sioux City
Larry & Gladys Graham
3131 Morgan Street
Sioux City, IA 51104
712-258-6240

Rev. Ronald J. Reicks
1122 Grandview Blvd.
Sioux City, IA 51105

MAINE
Joe & Kathy Lord
24 West St.
Fairfield, ME 04937
207-453-7796

Father Paul Ouellette
St. Paul's Center
136 State St.
Augusta, ME 04330
207-622-6235

MARYLAND
Mar-Va
Dick & Jean Wight
1914 York Drive
Woodbridge, VA 22191
VA #, 703-494-3287—Home
Wash. D.C. #, 202-550-9095—M.E. Line

Father Richard Cleary O.S.F.S.
5001 Eastern Avenue
Hyattsville, MD 20782
301-559-4022

MASSACHUSETTS
Springfield
Fred & Pat Roberts
32 Leonard Street
Agawam, MA 01001
413-786-8580

Father Bennet Kelly
Monastery Avenue
West Springfield, MA 01089
413-736-5458

MICHIGAN
Alpena
Joe & Doris Boyle
1110 Hinkley
Alpena, MI 49707
517-354-5406

Ann Arbor
Domenic & Del Bitondo
5 Manchester Court
Ann Arbor, MI 48104
313-971-4637

Detroit
Garry & Irene Heckman
20405 Gardendale
Detroit, MI 48221
313-341-2802

Father Allen Gruenke, O.F.M. Cap.
760 Boston Blvd.
Detroit MI 48202
313-579-2100—Office
313-867-5200—Home

Holland
Bill & Sharon Rocker
127 Sunrise
Holland, MI 49423
616-392-1966

Jackson
Rev. Bob & Marin Haldane
2524 Spring Arbor Road
Jackson, MI 49203
517-784-0785

Father Keith Krusky
1013 Carleton Blvd.
Jackson, MI 49203
517-783-2784

Saginaw
Moe & Fran Brandon
804 South Chilson
Bay City, MI 48706
517-893-5810

Father Malcolm Maloney
Blessed Sacrament Church
3206 Swede Road
Midland, MI 48640
517-832-2571

Upper Peninsula
Louis & Jane Carr
1100 Cleveland
Marquette, MI 49855
906-225-0081

Father Matt Nyman
Marygrove Renewal Center
Garden, MI 49835
906-644-2771

MINNESOTA
Minnesota M.E. Center
Roy Wolff, Coordinator
953 Lake Drive
St. Paul, MN 55120
612-454-3238

Alexandria
Dave & Linda Wenzel
Route 5
Alexandria, MN 56308
612-763-6198

Duluth
Tom & Marilyn Privette
2205 West 8th Street
Duluth, MN 55806
218-727-7720

Father Bill Fournier, O.M.I.
West End Catholic Parishes
2423 West Third
Duluth, MN 55806
218-722-4445

International Falls
Bill & Theresa Grimsell
719 - 5th St.
International Falls, MN 56649
218-283-3684

Father Roger Bergkamp, O.M.I.
Box 49
International Falls, MN 56649
218-283-3553

Mankato
Jerry & June Rooney
528 Hickory
Mankato, MN 56001
507-387-2720

Marshall
Bob & Dorothy Walser
Route 2
Marshall, MN 56258
507-532-3081

Father Dennis Becker
St. Mary's Catholic Church
Cottonwood, MN 56229
507-423-5220

Rochester
Jim & Bev Pluth
2533 Summit Drive N.E.
Rochester, MN 55901
507-288-1172

Father Frank Galles
Assisi Heights
Rochester, MN 55901
507-282-8127

St. Cloud
Dave & Joleen Hoeschen
RR #5
St. Cloud, MN 56301
612-252-3679

Twin Cities (Mpls. & St. Paul)
John & Cel Dahlmeier
3501 Ensign Ave. No.
New Hope, MN 55427
612-544-7909

Father Burt Pratt, S.J.
2201 Pillsbury Ave. So.
Minneapolis, MN 55404
612-871-1612

MISSOURI
Jefferson City
Jay & Dolores Prost
3122 Country Club Drive
Jefferson City, MO 65101
314-893-3160

Fr. Francis Gillgannon
2301 West Main
Jefferson City, MO 65101
314-635-7991

St. Louis
Ray & Gina Einig
9761 Ridge Heights
Fairview Heights, IL 62208
618-397-3778

MONTANA
Helena
Jim & Ruth Wilkins
1618 Winne
Helena MT 59601
406-442-5134

Fr. John Redman
Carroll College
Helena, MT 59601
406-442-3450

Billings
Bill & Irene Osborne
5411 Gene Sarazen Drive
Billings, MT 59101
406-656-2538

Fr. Charles Gorman
18th St. West & Yellowstone Ave.
Billings, MT 59102
406-656-2522

Great Falls
John and Barbara McNaught
1103-4th Ave. No.
Great Falls, MT 59401
406-453-8500

Fr. John Houlihan
413 - 22nd Ave. N.E.
Great Falls, MT 59404
406-727-4757

NEBRASKA
Hastings
Fr. Ernie Martello, O.S.C.
Crosier Workshop Center
Crosier Monastery
223 East 14th St., Box 789
Hastings, NE 68901
402-463-3188

NEW HAMPSHIRE
Manchester
Harry & Priscilla Myers
RFD #1, Box 78
Chester, NH 03036
603-483-8657

NEW JERSEY
North N.J.
Joe & Barbara Schenk
32 Lake Street
Ramsey, NJ 07446
201-327-6246

Fr. Frank McNamara, S.J.
144 Grand Street
Jersey City, NJ 07302
201-434-4400

NEW MEXICO
Albuquerque
Jack & Agnes Conroy
4915 - 14th St. NW
Albuquerque, NM 87107
505-344-1333

Albuquerque (Protestant)
Herman and JoEllen Leopold
1421 Luthy Circle NE
Albuquerque, NM 87112
505-299-9358

NEW YORK
Bayville - (Protestant - Episcopal)
Bruce & Virginia McMorris
102 Godfrey Avenue
Bayville, NY 11709

Buffalo
Bob & Judy Carrick
226 California Drive
Williamsville, NY 14221
716-632-8961

Catskills
Bob & Lynne Freedman
RD #2, Johnston Road
Livingston Manor, NY 12758
914-439-5708

Chemung Valley (Elmira)
John & Dorothea Watts
119 Scenic Drive So.
Horseheads, NY 14845
607-739-4805

Ithaca
Norris & Barb Danningburg
2 West Lake Drive
Dryden, NY 13053
607-844-9416

Nassau County
Bill & Betty Fox
181 Friends Lane
Westbury, NY 11590
516-333-6152

Olean
Ed & Linda Eckert
60 South Street
Cuba, NY 14727
716-968-3879

Fr. Bob White
St. Bonaventure University
St. Bonaventure, NY 14778
716-375-2000

Rochester
Gene & Karoly Edwards
70 Blackwell Lane
Henrietta, NY 14467
716-334-9658

Suffolk County
Ken & Claire Rathjen
Spring Hollow Hill
St. James, NY 11780
516-862-8726

Fr. Cronan Maxwell, O.F.M.
St. Johnland Road
Smithtown, NY 11787

Susquehanna Area
Dennis & Gail Abraham
3607 Beatrice Lane
Endwell, NY 13760
607-754-3174

Syracuse
Bill & Nancy Vaverchak
Rd #1, Box 108
Co. Rt. 10
Pennellville, NY 13132
315-668-7335

Watertown
Paul & Beverly Donahue
928 Academy Street
Watertown, NY 13601
315-788-5670

Fr. Rolland Hart
St. Rita's Church
Deferiet, NY 13628
315-493-1275

OHIO
Akron
Bob & Mary Ann Fabbro
2775 Serfass Road
Clinton, OH 44216
216-882-4348

Fr. James Becherer
c/o Family Counseling
1027 Superior Avenue
Cleveland, OH 44114
216-696-6525, ext. 215

Cincinnati
Jack & Jane Katenkamp
3856 Lincoln Road
Cincinnati, OH 45239
513-522-0222

Fr. Conleth Overman, C.P.
1055 St. Paul Place
Cincinnati, OH 45202
513-241-6218

Central Ohio (Columbus)
Dick & Annette Schorr
7043 Brennan Place
Worthington, OH 43085
614-846-3631

Fr. Jerry Stluka
Director, Family Life Bureau
197 East Gay Street
Columbus, OH 43215
614-221-5891

Dayton
Barry & Nympha Clark
7626 Cloverbrook Park Drive
Dayton, OH 45459
513-433-6115

Fr. John Tonry
Bergamo Center
4100 Patterson Road
Dayton, OH 45430
513-426-2363

Northwest Ohio
Don & Linda Worland
208 Riverside Drive
Tiffin, OH 44883
419-447-5813

Fr. Ed Schleter
501 Cherry St.
Toledo, OH 43604
419-243-4242

Maria Stein
Jerry & Kathleen Pulskamp
77 Circle Drive
New Bremen, OH 45869
419-629-6394

Fr. James Dugal
Maria Stein Retreat House
P.O. Box 128
Maria Stein, OH 45860
513-925-4538

OKLAHOMA
Oklahoma City
David & Jane Best
P.O. Box 60155
Oklahoma City, OK 73106
405-751-5285

Sister Judith Tate
P.O. Box 60155
Oklahoma City, OK 73106

Tulsa
Michael & Maryanne Murphy
7255 S. Pittsburg Ave.
Tulsa, OK 74136
918-402-6592

Fr. James McGlinchey
Catholic Social Services
739 No. Denver
Tulsa, OK 74106
918-585-8167

PENNSYLVANIA
Altoona-Johnstown
Herm & Nancy Clauto
606 West Sample Street
Ebensburg, PA 15931
814-472-6038

Fr. Paul Turnbull
2529 Broad Avenue
Altoona, PA 16601
814-943-6185

Harrisburg
Joe & Nancy Redington
135 McDermott Street
Chambersburg, PA 17201
717-352-7319

Pittsburgh
Jack & Joanne Ladish
531 Dugan Way
New Kensington, PA 15068
412-335-5327

Philadelphia (Southeast PA)
Bud & Kathy Carey
1010 Concord Avenue
Drexel Hill, PA 19026
215-853-1672

Williamsport
Nick & Susan Green
RD #1
Williamsport, PA 17701
717-322-0631

RHODE ISLAND
Rob & Winnie Sullivan
25 Williams Street
North Kingstown, RI 02852
401-295-8187

Fr. Jerry Haladus, O.P.
Providence College
Providence, RI 02918
401-865-2308
401-865-2487

TENNESSEE
Memphis
Ken & Shari Lee
3247 Bluefield Street
Memphis, TN 38128
901-386-8008

Fr. Ray Mullin
190 No. Adams
Memphis, TN 38105
901-526-6882

TEXAS
North Texas
Tom & Mona Peterson
4916 Carol Court
Fort Worth, TX 76118
817-485-1323

Fr. Baltazar Szarka
P.O. Box 56
Grapevine, TX 76051
817-481-2685

VIRGINIA
Portsmouth (Tidewater)
Dick & Mary Ann DeLuca
4499 Steeplechase Drive
Virginia Beach, VA 23462
804-499-2893

Richmond
Neal & Marge Schmitt
9701 Redbridge Road
Richmond, VA 23235
804-320-1284

Roanoke
John & Sandy Bedillion
4740 Player Drive
Roanoke, VA 24019
703-362-8062

WEST VIRGINIA
Charleston
Don & Ann Wobser
618-Churchill Drive
Charleston, WV 25314
304-342-0886

Fr. Jonathan Williams, O.F.M. Cap.
P.O. Box 172
Madison, WV 25130
304-369-0362

Morgantown
Oz & Rita Ann Schultz
651 Southview Avenue
Morgantown, WV 26505
304-599-1020

Fr. Jude J. Mili, OFM
Good Counsel Friary
P.O. Box 3377
Morgantown, WV 26505
304-296-1714

Parkersburg
Mike & Rosemary Deitch
535 Lakewood Circle
Washington, WV 26101
304-863-6125

WISCONSIN
Appleton
Jack & Eunice Klug
Rt. #3, Box 312
Appleton, WI 54911
414-733-6339

Fr. Bob Lexa, OFM Cap.
Family Life Office
921 Midway Road
Menasha, WI 54952
414-734-2601

Fond du Lac
Dick & Betsy Haskett
RR 4 #2561 Co. Trk. Q.
Fond du Lac, WI 54935
414-922-2545

Fr. Brian Braun, O.F.M. Cap.
St. Lawrence Seminary
Mount Calvary, WI 53057
414-753-3911

Green Bay
Jack & Betsy McCool
328 Terraview Drive
Green Bay, WI 54301
414-336-2820

Fr. Jim Habelwitz
Family Life Office
P.O. Box 38
Green Bay, WI 54305
414-437-6541

La Crosse Diocese
Fr. Joe Visse, S.M.
Marynook, House of the Lord
500 So. 12th Street
Galesville, WI 54630
608-582-2789

Fr. Joseph Bilgrien
Family Life Office
Box 1102
Wisconsin Rapids, WI 54494

Madison
Bill & Jan Nieft
5500 JoyLynne Drive
Madison, WI 53716
608-222-1036

Fr. John Satterlee
113 E. Division St.
Mazomamie, WI 53560
608-795-2277

Milwaukee
Marriage Encounter Office
2021 No. 60th St.
Milwaukee, WI 53208
414-258-2060

Dick & Jan Johnson
1001 Lynne Drive
Waukesha, WI 53186
414-542-7377—M.E. Line
414-542-8309—Home

Fr. John Furtmann
2021 No. 60th St.
Milwaukee, WI 53208
414-771-1200

Wausau
Bob & Lucy Hall
710 Henrietta
Wausau, WI 54401
715-845-4082

Fr. Terrence Heiden, O.F.M. Cap.
St. Anthony Retreat Center
Marathon, WI 54448
715-443-2236

NATIONAL M.E. CONTACT COUPLES AND PRIESTS

The following M.E. groups are affiliated with National Marriage Encounter but are not now presenting weekends. Many of those listed are well organized and offer various follow-up programs. Some hope to be offering weekends in the near future. If you wish to organize a National Marriage Encounter group in your area, you are invited to send in your name to be listed as a Contact. Please send to the National M.E. Office, 955 Lake Drive, St. Paul, MN 55120.

CALIFORNIA
Bob & Carol Ann Schultz
8440 Montana Drive
Paradise, CA 95869
916-877-8106

COLORADO
Pueblo
Bob & Eileen Comiskey
2108 N. Elizabeth St.
Pueblo, CO 81002
303-545-2353

HAWAII
Capt. Marvin & Harriet Weissman
45 Halawa Drive
Honolulu, HI 96818

IDAHO
Moscow
Neil & Carol Meyer
850 Cleveland Ave. No.
Moscow, ID 83843
208-882-0658

LOUISIANA
Baton Rouge
Ron & Evonne Holloway
10358 Cedarlane
Baton Rouge, LA 70816
504-924-3167

MAINE
Brewer
Charlie & Lorraine Roberts
34 Edgewood Drive
Brewer, ME 04412
207-989-3195

MASSACHUSETTS
Boston
Don & Roxanne Nickerson
6 Hampton Lane
Andover, MA 01810
617-475-4450

Plymouth Area
Bill & Chris Strong
South Meadow Road
Carver, MA 02330

MICHIGAN
Lansing
Frank & Linda Traviglia
3318 Snowglen Lane
Lansing, MI 48917
517-372-7366

Monroe
Marvin & Reatha Meyer
221 No. Roessler St.
Monroe, MI 48161
313-242-3615

Petoskey
Gary & Colleen Klingler
910 Grove St.
Petoskey, MI 49770
616-347-1113

MINNESOTA
Worthington
Jerry & Gladys Weibel
P.O. Box 293
2130 East Oxford St.
Worthington, MN 56187
507-372-2546

MISSOURI
Northeast
Bob & Veronica Buben
3254 St. Mary's Ave.
Hannibal, MO 63401
314-221-6849

NEBRASKA
North Platte
Don & Leona Suedmeier
314 West 1st Street
North Platte, NE 69101
308-534-2169

NEW YORK
Brooklyn
Tony & Rose Incorvaia
914 East 28th St.
Brooklyn, NY 13901
607-722-5254

Fr. Ed Hogan
Apostolic Formations Program
345 Adams Street
Brooklyn, NY 11201
212-855-2534

Queens
Patrick & Alice Hughes
85-04 - 122nd St.
Kew Gardens, NY 11415
212-441-7225

Rockland County
John & Marsha Abrams
19 Grand St.
Tappan, NY 10983
914-359-4175

Staten Island
Joe & Camille Auci
345 Katan Avenue
Staten Island, NY 10308
212-984-3837

Westchester County
Bill & Dianna Mealey
48 Pershing Avenue
Ossining, NY 10562
914-941-5687

OHIO
Steubenville
John & Mary Ann Shanley
226 Alfred Drive
Wintersville, OH 43952
614-264-2734

PENNSYLVANIA
Bloomsburg
Chuck & Muriel Brunke
R.D. #4
Summit Avenue
Bloomsburg, PA 17815
717-784-9463

SOUTH CAROLINA
Charleston
Dave & Ginny Lovett
110 Mallard Drive
Goose Creek, SC 29445
803-553-4233

TEXAS
Wichita Falls
Fr. Tom E. Gallenbach
2202 Harrison, Apt. 171
Wichita Falls, TX 76308
817-322-8566—Home
817-852-2912—Office

WASHINGTON
Spokane
Joel & Carole Sargent
N. 7130 Winston Drive
Spokane, WA 99208
509-328-3274

GROUPS NOT AFFILIATED WITH NATIONAL M.E.

WORLDWIDE MARRIAGE ENCOUNTER
(Roman Catholic-Chapters in most states)
Dick & Barbara McBride and Fr. Paddy Colleran
Executive Secretary Team
3711 Long Beach Blvd., Suite 207
Long Beach, CA 90807   Ph: 213-595-5336

CHRISTIAN MARRIAGE ENCOUNTER
(predominantly Protestant-groups in Southwest)
George & Emily Walther, QTRS 8010
USAF Academy, CO 80840   Ph: 303-472-1738

DIOCESE OF WORCESTER, MASSACHUSETTS
Nick & Jan Cappello, 84 Tarrytown Lane
Worcester, MA 01602   Ph: 617-753-5796

237

ERIE, PENNSYLVANIA M.E.
Tom & Diane Rutkowski, 2641 Sassafras St.
Erie, PA 16508   Ph: 814-456-9464

JOLIET, ILLINOIS M.E.
Joe & Mary Cannizzaro, 546 Hampshire Lane
Bolingbrook, IL 60439   Ph: 312-739-6380
Fr. Jim Curtin, Marmion Abbey
Aurora, IL 60504   Ph: 312-859-0856

CENTRAL INDIANA M.E.
Lou & Louise Firsich, 7215 Moorgate Road
Indianapolis, IN 46250   Ph: 317-849-3922

OUTSIDE U.S.A.

OVERSEAS U.S. MILITARY
Fr. Frank Hajtas
Department of the Army
Office of the Chaplain
HQ VCA
APO New York 09175
06151-52322

ICELAND
Ray & Eileen Andrieu
AFI Box 854
FPO, New York, NY 09571

SEOUL, KOREA
Maj. & Mrs. Charles B. Hodell
HQ UNC/USFK/EUSA
JCIS Division
APO San Francisco 96301

JAPAN
Fr. Donnon Murray, O.F.M.
Catholic Church
Higashi Honchoo 46-20
Ota Shi, Gumma Ken
Japan 373

BERMUDA
Rev. D. A. Kirwan, C.R.
St. Michael's Rectory
Page, Bermuda 6-03

PANAMA CANAL ZONE
Ed & Bonnie Dolan
P.O. Box 1621
Balboa, Canal Zone

CANADA M.E.
Winnipeg
Dick & Marge Lebrun
195 Elm Street
Winnipeg, Manitoba
Canada R3M 3N5

Fort Francis
Dave & Eva Thornton
840 Fenette
Ft. Frances, Ont., Canada
807-274-3132

Montreal
Ray & Jean Brooks
1805 Du College
St. Laurent, P.Q.
Canada H4L 2N1

OTHER ORGANIZATIONS RECOMMENDED BY FATHER CALVO

International Confederation of Christian Family Movements
Mrs. Patty Crowley
175 E. Delaware Pl. Apt. 8804
Chicago, IL 60611

Christian Family Movement
Ray & Dorothy Maldoon
1655 Jackson
Chicago, IL 60612   Ph: 312-829-6101

Family Life
Father Don Conroy
1312 Massachusetts Ave. N.W.
Washington, DC 20005   Ph: 202-659-6672

Movimiento Familiar Cristiano
Raul y Milagros Rivera
2401 E. Holcombe Blvd.
Houston, TX 77021   Ph: 713-695-0162
Gaston y Genoveve Ponce
6932 Thrust
Houston, TX 77026   Ph: 713-643-6233

Marriage Encounter and Encuentro Conyugal International Coordination
Armando and Barbara Carlo
8331 East Monterey Way
Scottsdale, Arizona 85051   Ph: 602-947-0565

Marriage Retorno
Gene & Mary Lou Ott, Father Gerry Koob
4506 Golf Terrace
Edina, MN 55424   Ph: 612-922-5636

Association of Couples for Marriage Enrichment
David & Vera Mace
403 S. Hawthorne Road
Winston-Salem, NC 27103

Divorced Catholics Group
Rev. Jim Young
Paulist Center
5 Park Place
Boston, MA 02108

Families for Prayer
Rev. John Gurley, Sister Angelita Fenker
773 Madison Ave.
Albany, NY 12208

Teams of Our Lady
Bill & Claudette Reagan
12 Maplevale Drive
Yardley, PA 19067

Widows and Widowers
Clarence & Kathleen Enzler
Family Life Bureau
717 Fifth Street, N.W.
Washington, DC 20001

National Marriage Preparation Committee
Rev. Carl Arico
2032 Westfield Ave.
Scotch Plains, NJ 07076

JEWISH MARRIAGE ENCOUNTER

NATIONAL COORDINATORS
Joe and Deanie Crane
199 Boston Ave.
Massapequa, NY 11758
516-798-4136

ARIZONA
Mike and Brenda Katz
8533 E. Colette
Tucson, AZ 85701
602-886-2974

COLORADO
Howard and Sue Flingold
1521 S. Titan Ct.
Aurora, CO 80012
303-755-5116

CALIFORNIA
Jewish M.E. of California
c/o University of Judaism
6525 Sunset Blvd.
Los Angeles, CA 90028
213/463/1161

Len and Sherry Minowitz
23244 8th St.
Newhall, CA 91321
805-255-6759

CONNECTICUT
Buz and Shirley Smuckler
33 Clover Lane
E. Hartford, CT 06118
302-568-2155

DELAWARE
Jay and Nancy Blumberg
2629 Pennington Drive
Wilmington, DE 19810
302-475-6839

FLORIDA
Bill and Hinda Finn
11463 A SW 109th Rd.
Miami, FL 33156

GEORGIA
Gerald and Sue Epstein
901 Edgewater Dr. NW
Atlanta, GA 30328
404-255-1497

ILLINOIS
Gene and Judi Arbetter
1130 W. North Shore Ave.
Chicago, IL 60626
312-262-9813

INDIANA
Ave and Barbara Herman
1320 Darby Lane
Indianapolis, IN 46260
317-255-2039

LOUISIANA
Alvin and Ruth Cohen
758 Emerald St.
New Orleans, LA 70124
504-288-5195

MARYLAND
Arthur and Gloria Goldman
5764 Sweet Wind Place
Columbia, MD 21045
301-997-3838

MINNESOTA
David and Mary Ann Silber
2736 Ewing Ave. So
Minneapolis, MN 55416
612-920-6550

MISSOURI
Harvey and Renee Dobkin
1542 Gold Leaf St.
St. Louis, MO 63141
314-432-8968

NEW JERSEY
Ben and Florence Levey
42 Old Hook Rd.
Westwood, NJ 07675
201-664-5280

240

NEW MEXICO
Ralph and Louise Warschauer
209 Cabeza Negra SE
Albuquerque, NM 87124

NEW YORK
Albany
Marty & Shelley Somerdin
95 Miller Road
Watervliet, NY 12189
518-785-0132

Brooklyn, Staten Island, Manhatten
Norman and Barbara Goldman
5208 Av K
Brooklyn, NY 11234
212-251-7084

Buffalo
Mike and Ellen Roben
101 Tudor Rd.
Buffalo, NY 14215
716-836-2559

Orange County
Allen and Eden Rich
238 Summit Dr.
New Windsor, NY 12550
914-565-5428

Long Island, Queens
Noel and Ruth Selig
1168 Albert Rd.
N. Bellmore, NY 11710
516-221-7532

Rochester
Dick and Ruth Levin
50 Ashley Dr.
Rochester, NY 14620
716-442-1075

Hudson Valley
Vinnie and Madelyn Crain
3617 Flander Dr.
Yorktown Heights, NY 10598
914-245-7628

NORTH CAROLINA
Dave and Kitten Bart
6511 Farmingdale Ave.
Charlotte, NC 28212
704-535-6130

OHIO
John and Olivia Pike
7494 Essex Dr.
Mentor, OH 44060
216-946-5278

PENNSYLVANIA
Harry and Claire Shapiro
1206 Hale St.
Philadelphia, PA 19111
215-535-4706

TEXAS
Houston
Alan and Jan Selbst
2622 Fairway Dr.
Sugarland, TX 77478
713-494-6258